Learning
to
CHANGE

Learning to CHANGE

A Guide for Organization Change Agents

Léon de Caluwé
Twynstra Group and Free University, Amsterdam

Hans Vermaak
Twynstra Group

SAGE Publications
International Educational and Professional Publisher
Thousand Oaks ▪ London ▪ New Delhi

Copyright © 2003 by Sage Publications, Inc.

For information:

Sage Publications, Inc.
2455 Teller Road
Thousand Oaks, California 91320
E-mail: order@sagepub.com

Sage Publications Ltd.
6 Bonhill Street
London EC2A 4PU
United Kingdom

Sage Publications India Pvt. Ltd.
M-32 Market
Greater Kailash I
New Delhi 110 048 India

Printed in the United States of America

Library of Congress Cataloging-in-Publication Data

Caluwé, Léon de, 1950-Learning to change : a guide for organization change agents / by Léon de Caluwé and Hans Vermaak.
p. cm.
Includes bibliographical references (p.   ) and index.
ISBN 0-7619-2702-6
1. Organizational change. 2. Organizational change-Case studies.
I. Vermaak, Hans. II. Title.
HD58.8 .C29 2002
658.4´06--dc211

2002005210

02 03 04 05 10 9 8 7 6 5 4 3 2 1

Acquiring Editor:	Marquita Flemming
Editorial Assistant:	MaryAnn Vail
Production Editor:	Claudia A. Hoffman
Copy Editor:	Kris Bergstad
Indexer:	Molly Hall
Cover Designer:	Michelle Lee
Cover Art:	Ria Lap, *Landschap met bleke zon*, 1996
Interior Art:	Desirée Langenbach

Contents

Preface

Early in 1997, four people got together with the challenging idea of mapping out the field of change management for the benefit of their colleagues in the consulting profession. After all, change does lie at the heart of our profession, and it seemed like a good move to make any available wisdom more explicit. Thus began a year of collecting and exchanging theories, models, and experience from many kinds of sources, including gems picked up from our clients and fellow consultants in the course of our work. It was a year of sifting through and collating a wealth of material and arguing about the differences. It made for inspiring discussions. Over time it turned into a process of seeking common language, images, and nuances. We did not always find them, but by and large our efforts were rewarded, and at the end of the year we were able to launch a change management course accompanied by a substantial course book. We switched our efforts to teaching, bringing together groups of twenty people for a few days at a time every couple of months to discuss change processes, and to apply and test our concepts. The responses in these meetings strengthened our belief that the concepts are valuable and practical. The meetings also gave us new food for thought.

Two of us wanted to detail our collected insights further and decided to write a book. We wanted to offer the reader a variety of change theories and practices without making (too many) value judgments, knowing that there are often multiple approaches possible to the same problem. At the same time we wanted to furnish change agents with common and practical language and concepts, while guarding against expounding personal ideologies. In short, we wanted to create a concise and state-of-the-art overview of change management. This guide for organization change agents is the tangible result. But that is not all; we discovered that the very process of writing changed us, and we hope that our book might change you a bit as well. This is why we have chosen to call it *Learning to Change*. Perhaps the essence of being a change agent is the endless quest to learn what change is, how it works, and where we can contribute. This book marks a milestone in our thinking, even though we are not done learning about change, nor would we want to be.

This book would never have been written without the help of Hanneke Elink Schuurman and Wilma Terwel, the other two members of our original group. Much of what is written here is also the result of their work. In addition, Jan Bas Loman, Gert Wijnen, Hein Abeln, and Anneke Mensink supplied their energy and wisdom. We were also supported by Herman Grootelaar, Anna Bicker Caarten, Huub Vinkenburg, Jac Geurts, Marc de Roos, Rob Schutte, and Gerton Heijne. To make the ideas accessible to an international audience, we have sought to translate this book. Through inspiring colleagues at the Academy of Management, we met Marquita Flemming of Sage Publications and, with her help, that of her colleagues, and of Eileen Moyer, we were able to adapt the book for an international audience—a more difficult task than we had expected beforehand.

In conclusion, this book also owes a great deal to the inspiration gained over many years of working with clients, colleagues, scholars, and friends. There is no better way to learn than through experience.

Regular visits to the peaceful and inspiring surroundings of the Koningshoeven Abbey in Tilburg (The Netherlands) provided us with the ideal conditions to collect and record our thoughts. It was a location where we could leave the everyday world behind and give our thoughts free rein.

— Léon de Caluwé *and* Hans Vermaak

May, 2002

Learning to
CHANGE

1 Introduction

Confucius said, "Only the wise and the simpleminded never change." There are those peaceful moments when we dare to number ourselves as being among the wise. Lying in the grass staring up at the clouds, we realize that nothing really changes and never will. This is a comforting thought. When we take a break in the monastery where we work on this book, we hear the sounds of the monks going about their daily affairs as they have done for centuries, and realize that many a new management method is simply vintage wine being decanted into new bottles. *Capitulum* is the Latin root for the practice among these monks and many before them of discussing rules and problems and disciplining where needed. This is called feedback these days, and St. Benedict's rules of life are now being peddled as words of wisdom for the management of professionals.

Unfortunately, we usually operate in the middle ground between wisdom and stupidity and, just as Confucius philosophized, we witness change in both ourselves and in all that surrounds us. We can assume that this happens to most people and with such intensity that it is often difficult to manage and control it all. One of the greatest insights must surely be that it is not necessary to do so. You should let fate do some of the work for you. If change is the only constant in the universe, managing it would be Sisyphean. To undertake it would be rather presumptuous, even pretentious, not to mention exhausting.

What Is This Book About?

This book is not about all types of change; it deals solely with *planned change*. It is about that tiny fraction of change processes that you or we could or would want to influence, where we wish to believe that we can to some degree mold our lives, our organizations, or our societies. And where we think we perceive causal relationships between actions and reactions and try to make use of them.

Besides this, we also observe the occurrence of *unplanned* change—that things happen spontaneously and that you can benefit from that too. In this book we explore a number of fields of tension about which the final word has certainly not yet been written: the dilemma between autonomy and being managed, for example; the creation of intentional versus unintentional effects of change approaches; whether or not the interests of change agents and change objects overlap during change processes; regarding resistance as a force that assists rather than obstructs change (even if in a different direction). It is all quite complex, and we can do no more than attempt to observe and understand as much as possible. These fields of tension have shaped this book as much as we have, and so they should. Certain parts, the chapters describing method, steering, and tools, in particular, appear to be ordered in a rational and planned ("blue") fashion; but here, too, we are attempting to do justice to these tensions and diverse points of view.

Throughout the text however, the underlying need to understand and influence remains a powerful motive both for change agents and for us.

For Whom Is This Book Written?

This book is written for managers, consultants, and students. In fact, it is written for anyone taking responsibility in whatever form for directing change—for our colleagues who, like us, find themselves on the road between "wisdom and stupidity." In order to understand this book, it will help to be familiar with basic business science and organizational science jargon, either by having had training in these fields or having had several years experience in a consulting, management, or similar position. Specific knowledge about "learning" and "changing" is not required beyond what has been gained through general education or implicit observation.

How Is This Book Put Together?

The book is made up of nine chapters. Each chapter has a different purpose, is written in a different style, and contains a specific message for the change agent. This first chapter will help guide you through the whole book.

What is so difficult about directing change, anyway? Why is it relevant to acquire skills in this field? In Chapter 2 we share with you some ideas that influenced our thinking on this subject. We do this by putting forth twelve theories. These theories are about loosely coupled systems, managing and being managed, sociopolitical mechanisms, and chaos. Avoiding going into too much detail, we will discuss them just enough to elicit the response, "Yes, that frustrated our last change process as well." The message in this chapter is that change processes are often irrational and the theories help to explain this. The message is also that change agents must have more to offer than just

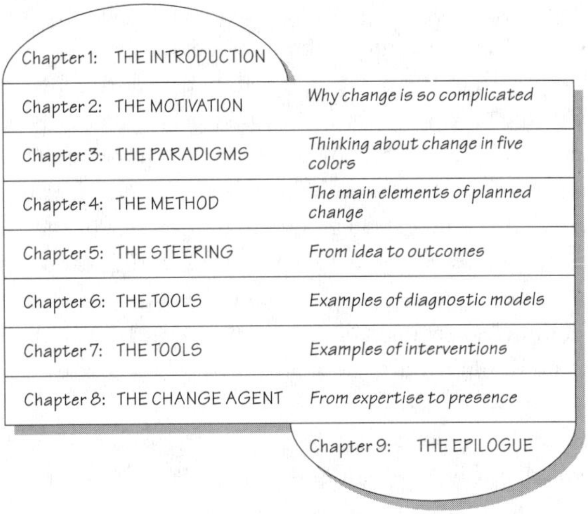

Chapter 1: THE INTRODUCTION	
Chapter 2: THE MOTIVATION	Why change is so complicated
Chapter 3: THE PARADIGMS	Thinking about change in five colors
Chapter 4: THE METHOD	The main elements of planned change
Chapter 5: THE STEERING	From idea to outcomes
Chapter 6: THE TOOLS	Examples of diagnostic models
Chapter 7: THE TOOLS	Examples of interventions
Chapter 8: THE CHANGE AGENT	From expertise to presence
Chapter 9: THE EPILOGUE	

Figure 1.1 The Book's Structure

rational top-down and contingency approaches, because the more irrational the change process is, the less fruitful these approaches turn out to be.

What exactly do people mean when they talk about "change"? What is there besides rational and contingency approaches? Why are there so many different schools of thought among change agents, and what are the differences between them? In Chapter 3 we explore five paradigms about change, each associated with certain beliefs and worked out in terms of their characteristics, ideals, and pitfalls. These five paradigms, each typified by a color, cover most change processes we see in real life and most theories about them in literature. The message in this chapter is that communication about change can be clear only if we are aware of our own as well as other people's paradigms. "Thinking in colors" provides a suitable framework for doing this. Another message is that change processes succeed more often when the change agent decides beforehand on a focused one-color approach suited to the situation rather than on an all-purpose mishmash.

Do change processes have standard elements? Are there things that always crop up regardless of what type of change process it is? Is there a road map of essential elements? In Chapter 4 we present such a road map, containing six elements. We have drawn up a checklist for each of the six elements that change agents should be aware of, and we have indicated how the checklists can help them irrespective of the "color" in which they think. The message in this chapter is that there are certain elements that appear in every change process and that you can both design and describe change processes well with them.

What are a change agent's most important activities? In Chapter 5 we describe four main steps: diagnosis, change strategy, the intervention plan, and interventions. We explain in detail how each of these steps is taken. In a sense this forms the heart of the book, a place where the previous more contemplative chapters and the following more instrumental and personal chapters come together. The message in this chapter is that many change agents are occupied with interventions and planning, but give little thought to diagnosis and change strategy, and that this is one of the main reasons why change programs are so ineffective. Another message in this chapter is that it is very easy and just as undesirable to carry out one-sided diagnoses and interventions. Anyone with a hammer looks for nails, no matter what is being built. This chapter gives some hints and tips to thwart one-sidedness.

If one wants to avoid one-sided diagnoses or interventions, what are the options? From which range of possibilities can one choose? What is available out there, and what would add nicely to one's individual repertoire? Chapter 6 gives a good start. In it almost forty diagnostic models are categorized. We describe these models and characterize them by their nature (business aspects, organizational aspects, or change aspects) and their level (from individual to the environment). The message here is that if you diagnose from a myriad of different viewpoints and are able to make sense of the information that results, which is often conflicting, you will miss little of importance. The more diverse the models you use, the greater your chances will be.

Chapter 7 categorizes forty-five interventions, which we describe and characterize in relation to one of the five colors and one of three levels (individual, group, or organization). The message here is that you can choose suitable interventions for change only when you are aware of many of the interventions available. If you do not know what is available, choosing the right intervention is a matter of chance. Both Chapters 6 and 7 are more suitable for reference purposes; they are designed to be browsed through or consulted rather than read from front to back.

Who, then, are these change agents and in what kinds of shapes and types do they appear? What makes someone "top notch," and how can we achieve this state of professionalism? Chapter 8 discusses styles, competencies, career lines, and development tips for change agents. The message in this chapter is that good change agents can be one-sided, but they have to be aware of their own limitations and incompetencies. This chapter also makes clear that the best guarantee for professional behavior and growth is continuous reflection and learning. And that both doing and organizing this is part of being a change agent—possibly even the best part. In Chapter 9, the epilogue, we reflect on this book both as change agents and change objects.

What Good Will This Book Be to You?

We would be very interested to find out. The book was created in a context of heated discussion among a large group of change agents working both nationally and internationally in the public and private sectors. The ideas have been tested for use in construction projects, conflict management, restructuring, mergers, coaching, gaming, interactive policymaking, competency management, training and education, and much, much more. We feel that this has enabled us to set out change management ideas without promoting or subscribing to any one particular school of thought and in a way that shows what is available "out there." On one hand, the book contains contemplative parts that have been an inspiration for certain people, while on the other hand, it contains tips, hints, and tools of a more practical value. This is reflected in its title and subtitle: *Learning to Change* indicating the contemplative and theoretical elements and *A Guide for Organization Change Agents* indicating its more practical applications.

2 Why Change Is Complicated

In this chapter, we describe theories and images illustrating why change is complicated. These theories and images, which we have observed in the course of the past years, have considerably widened our insight and will hopefully provide more in-depth knowledge of how change works and, more particularly, why it often does not work. These are theories that are recognized by and useful for people in our profession, and every change agent would do well to be familiar with them and take them into account. We discuss twelve theories. With a degree of poetic license, we give an outline of each theory together with one or more examples. For each of the clusters of three related theories, we discuss the consequences for change processes.

In the first cluster we describe Karl Weick's well-known theory regarding loosely coupled systems. He explains the ambiguities and, in part, the irrationality in organizations (see section 2.1.1). Weick once said, "Organizations keep people off the streets, provide an alibi for holding meetings, simplify social contact but further, they have little to offer." One essential element of his theory is the inadequate coupling of opinions and behavior (2.1.2). Organized anarchy, in the form of garbage-can decision making, provides a perfect insight into the ineffectiveness of rational planning and holding meetings to bring about change (2.1.3).

In the second cluster we describe the autonomy and cocksureness that characterize many staff members, and the problems that arise in their organizations (2.2.1). In section 2.2.2 we examine the basic conflicts between managers and professionals that can be reduced only by separating their domains and redefining their ways of dealing with each other. The "pocket veto" (2.2.3) illustrates how staff evade the manager's power the moment the manager pulls rank and tries to enforce changes. People change their behavior first and foremost because they want to, not because their boss wants them to. The cluster's theme is all about managing versus being managed.

In the third cluster we describe the insights that arise from chaos theory or are related to it. This deals, first, with the degree to which an organization does or does not maintain a dynamic balance with its environment (2.3.1): that sometimes, organizations are driven by various underlying patterns that, if not fully understood and taken into account, mean that change processes will be doomed at the outset. Zuijderhoudt and Greiner state that dysfunctional patterns do not materialize out of thin air but result from an organization's history (2.3.2). Dysfunctionality is often expressed by oscillating behavior: organization progress on some aspect is invariably followed by actions to nullify it and vice versa. Fritz (2.3.3) examines the structural laws, which help explain why some organizations end up in this fix and some happily advance.

The fourth cluster deals with the theme "socio-politics." We describe Parsons's action theory, which provides an insight into how people use their power to defend their interests (2.4.1). We then examine formal and informal aspects of organizations and demonstrate how influential the informal organization can be (2.4.2). The last theory concerns the economy of group behavior: "You scratch my back, and I'll scratch yours" (2.4.3).

In the final section (2.5) we summarize the clustered theories in one diagram. Here we discuss the most important mutual characteristics of the theories: the seeming irrationality of change processes. It is this irrationality that prompted us to write this book and that possibly prompts you to read it. That is why we open the book with these theories. In addition, this apparent irrationality casts doubts on the dominance of rational and contingency approaches to change and provides a legitimate reason to search for a broader spectrum of approaches to change and a description of the components, activities, tools, and styles that do justice to this broader spectrum. This is, in short, the content of the remaining chapters.

2.1 On Loosely Coupled Systems

The theory of "loose coupling" was developed by Weick. He considers it applicable at the organizational level (2.1.1) as well as at the individual level (2.1.2). The garbage-can theory by Cohen, March, and Olsen (2.1.3) demonstrates that a similar phenomenon can occur at group level.

2.1.1 Ambiguities in Organizations

"Imagine that you are either the referee, coach, player or spectator at an unconventional soccer match: the field for the game is round; there are several goals scattered haphazardly around the circular field; people can enter and leave the game whenever they want to; they can throw balls in whenever they want; they can say "that's my goal" whenever they want to, as many times as they want to, and for as many goals as they want to; the entire game takes place on a sloped field; and the game is played as if it makes sense.

"If you now substitute in the example above principals for referees, teachers for coaches, students for players, parents for spectators and schooling for soccer, you have an equally unconventional depiction of school organizations. The beauty of this depiction is that it captures a different set of realities within educational organizations than are caught when these same organizations are viewed through the tenets of bureaucratic theory."

The above passage is quoted from the opening lines of Karl E. Weick's (1976) article, "Educational Organizations as Loosely Coupled Systems."

In our opinion, this passage can be broadly applied to most of the organizations we are familiar with, certainly where knowledge workers or professionals constitute the majority of the workforce of the organization. What is striking in the passage is how ambiguous many organizations are. There are a number of features that show these ambiguities:

Ambiguous objectives. This is the case when an organization functions with various badly or vaguely defined, sometimes even conflicting, goals. These goals can be interpreted in a variety of ways and act as a "cover" for a mixed bag of activities. Everyone can say "that is my goal" whenever they want to, as often as they want to, and for as many goals as they want to. Many strategic documents and mission statements have these characteristics: They are often very ambiguous (see also 2.3.3.). Sometimes they camouflage disagreement (vague goals as a means of reaching compromises about differences of opinion), sometimes the words and sentences are interpreted in contrasting ways. The formal objectives might have some relationship with shop floor reality and working methods, but might equally well be entirely separate from them (loosely coupled).

Ambiguous technology (work processes). Many employees have little insight into the work processes that determine the output and value their organization produces. That causal connection between activity and value is difficult to define and to articulate. What makes good education? What factors contribute to effective medical treatment? What constitutes good consultancy? Both consensus and objective answers to these questions are hard to find. People often do things to the best of their ability and their comprehension, but such mixtures of effort and opinion do not necessarily produce tangible results. In truth, our knowledge about what works and what doesn't is limited.

This explains why different teachers and doctors speak and act so differently and get away with it. What is good and what is not?

Ambiguous participation. The involvement of persons or groups in any activity within an organization generally varies and thus is hard to pin down. Who participates in the decision making about what and with what mandate? Who belongs to which group, department, or commission? Who is supposed to attend which meeting? If we work together, does that mean we make all the decisions together? If we want to increase participation, does this imply that people can sit in and listen to us, contribute ideas, have a vote, or change the whole agenda? The answers to these types of questions vary considerably depending on whom you ask, and furthermore, the answers can vary from day to day.

In this view it is hard to see system goals that can be achieved along predictable and well-planned routes. The situation is one of ambiguity and variability, many loosely coupled elements that react to one another only slowly, infrequently, or not at all. This view is at odds with the idea of an organization as a consciously designed machine with all its parts geared to one another, with the intention of producing predictable outcomes. Weick's theory is a reaction to the systems approach where rational principles dominate (see, e.g., Knip, 1981).

2.1.2 Loose Coupling Between Intentions and Behavior

Loose coupling, according to Weick (1969), plays a role not only at the organizational level but also at the individual level: the way in which intentions and behavior influence each other. There is a growing awareness that opinions and intentions have little influence on behavior; the opposite seems to be the case. In other words, intentions and opinions are stated rationally after the event. Weick says that, consequently, behavior and opinions at the individual level are as much uncoupled as systems are at the organizational level. Behavior appears to function quite independently of opinions. If you ask people what the reason or motive was for their behavior, they will construct something on the spot.

> "There is a developing position in psychology which argues that intentions are a poor guide for action, intentions often follow rather than precede action, and that intentions and action are loosely coupled. Unfortunately, organizations continue to think that planning is a good thing, they spend much time on planning, and actions are assessed in terms of their fit with plans. Given a potential loose coupling between the intentions and actions of organizational members, it should come as no surprise that administrators are baffled and angered when things never happen the way they were supposed to." (Weick, 1976)

In order to clarify intentions, many organizations invest a great deal of time in developing plans. However, the theory suggests that this is a dead-end street: the coupling becomes even looser than it was. Examples of this can be found in approaches to change where people first hold numerous meetings to decide exactly what it is that needs to be changed and how the change will be tackled. The result is a mass of memos and documents but seldom an actual behavior change. Worse still, the contents of these memos bear little relationship to how people actually work and behave. In the following theory (section 2.1.3) there is another vivid illustration of this phenomenon— so-called garbage-can decision making. This examines the gap between the theory in use, that is, what people actually do, and espoused theory, or what people purport to do but don't.

Instead of concentrating on plans, intentions, and opinions it is also possible to ask people to make explicit their behavior and to reflect on it. This lays bare the implicit opinions that underlie their actions. The difference between their implicit and explicit opinions becomes clear as it scrutinizes the loose coupling between behavior and opinions. Weick regards this consciousness raising as an important exercise, the best way of creating a "tighter coupling" between behavior and opinions.

2.1.3 Garbage-Can Decision Making

A vivid illustration of the ineffectiveness of meetings and decision making is demonstrated in the garbage-can decision-making theory of Cohen, March, and Olsen (1972) and in de Caluwé and Petri (1985). The former give the following definition of an organization:

> An organization can be viewed for some purposes as collections of choices looking for problems, issues and feelings looking for decision situations in which they might be aired, solutions looking for issues to which they might be an answer, and decision makers looking for work.

"Garbage cans" full of unresolved issues, unrealized solutions, and potential decisions are to be found everywhere and instead of being emptied, they are transferred into new, larger garbage containers.

Let us consider an example from an imaginary school (but it really did happen).

> In a plenary staff meeting a proposal is discussed that would mean that all lessons would be shortened by five minutes from fifty to forty-five minutes. The five-minute lesson time would then be used for individual pupil guidance.

The modern-language teachers think that they cannot spare this time and wonder out loud what the consequences for their teaching methods would be if the proposal should be accepted. Other teachers ask themselves just how this extra time for pupil guidance should be spent: They would not like this to be unspecified and open ended. Some teachers consider it best to accumulate the time in order to organize a collective work-week in the countryside for all students and teachers, while others have concerns regarding the organization and management of these work weeks. One teacher who does not see the usefulness of work weeks warns about the inferior quality of the material of the rented tents, for this will certainly give rise to problems with parents. Others see problems in the fact that parents would be granted a say in these matters and would first like this to be discussed. A few are unhappy about logistics: the layout of the room in which the children eat their packed lunch as well as the surveillance roster. They are afraid that things will get worse if the educational aims outstrip the other aims in the school to a greater degree. A few think that the deputy director responsible for pupil guidance is already overworked and they feel, in light of his family circumstances, that the organization of the school should be adapted before such a proposal is adopted.

In brief, the five-minute pupil-guidance garbage can is getting fuller and fuller: Hobbyhorses keep rolling in. The longer the moments of choice last, the more problems can be thrown in. Someone thinks that too little consideration is given to the wishes of the pupils themselves and would like to add this to the agenda. Someone else has heard that pupil guidance at another school has been a failure and would like to see more research on this. The garbage can is full and consequently it becomes increasingly difficult to empty it. As a result of the discussions and the proposals, involvement has increased and the decision that must be taken has become weightier. The risk that a "wrong" decision will be made also increases: where nobody really gets what he wants and nobody really gives his support. The best recourse then seems to be to postpone the decision and take stock. However, the risks keep on increasing. The longer the moments of choice remain open, the more unsolved issues can once more be dragged in. "Communication between the different subject departments also gives rise to problems," adds someone. Another option would be to make a decision that circumvents the problem; "Let's hold a study conference." Now there is a new garbage can in place, still empty, but that won't last long.

Should it be a one-day or a two-day conference? Where? Who will take part, some pupils too? During school time? Also in the evenings? Do we have to bring in external expertise? Who will carry out the preparations? Will the conference

> program first have to be approved in a plenary meeting? What subjects will be discussed? Will we make decisions or will we stick to a general discussion or brainstorm? Will the subgroups be made up of similar people or will the subgroups be heterogeneous?

In the meantime, the first garbage can is still full of issues waiting to be solved, but because of the complexity and risks involved no decisions are taken. People run away from this first garbage can and install a new, empty one by deciding on a study conference. The result is that the old problems are transferred to the new garbage can and there are great expectations all around.

In this way, problems and decisions float around in the organization as elements seeking and avoiding each other and new moments of choice are highlighted. The "organization" carries on without really solving any problems and, more important, also without creating new, collective problems that would challenge the organization.

2.1.4 Implications for
Change Agents and Change Processes

Weick's observations that ambiguities increasingly occur mean that it is difficult to characterize organizations as entities that follow a univocal course and a clear rational approach. They can much better be characterized as networks of autonomous centers (sometimes right down to the level of the individual staff members) that, in their dealings with each other, are continually searching for an identity and a direction. For change agents, the loosely coupled character of organizations means that, in many cases, they cannot limit themselves to a top-down rational approach. Expanding the coupling between the parts means that the staff members must be involved in the discussions concerning objectives, in carrying out the activities, and in mastering the most important competencies.

The garbage-can theory implies that this involvement can degenerate into an interminable and fruitless cycle of meetings. It was once said, "There's only one thing worse than dreaming that you are asleep at a meeting and suddenly waking up; it's being at a meeting and not being able to sleep." There is little chance for organizational development when there is a high degree of garbage-can decision making as these organizations are plagued by little coherence, acceptance of noncooperation, and counterproductive communication. Meetings become mere frustrating rituals. The inventors of the garbage-can theory do not see the point of attempts at improvement. They tend to advise management to add to the chaos and use it to their advantage, as nothing else will work anyway. We are a little more optimistic but think that improvement cannot be realized spontaneously from within. A breakthrough in the garbage-can mechanism will come about only as a result of external causes: a shrinking market share, mergers, a chance to make a great leap forward, or a top-down reorganization. If discussions have not deteriorated into a garbage-can situation, however, there are more possibilities. The theory of a loose coupling between intentions and behavior warns us not to focus discussions on intentions, for they might then have no effect on behavior. If one wants to influence behavior during the change process it is best to first make people aware of their actual behavior and how it contributes to the problems at hand. This involves making this behavior visible. Only then can one make explicit the underlying opinions and intentions. Others must be involved in this endeavor: It is difficult, if not impossible, to observe one's own behavior. By making it explicit, a tighter coupling between behavior and opinions is created. There are approaches to change or interventions that further the realization of a tighter coupling between opinions and behavior. These are approaches in which

◆ behavior is made visible
◆ there is sufficient safety for people to give and receive feedback on their behavior
◆ the people involved are committed to learning about their own behavior
◆ the skills that enable people to learn from and about each other are present

2.2 On Managing and Being Managed

The trend of ongoing professionalization places new demands on the working methods of managers and staff, but these working methods do not develop at the same pace. This gives rise to a fixed set of problems (2.2.1). The conflicting orientations (2.2.2) of professionals and managers create a basic conflict that arouses avoidance tendencies like the pocket veto in the staff (2.2.3).

2.2.1 Autonomous Workers and Hierarchical Managers

(Not) managing oneself and (not) being managed is a theme that is much in evidence in professional organizations, where it can take exceptional forms. Therefore, the focus of our descriptions is on professional organizations, but the phenomena described can be found in nearly all types of organizations.

The similarities among Erasmus, a violin maker, and a teacher include the following:

◆ each of them is learned/has learned a lot
◆ each of them knows best how to practice his profession
◆ each decides himself how his relationship with his clients will be

- each identifies himself more with his profession and his fellow professionals than with the organization of which he is part
- each learns through his own experience and shapes his own professionalization

In other words, they all have a high degree of autonomy in their work and their own development and in their relationship with colleagues and clients. When there are many people like this in an organization, typical phenomena will surface. We call this the professional organization. Much has been published concerning the management and changing of professionals (Van Delden, 1995; Weggeman, 1992; Vermaak, 1999). The vein is fairly skeptical. Can professionals be managed, steered, or changed? Professionals are not keen to renounce their independent and cocksure nature, and they behave as if they are still self-employed. Hobbies and solo performances are considered legitimate, so collectivity in products and services is usually difficult to detect. What is more, good professional quality is considered to be of overbearing importance. Correspondingly, commercial result orientation is often lacking. Another factor is that professionals do not easily agree among themselves about the current or desired quality of their work. As a rule, the opinion of someone else is valued less than their own opinion, for why should a colleague know better? The opinion of a customer or a boss is often taken even less seriously, for they are considered to have little or no professional background. Learning together and innovating prove difficult, and knowledge is regarded as personal property and remains locked in the head or in a cupboard. And so three core problems often arise:

- fragmentation as a result of everyone following his own direction;
- mediocrity because people do not learn from one another;
- and noncommitment because there is no focus on results or deadlines.

These core problems occur in most professional organizations. Professionals can hold long, emotional discussions about these problems but here, too, they act as typical freelancers: Everyone has his own shrewd solution. Splendid democratic decision-making processes are often doomed when faced with the reality of too many cooks spoiling the broth. "I cannot force a colleague to do something against his will, let alone vice versa," the professional will say. A common metaphor for this is "a wheelbarrow full of frogs." The pursuit of a consensus can paralyze an organization, thanks to the earlier discussed garbage-can model of decision making. Frustrated by the persistence of all these problems, professionals often suddenly behave like old-fashioned wage laborers: Problems are laid at the manager's door.

The pharaohs, Henry Ford, and classic governmental organizations have the following in common regarding their thinking about organizations:

- the favorite way of thinking about organizations is to imagine a pyramid, with the boss at the apex

- management's authority is legitimate and is not open to discussion
- rationality and rational argumentation are the dominant principles in organizing
- planning and control form the basis for steering the employees
- employees are regarded as expendable/replaceable production resources

According to Feltmann (1993), managers have a natural disposition to view possession and control, definition and overview, planning and evaluation as guarantees of good fortune. The news media, the shareholders, and the managers themselves refer to "the man at the helm," "the man pulling the strings," someone who can be held accountable for the results. Thus it is implied that there is such a thing as actually managing and controlling an organization and that there can be one person with sufficient power to do all that. This approach has proved its worth in sectors with standardized working methods and where efficiency is prized above all else. Transportation, industry, traditional government organizations: it was here that this management wisdom evolved, a wisdom later canonized in management literature. But bureaucracy also appears to provide us with a number of inherent problems and, in the meantime, "We have almost reached the point where the term *bureaucracy* is used to illustrate everything that is wrong with organizations; inflexible, not client-oriented, inhuman, ineffective, and lacking in innovative ideas" (de Leeuw, 1997).

In short, the combination of the bureaucratic manager and the autonomous professional is troublesome. A boss who attempts to give strong leadership is faced with a lack of understanding. Top down leadership is taboo; professionals are allergic to everything that even hints at the dreaded threesome of "Bureaucracy, Bosses, and Policies." They follow their managers' activities not only with Argus's eyes but consider it perfectly legitimate to express unsolicited criticism. They think that they are permitted to publicly discuss the incompetence of the management, but of course, managers are forbidden to do the same about them. Furthermore, they feel that they have the right to ignore any management decision that clashes with their professional standards and, before you realize it, they try to extend their authority to cover such management matters as budgets and personnel policy. They'll show the boss how it should be done.

2.2.2 The Basic Conflict

The previous section explains that in many, if not all, organizations there are conflicting orientations. Bureaucrats attempt to steer and control change and compel employees to carry out their wishes. Employees, on the other hand, try to avoid being steered and controlled, certainly when this interferes with their own plans and ideas. This is what we call the basic conflict; it is always present in any organization, to a greater or lesser degree. It keeps popping up in one form or another. Sometimes it has an

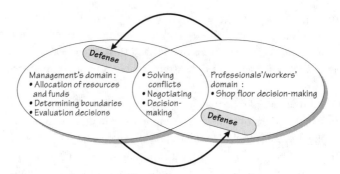

Figure 2.1 Interacting Spheres Model

organization completely in its grasp; all activities are then geared toward it and can be explained by it. Managers keep thinking up shrewder arguments and clever means to provide them with more influence over their staff's activities, and the staff think up better ways of wriggling out of them. This can sap all the life out of an organization; we are regularly faced with the situation where managers employ strategies to increase their hold on the staff and the staff employ theirs to evade this hold and sabotage their manager's efforts. In this way, everyone is kept off the streets. All are busy.

Mark Hanson (1996) describes this basic conflict in his Interacting Spheres Model (see Figure 2.1). He states that managers and professionals/workers each have their own domain over which they make decisions. For example, managers make decisions about budgets and resources, or entering into a strategic alliance with another organization. Professionals/workers make decisions that have a direct bearing on their work and how they carry it out. This is the type of decision that the teacher in front of a class makes or the employee at the counter when dealing with a client, and so on. Each "party" cherishes his or her own domain, and if another party tries to trespass, they defend it fiercely and things do not run as smoothly as before.

Of course, there is also a gray area. Hanson calls this the contested zone, the zone in which professionals and management need each other and are dependent upon each other and where joint decisions have to be taken.

2.2.3 Pocket Vetoes

Life is not that simple in this gray area, however, for the members of staff want their exclusive domain to be as large as possible and to push the manager (and other professionals) out. Here, the term *pocket veto* is instructive. This term, originating in Political Science, describes the right the president of the United States has to not approve a bill that has already been passed by Congress, by not signing it into law. The president can put it, metaphorically speaking, in his back pocket until the time for approving the bill has expired. Congress is aware of this and has no choice but to accept this prerogative.

In his book *Educational Administration and Organizational Behavior,* Mark Hanson (1996) uses the term pocket veto to describe the power teachers (professionals) have when innovations for classroom interaction are introduced from "above." He uses the concept pocket veto because "its power is exerted through inaction; in other words, the teachers simply did not respond to requests or mandates for change" (p. 97).

We think that the following example is a good illustration of a pocket veto. Boss John sees employee Pete doing something that he does not agree with. It could have to do with the way Pete is dealing with a customer or a colleague. John finds Pete's behavior "unacceptable in this day and age" and asks Pete to come and have a talk with him about it.

In that discussion, John explains why this just won't do and, in turn, Pete explains why he does what he does. John then restates his point of view and Pete does the same.

The discussion is closed and both go away thinking that they have made their position perfectly clear to the other.

Two weeks later Boss John sees employee Pete doing exactly the same thing and immediately takes the initiative and arranges a new discussion. Then he explains his point of view once more, in slightly stronger language and with a little more power. Pete replies in the same vein and the atmosphere becomes frosty. Afterward, John says to himself, "I think he has finally gotten the message." Pete, too, thinks that his boss has understood at last.

What happened represents only the tip of the iceberg, for below the surface lies a learning process that can be easily assimilated by the average employee.

That learning process is as follows:

1. Make sure that the boss doesn't see what you do; if he cannot observe it, he will have nothing to say about it.
2. Always agree with your boss. Hum empathically. Compliment him on his way of thinking; say, "That's what we'll do or try," but go ahead and do just

> what you want to or what you think suits best your professional environment, which by now you have carefully shielded from your boss. That is the principle of saying one thing and doing another. It makes the boss believe that his staff is doing things the way he wants. He feels himself a lucky man. The staff is also happy; they carry on in their own way in their own little world.

Pocket vetoes can be found in every organization. There is likely to be a particularly high incidence of pocket vetoes where managers are convinced that their staff has exactly the same view as they themselves do. Such convictions raise alarm bells in us as consultants, whereas it is still the dream of many managers. In our view, managers should be continually aware of the presence of pocket vetoes. Pocket vetoes result from too great a recourse to hierarchy, from serious differences of opinion, or from too little discussion, respect, and acceptance. They are also often the result of staff members regarding the pocket veto as their prerogative given how work is organized. Think of the teacher who shuts the classroom door, the doctor who closes the examining room door, the consultant who spends time with the client away from a home office, the salesperson on the road, and so on. Many employees have the opportunity to make things invisible when it comes to certain areas of their work, and use the opportunity with zeal when the boss asks them to do something that they do not agree with.

The situation can become particularly unhealthy when lots of employees employ the pocket veto. The top then becomes completely detached from the work floor and two separate "realities" arise: The reality of the apex and the reality that exists on the work floor. You encounter this to some extent when you join a new organization, where, after a couple of days, the booklet with the internal rules no longer seems to apply. The rules are different. Your new colleagues say, "OK, that's what is written, but you will have to do it differently or it won't work."

However, this can occur in various degrees, right up to the pathological. In the worst possible scenario the real communication channels are fully clogged up or are used only for irrelevant matters. A crisis or confrontation is then lurking.

2.2.4 Implications for Change Agents and Change Processes

Tensions in (professional) organizations are unavoidable, and change agents should be aware of this. As a result of the distribution of power and competence in these settings, by definition an arena is created where differences of opinion arise. Each professional or employee has his own ideas and is not afraid to express them. Without a meeting of minds everyone goes his or her way, which is exactly why the three core problems in this sort of organization arise: fragmentation, mediocrity, and non-commitment. Any manager who thinks that all is going well in her organization because everything is ticking along quietly probably has much pocket-vetoing among the staff. One important implication is that coherence is necessary but cannot be enforced by hierarchy or by rational arguments. There is a tendency to forget the human factor and to pay a lot of attention to decisions about the outcomes of change but little to the change process and implementation. In this way new problems arise, such as a lack of support, unnecessary resistance, and so on.

The theory about basic conflict provides a first foothold: Divide the domains of managers and staff into those they are best equipped to deal with. Allow the staff to rule over the primary process: their craft, their contact with clients, their development. In this domain the role of managers is best confined to providing support, coaching, recognition, and challenges while insisting on accountability for the professionals' output. Conversely, managers may claim the secondary processes as their own. Professionals should not meddle here, as they do not understand these processes, have no aptitude for managing them, and do not enjoy doing it, either. The managers look after the facilities, take care of support services, and consult with bodies from the surrounding environment. This division of domains ensures a considerable reduction of possible conflicts.

What remains is what Hanson calls the "contested zone." This is the region where cooperation must be achieved in areas affecting every professional: for example, strategy formation, training, marketing, and output agreements. Hanson suggests that the basic conflict also makes itself felt here, but can be resolved through effective negotiation. This will succeed if

- both parties are conscious of the basic conflict
- people respect each other's domain and do not trespass
- people are willing to recognize that they depend upon each other
- there is a negotiating/communication forum
- there are positively accepted agenda items to be discussed
- there is agreement about the consultation procedures
- there is mutual, legitimate coordination concerning decision-making and the execution of the decisions

In other words, the realization that there is a basic conflict and mutual respect is an important basic principle for a productive relationship between managers and staff.

In this "contested" zone it is important to be aware of the pocket veto. In the first place, managers or change agents must realize that they, too, can become "victims" of the pocket veto. At first, everything seems to be going well: the staff appears to be in agreement with you . . . but wait. Then the anxiety begins, you see so little of them these days . . . A second message is that it must be obvious to all that you are rewarding transparency, even when what surfaces are things that you yourself do not agree with or that are, in your opinion, indisputably wrong. The staff must be encouraged to carry out their activities openly, to be open to discussion and accountable. They must be discouraged from staying out of sight, not being available to have their actions screened and discussed. In many cases it might be recommended to create horizontal groups where peers show their work, explore its quality, and are willing to learn from this and, if necessary, to adapt their ways. Examples of this type of collective learning include intervision groups, working in teams, clinics, gaming, and intercollegial review. Where much learning and experimentation is allowed and supported, there is little need for pocket vetoes. As a change agent, you seek mechanisms to couple tighter what professionals think and do: their cognitions and actions; their opinions and behavior. We discussed this in section 2.1.2. If there is one thing you should stay clear of during change processes, it is holding lots of meetings about the intended change. Instead, just embark on the change by acting together, exchanging experiences, reflecting together upon what works, and committing to the next step.

2.3 On Chaos Thinking

Chaos thinking emphasizes a focus on the underlying patterns in an organization that determine its behavior. These patterns come in many shapes and sizes. There are patterns that upset the dynamic balance between an organization and its environment by creating either chaos or a steady state (2.3.1). Oscillating patterns of behavior emerge when organizations pursue conflicting goals, be it consciously or not (2.3.3). These patterns can often be regarded as a product of an organization's history; they do not appear out of thin air (2.3.2). They have become, as it were, part of the culture and identity of the organization: "That's the way we do things around here and it has worked so far." What all these patterns have in common is that they are not in plain view but need some unearthing.

2.3.1 Dynamic Balance

Chaos theory has many "fathers," particularly in the sciences. One of these fathers is the theoretical physicist Bohm (1992), who reasons that we often unjustly distinguish between the thinker, the thought, and what is being thought about. Bohm sees "everything that exists" as an explicit order, a temporary, creative swelling in a "universal stream," which is the implicit order, for which there is no explicit description but can only be implicitly known and recognized. According to Bohm, all of our knowledge and science is directed at explaining the explicit order and, in so doing, we make the mistake of not seeing our theories as representations of reality but as part of reality itself.

This explicit order is often equated with steady states, structures and systems, predictability, and controllability. Organizations are orderly constructions consisting of clear-cut elements (objects) that behave in an understandable manner. Such explicit order is in line with a mechanistic worldview that many of us became quite familiar with growing up, and one that is still dominant in management literature, stacked as it is with quick fixes and proven remedies. In contrast, chaos theory views systems such as organizations as adaptive networks or *holons,* whose characteristics cannot be traced back to the characteristics of the constituent parts alone.

Holon

It was biologists who first described the remarkable ability of all life to form structures with different "layers." Each of these systems forms a whole with regard to its parts and is at the same time part of a (bigger) whole (see Capra, 1996). Koestler (1967) coined the word *holon,* which represents an entity that is a whole itself and at the same time part of another whole. In his view, the world consists of trillions of holons: a whole atom is part of a whole molecule, a whole molecule is part of a whole cell, the whole cell is part of a whole organism, the whole organism is part of a (social) system. In the sense we will never see *the* whole; there are only whole/parts.

Just like a hologram, which you can cut without losing the total image, every single holon contains an image of the bigger whole. Holons have four capabilities: the capability to act independently as an entity, the capability to unite with other holons, the capability to transcend itself, and the "capability" to decompose itself. (from Cornelissen, 1999)

According to chaos theory, people do not focus on individual objects but rather on the relationships between these objects and the patterns that emerge from these relationships. People do not recognize reality on the basis of familiarity with objects but discern reality from observing the emerging patterns between them. In organizations, people weave these patterns into a continual cycle of sense-making. The more patterns being woven, the more dynamic the system. When an organization is extremely dynamic or in flux, then structures, systems, and strategies provide fewer footholds to a change agent than the people who create them. The borders and the identity of the organization become open and fluid: people flow through, cooperative external relationships are sometimes more important than internal ones, old and new ideas coexist, and so on.

Such an "adaptive network" is susceptible to many forces: complexity and turbulence are considered to be the primary external forces. Dominant internal forces include both the increased autonomy and mutual dependence of the staff and the diversity of their views about the work and their own contribution to it. The relevance of chaos theory increases as organizations are confronted with an increase in these forces. What are the consequences? Linearity decreases: a single, minor cause can have more and bigger consequences because self-reinforcing feedback loops make the organization more sensitive as a network than it was as a traditional, stable organization. The behavior of this type of system becomes unpredictable. The most familiar example of this is Lorenz's (1963) butterfly theory. To his surprise, he discovered that in his meteorological model a minute change in one of the parameters in the preliminary stage could lead to entirely different types of weather. He published his findings under the significant title, "Could the Flapping of a Butterfly's Wings in Brazil Cause a Tornado in Texas?"

However, Lorenz also indicated something else; even the most chaotic systems, such as weather, vary within certain boundaries. They have a certain balance. This balance is not static like a marble in a glass and neither is it a periodic balance like the pendulum of a clock. It is a dynamic balance in which the speed of the development within the organization keeps roughly the same pace as the development speed of its ecosystem. If the speed of development is much faster outside the system than inside, the organization moves far from equilibrium: This may sound quite grim but the biologist Prigogine (1985) states that there is hope in this murky chaos; a type of self-organizing ability emerges that, precisely in this type of situation, is capable of creating a new order.

In its functional form, this situation demonstrates the characteristics of a learning organization, where the ability of the organization to adapt to its ecosystem is greatly increased.

Loman (1998) recognizes five areas in which an organization can find itself. The areas are specific to an organization as they are a function of the degree of the complexity and the dynamics in and around that organization:

◆ on the edge of control: static equilibrium
◆ between the edge of control and dynamic balance
◆ dynamic balance
◆ between dynamic balance and the edge of chaos
◆ on the edge of chaos: out of balance

Dynamic balance, or as Stacey (1996) calls it, "bounded instability," may sound as if it is the "best" area. Appearances are deceiving. An out-of-balance situation, for example, can provide many opportunities for renewal. Chaos can be functional or dysfunctional. This too is specific to the holon in question.

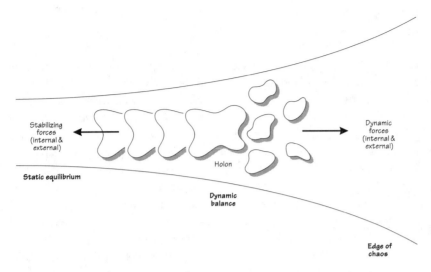

Figure 2.2 Five Areas

In environments with high-paced development, some organizations have difficulty finding the right adjustment to its dynamic surroundings.

Dysfunctional "static equilibrium"

Real life example: A health care insurer that loses contact with clients and staff. Its internal organization is characterized by centralized management with corresponding "bureaucratic layers": middle managers who are busy maintaining the status quo. The internal organization is an archipelago of small fiefdoms that enjoy a great degree of autonomy. The terms of employment are excellent, but people's mobility and eagerness to learn are largely absent. There is great resistance to making a clean sweep. This is an example of an organization that is too involved in keeping everything manageable while the environment of the financial sector undergoes dynamic changes. There is too much emphasis on:

♦ internal matters, leading to navel-gazing
♦ material aspects, leading to firefighting based on facts and figures
♦ business processes, leading to "more of the same" improvements that are too rigid to make a difference,
♦ continuity, leading to a compulsion to reach consensus and keep things together
♦ problem solving, which leads to reactive measures

Dysfunctional out-of-balance situation

Example: An IT department in a bank is under great pressure from the front office to introduce all kinds of adaptations to the IT systems. The department caves in under this pressure and all involved step up their work tempo. Client orientation (the front office is the internal client) is, after all, the number-one priority. As a result of the enormous workload, the staff abandons the quality handbook and the project management procedures. Mistakes start creeping in. Via various improvised adaptations to the system and cooperation with other departments, an attempt is made to create new patterns in the applications system without these being understood by management, partly because they have not been involved in the process. The bank is confronted with an increasing and predictable operational risk. Managers come to regard the organization as a "twilight zone." Here, we have an organization that finds itself regularly on the edge of chaos, as if it wants to make a great leap forward in adapting itself to the dynamics of the environment. In total contrast to the previous example, in the IT department there is too much emphasis on

♦ external aspects, which leads to "overheating"
♦ immaterial aspects, leading to day dreaming
♦ mental processes, causing unpredictability
♦ evolution, with the risk of things falling apart
♦ reframing, causing lots of new ideas but little being completed

In both examples there is no dynamic balance. The health care insurer tries to control a world where this is no longer possible. In a manner of speaking, it has fallen behind the dynamic balance. The computerization department becomes unmanageable because it is unable to create (new) order in an uncontrollable world. It is too far ahead of the dynamic balance. We see many organizations struggling with these kinds of dilemmas, and have seen that their reactions, especially when based on their own previous successes, do not guarantee successful adaptation. Making a clean sweep in the bank could result in the organization becoming more stable and their risks more controllable, something that would not be impossible along traditional, bureaucratic lines. The health care insurer can scratch the surface of the problem by providing courses in client-oriented behavior for its personnel. Skills would improve, but this does nothing to create the kind of decentralized decision making and self-steering that is instrumental for dealing flexibly with the turbulent environment they are in.

2.3.2 Autonomous Development

The previous section dealt with the extent to which an organization has lost its dynamic balance, but other authors have focused their energies on discovering how an organization lands itself in that predicament. Is an organization born out of balance, or is this something that happens to all organizations sooner or later? Zuijderhoudt (1992) applies himself to this question in a model of the life span of organizations. He argues that organizations move autonomously toward greater complexity and quality. If an organization wishes to maintain a dynamic balance, its internal development must keep pace with external development and, therefore, become more dynamic and complex. But, according to Zuijderhoudt, this is not usually the case. After a shorter or longer period of growth, the internal speed of development usually progresses at a pace different from external development; in most cases slower. The organization attempts to maintain predictable behavior patterns in its staff according to the old recipes, but the old rules no longer apply, and as a result the behavior of the staff shows unpredictable but increasing fluctuations. If, for example, the organization is fragmented because of "little kingdoms," control from above is tightened. However, when this results in more pocket vetoes, disobedience, and demotivation, control is relaxed again. This is one example of fluctuating behavior, but the theory states that several specific "preferred" fluctuations will occur parallel to one another. This set of fluctuations is perceived as typical for the organization—"That's how things always turn out here"—and, what's more, the set becomes stronger over time. At a certain point, these fluctuations lead to the awareness that the existing reflexes and recipes won't help: There is a crisis at hand.

Zuijderhoudt distinguishes three possibilities in such situations:

♦ The organization stagnates and fossilizes. Various attempts are made to temporarily divert the tensions for a time while people long for the old situation and hope for the better. This is only a short-term solution and offers no long-term prospects (static equilibrium).
♦ The organization renews itself. In times of need, innovators turn out to be present at unexpected places throughout the organization. They were not called on before but now form an undiscovered reservoir (redundancy) of ideas and initiatives for a new organizational set up. New mental models of the organization are developed and new management patterns are created. (In an out-of-balance situation, the organization evolves toward a new order/a new dynamic balance.)
♦ The organization dies. No room, time, or strength for renewal can be found and regression is the outcome. This is the most common association we have with chaos, probably because we can see no links between chaos and the possible seeds for renewal. However, this death is not always total. A "healthy" part of the

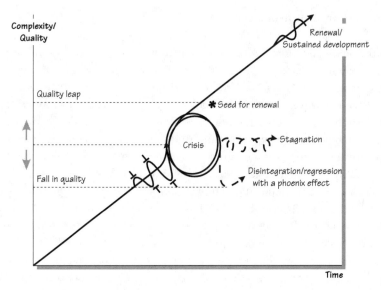

Figure 2.3 Autonomous Development (Zuijderhoudt)

organization can carry on; in a phoenix effect, a holon rises from the ashes. An example of this is the restart of DAF trucks as a viable small part of the previous, much larger organization (a Dutch company that made a wide range of vehicles).

Zuijderhoudt is not the only one to discuss life spans or life cycles of organizations. Greiner (1972) developed a similar model, although it had no link with chaos theory at that time. He argues that there is a specific set of crises that can be expected in the development of any organization. Each of these crises can lead organizations to downfall or renewal, but nothing in between. Others have later expanded on his model.

The following crises are often identified:

♦ A leadership crisis follows the growth after the birth of an organization. More than anything this growth was fueled by (the founder's) creativity. However, the informal communication, indirect management, and entrepreneurship of the founder are, after a certain time, insufficient. The seeds of renewal often lie hidden in more formal leadership.
♦ An autonomy crisis follows a period of growth through leadership and "proper" management. Formal structures, systems, and communication have put things in order and efficiency reigns. But the growth of the organization

has left middle management feeling restricted; they feel over-qualified for their jobs and want to take more initiative. The seeds of renewal often lie in delegating responsibilities.

♦ A management crisis follows a period of growth through delegation. The organization has felt the need to create more room for autonomy by means of decentralized units with far-reaching tasks and responsibilities. However, units that "run their own show" have since arisen, while the central board of directors practices "management by exception." The grasp on the organization's performance as a whole gets lost in the process, and recentralization is not acceptable. The seeds of renewal often lie in coordination.

♦ A bureaucracy crisis follows a period of growth through coordination. The top of the organization has introduced large-scale systems in order to improve coordination. There are new product/market groups while the technostructure and support staff do their best to glue all the organization's parts together. However, all the systems do not merely coordinate, they also choke the life out of the organization. Too much gets suffocated in procedures. The seeds of renewal lie in cooperation.

♦ A democratization crisis follows a period of growth through cooperation. Coordination via systems has been exchanged for coordination via interaction. Personal cooperation has done the job: Working in (multi-disciplinary) teams, bridging differences of opinion, and flexibly dealing with conflicts have taken preference over formal control. However, all this interaction and flexibility becomes too much for some. They have reached a mental saturation level and start experiencing the democracy as stressful. They ask themselves if they would not be more at home in a much smaller organization with lots of informal communication. And then everything starts all over again.

An attractive feature of theories on life cycles is that they can be regarded as putting the chaos theory, with all its ideas on fluctuations and crisis, into a historical, diachronic, perspective. An organization is not manufactured "here and now" but is, to a large extent, the product of its past. Crises are not accidents but are to-be-expected growing pains that are necessary for its further development, even though that does not make them controllable. It is not a matter of good and bad but of owning one's own history. Too many organizations are unaware of their own history and strive toward perfection—at least in our view. The assumption is still too often that the organization can be constructed as though it were a machine: You build it according to blueprints and the era or arena in which it must operate plays little role. Life cycle theorists, evidently given the chosen terminology, regard organizations as organisms that grow and perish and in between go through bouts of illness, pain, and recovery.

Organizations move throughout their lives between harmony and disharmony. When they die, often they bear within them the seeds of new life.

2.3.3 Structural Tension and Structural Conflicts

In 1996, Fritz wrote his book *Corporate Tides*, in which he explains "inescapable structural laws" that any organization is subject to. He states that organizations fall into two categories: They advance or they oscillate. That distinction depends on whether they take the structural laws into account in how they run their organizations. An organization that does, sees its actions crowned with success. An organization that doesn't, can undertake exactly the same actions—TQM, learning conferences, breaking down the hierarchy, information system, and so on—but it will not achieve lasting success. The structural laws are an often invisible, underlying pattern that drives an organization's performance. How does it work?

> "Every time we go through some major organizational change, our executive managers find 'tools' or methods to help. ABCM, reengineering, different process consultants bring in other methods—we implemented them, but then we find half way through the process the organization isn't taking them on. So then we abandon them, but later new tools are brought in. People are really up in the air about it all." (Fritz quoting Greenidge, a manager at BC Telecom)

Oscillation is a result of "structural conflict," people pursuing conflicting and competing goals. A posh term for this is *balance management,* and its characteristics can be found in the vision statements of many companies: It is a repository for all sorts of desirabilities but not for choices. Yet it is exactly by not making choices, by trying to please everyone, that you end up with oscillation. An example: An organization aims for both profit and expansion. First, the costs are cut, producing more profit, but then there is a reduction in growth, which is countered by more investment. As a result, the profits decrease and, once more, costs are cut. There are various types of this sort of structural conflict that bring organizations swaying from one measure to a juxtaposed one and then back again. For example:

♦ the organization wants to meet short-term demands ("quick fixes") but at the same time desires to strive toward long-term growth ambitions (the long haul)
♦ managers desire to control outcomes (centralized decision making) but, at the same time, management also wants to include and involve employees (delegation of decision making)
♦ there must be entrepreneurship (decision making) but, at the same time, risks should be avoided (avoid decisions)
♦ there should be growth (decentralization), but stability must be preserved (centralization)

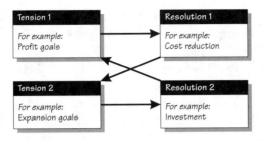

Figure 2.4 Structural Conflict

How can you recognize a structural conflict? In a structural conflict, actions that appear to be successful in themselves put the organization even more off balance: oscillation increases. In organizations that oscillate, success is neutralized.

Advancement works differently: There is structural tension but no structural conflict. The tension is between a desired state and the present reality. Conflict is absent, as there is only *one* desire or goal, not two (or more) competing ones. Some organizations are lucky enough to have a clear hierarchy of goals and can thus advance. Some have it only on paper and their oscillating behavior shows it to be fiction. There is only one way to stay clear of oscillation: Get to a situation where goals do not compete. This is not a cosmetic distinction. Sometimes this is achieved by a new overarching goal, more often by a (painful) choice to prioritize. Internet companies, for example, managed to stay out of oscillation several years back by putting growth before profit. It works if you are willing to pay the price. In structural tension the difference between goal and reality calls for action, action that is the logical consequence of structural tension. This time successful actions do not create oscillation, but bring the organization closer to its vision. Structural tension doesn't make life a breeze. For one, it can be confrontational to be honest about both reality ("This merger does not work") and goals ("We want a smaller company"). Second, actions might still fail, but if the desire is real and persistent, obstacles are there to teach lessons and failures show us what works and what doesn't. This is in contrast to structural conflicts where setbacks are often a reason to reassess efforts or to formulate new goals or visions.

Fritz states that these laws, certainly at the organization level, are often unknown or forgotten. The organization grows, but the forces that drive it often remain undetected. An organization that fails to recognize these forces, its driving "structure," will, he predicts, sooner or later end up oscillating.

2.3.4 Implications for Change Agents and Change Processes

All theories allied to chaos thinking emphasize diagnosis: recognizing the driving force and underlying patterns and giving them meaning. What drives this organization?

Why do things always end up the way they do? According to Zuijderhoudt, taking action without a full awareness of underlying patterns leads to fight-or-flight behavior. This statement is heartily confirmed by Fritz, who predicts that any reactive course of action leads to oscillation: The incentive to fix a problem diminishes with its success and thus makes the problem reemerge at a later date. The dominant analytical, diagnostic toolkit of change agents is, however, often insufficient to detect drivers and patterns. The reason is that it is used to diagnose rational, limited areas; it focuses on facts and objects, on the organization as a closed system, and on the current situation. The desired diagnosis would have a much broader focus: for example, also on the interpretations of those involved, on interaction between people, on relationships between objects, on the interchange between the organization and its environment, and on the organization's history. One of the most important principles is that the resulting insight into "why things are the way they are" must first be embraced, accepted, and acted upon. It is the same kind of process as in personal growth: Before you can move on to the next (life) phase, you have to take a hard look at your life up to this point, see it for what it is, and accept responsibility for it, however hard the facts may be. Crisis, from this point of view (compare a "midlife crisis"), is a warning that you can't carry on in the same old way. It is a call to reflect and to distance yourself from dysfunctional dreams and images. It is a time for a new start.

Another implication is that, on the basis of this insight, space must be created for new patterns. This usually requires breaking down barriers that block renewal and providing opportunities for new energy (ideas, initiatives, etc.) to manifest itself within the organization. It helps to challenge the drive and confidence of renewers; coaching and supportive leadership can further assist them to play the role of heralds and new heroes of a new organizational game. According to Zuijderhoudt and Loman, when an organization tries to achieve a dynamic balance in a turbulent and complex environment, still more is required: Raising individual self-confidence must go hand in hand with raising group consciousness. Typical interventions are examining the dominant mental maps, analyzing trends and scenarios, and applying dynamic system thinking. All this should preferably be done collectively in dialogue using team settings, networks, information rich environments, and by promoting diversity (in people, ideas, etc.). The aim is to somehow combine personal initiative and new perspectives with some kind of mutual commitment. This results in collective strategies, commitments, and choices.

Fritz is optimistic when it comes to crafting new patterns in an organization but emphasizes this final step before all others: Real heartfelt choices have to be made in term of a hierarchy of goals in order for there to be progress. This implies that common strategies have to be based on personal involvement and commitment instead of being socially desirable compromises. In this light, Loman emphasizes that any "new order" goes beyond compromising to actually reconciling apparent opposites. He mentions, among other things, the following dichotomies:

- internal and external focus: reconciling stability with super-pleasing target groups
- material and immaterial focus: reconciling matter-of-factness with experimentation and exploration
- business processes and mental processes: reconciling efficiency with innovation
- continuity and evolution: reconciling mutual adjustment with an optimal conflict level
- problem solving and reframing/breakthroughs: reconciling a drive for action with a drive for learning

2.4 Sociopolitical Mechanisms

Classic action theory introduces power and political processes as views on organizations (2.4.1). The informal organization may be stronger than the formal one and undermine it (2.4.2), and an unspoken economic exchange can be observed in groups and organizations (2.4.3). All three concern strong influencing mechanisms in the "invisible" world of the organization.

2.4.1 Action Theory and Power

Action theory (Parsons, 1977, 1978) argues that people have their own interests and goals and cannot help but pursue them. In order to achieve their goals and interests, they form coalitions and power blocks (see, e.g., Hanson, 1996; Cummings and Worley, 1993). Power is used as the instrument for meetings one's interests. The seeming irrationality of a situation may disappear if statements, actions, and interactions are analyzed by a change agent with an eye to the interests of members, departments, networks, or systems within the organization. This is when the action theory proves its worth: when the laws of the socio-political system come into action (see Hanson, 1996). Power is an important factor in organizations, it covers a much wider area than just the formal power of management, and can be a decisive factor in the start, the course, and the outcomes of change processes. The choice of whose definition of the environment is employed, including context and reason for change, is strongly influenced by who has the most power. The same applies to the definition of the content of the change, the appointment of an external consultant, and more. It can be extremely useful and insightful for a change agent to analyze the differences of opinion in a board of directors concerning an intended change program and to interlink this with how power and interests are distributed in the board.

Action theory argues that each individual or group tries to hold on or increase its influence This can be done in various ways: by behaving unpredictably; by concealing information or distorting it; by imposing rules for the game, or, on the contrary, simply ignoring them; by forming coalitions; or by blackening somebody's reputation.

Action theory sketches how individual interests and motives unavoidably lead to power blocks and conflicts. The organization as a uniform, cohesive system in no way fits into this picture.

The theory is highly relevant in professional organizations because there, by definition, power is widely distributed. Professionals possess informal power based on their knowledge, personalities, and contacts. Managers might draw on their own personality, but most of their power is generally derived from their formal hierarchic position. They are well-matched opponents, which means that conflicts flourish and victories are hard-won. An example of this is the way Dutch medical specialists have been able to voice their criticism of hospital management for many years. In the summer of 1997, the national organization of these specialists placed a full-page advertisement in the Dutch national dailies that was very illustrative. The ad's title parodied the health warning on cigarette packs and, underneath, in small letters, was added: "the new health bill forces us to be at the beck and call of the bookkeepers of hospitals and insurance companies. This development contravenes the principles of the Hippocratic oath and our medical ethics." The closing sentence in the advertisement was: "Our common sense does not allow us to comprehend present day hospital policies." We noticed that many hospital managers had an equally hard time making sense of medical specialists. In the dissension that results from interactions such as these, one of the parties is usually a victim, and in most cases it is the manager. Looking at the consulting assignments we have carried out over the years, it appears that a change of management takes place much more often in organizations of professionals and is often instigated by conflicts between management and professionals. However, power, and the processes aimed at obtaining and guarding power, play an important part in all organizations and provide an explanation for much apparent irrationality.

2.4.2 Informal Organizations

The Hawthorne studies brought about an important revolution in the school of thought about organizations (Mayo, 1933; Roethlisberger and Dickson, 1939). These experiments aroused interest in informal group processes and interpersonal relationships: "A happy worker is a productive worker." Roethlisberger and Dickson conclude:

> Many of the existing patterns of human interaction are nowhere to be found in the formal organization. . . . Too many people assume that the organization of a company is the same as a blueprint or an organization chart while, in fact, this is never the case.

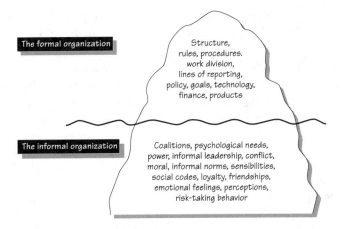

The formal organization

> Structure,
> rules, procedures.
> work division,
> lines of reporting,
> policy, goals, technology,
> finance, products

The informal organization

> Coalitions, psychological needs,
> power, informal leadership, conflict,
> moral, informal norms, sensibilities,
> social codes, loyalty, friendships,
> emotional feelings, perceptions,
> risk-taking behavior

Figure 2.5 Formal and Informal Organization

The informal organization can be seen as those processes and behavior that are not formally planned or anticipated but that occur spontaneously as a result of people's needs. People bring their hearts and minds to work, not just their hands.

The formal organization can be regarded as the tip of the iceberg. The informal characteristics of organizations form the huge hidden mass of the iceberg, out of sight but always present and often at least as influential. Figure 2.5 illustrates the characteristics.

There are always informal activities, and these activities appear to increase if the formal organization cannot or will not meet certain needs. It is as if a "shadow world" is formed that can both initiate and frustrate change. When the shadow world makes its presence felt, a bit more of the iceberg is revealed. Those involved often perceive this as an increase in informal activities, and because these activities are generally neither superficial nor temporary, they can cause quite a fright. Feelings, interests, loyalties, and other similarly difficult-to-control matters come out into the open. Managers start to wonder, "What else is going on?" and suspect that it is indeed only the tip of the iceberg that has become visible.

Informal activities can help to strengthen the formal organization. For instance, difficult decisions may have been "chewed over" in the corridors. A football tournament or a study trip can help a group of colleagues to get to know and trust one another, and the friendly atmosphere that ensues can do wonders to support much-needed cooperation in the office. However, informal activities can also hinder formal activities. A work-to-rule action by a group of secretaries can make it clear that they are no longer willing to tolerate the extra workload. Informal organization is neither good nor bad. Sometimes, opposition is a valuable warning: Change is necessary. If the warning is ignored, opposition can grow to destructive proportions, and then the informal organization no longer warns but undermines the formal one.

French and Bell (1984) sum up the characteristics of informal activities as the "culture of an organization": activities that better characterize the character of an organization than any set of formal activities. They claim that in many change processes these informal activities receive little or no attention during diagnosis and, because of this, what really matters is not taken into account in the change effort. Change processes then become more like a fancy lottery than a planned and professional endeavor.

2.4.3 Economic Exchange in Group Behavior

No social system can exist without a certain bond between the people that make up that system. A bond can be interpreted as the degree of mutual exchange within the group: members "give and take." For example, to be regarded as a group of friends, loyalty and trust have to be acknowledged and observed by all and concerns and support must be shared. If one party fails to live up to this, the group disintegrates. In that sense, "there is no such thing as a free lunch." Homans (1958) and Blau (1963) draw a parallel between exchange in social systems and in economic systems. In this view, social behavior in groups requires that people exchange immaterial goods such as prestige, signs of approval, information, or loyalty. Blau (1963) gives an example where the exchange process did not function properly between a group of law enforcement officers who required help and advice from their bosses or colleagues. The officers had the feeling that if they asked for advice too often, the boss might (start to) think they were incompetent and this would show up in their annual reviews. Neither did most officers want to consult with their colleagues: Not only would that keep the others from doing their own work, but the one asking would owe them a favor. These "favors" became the basis of the informal status differences in the group; the one who never asked advice was regarded as the top dog.

In this way, it would appear as if each member of a group has only a limited amount of "ready cash" to spend. If you have spent your cash and your reserves on favors, you can lose status and be banished from the group. You have to be sparse in asking for help: You cannot do something often without people forming a certain image of you as a result. A teacher can send one pupil out of the classroom without any problem, but if she does it too often, she gets a reputation as a poor disciplinarian. The principal can eventually even send pupils back to their teacher. However, if the teacher only rarely sends pupils to the principal's office, it is the pupils who get a bad reputation, not the teacher.

These exchange patterns have a great influence on the bonding and the disintegration of groups. They can vary greatly among various groups, even within one organization.

It is relevant to diagnose them: Suppose the change agent who has been brought in has little "ready cash" and has great difficulty in recruiting supporters. Or suppose that the aims of a change process are directed at learning together and supporting each other, although this puts pressure on existing relationships and upsets status differences: People will only pay lip service to the proposed changes.

2.4.4 Implications for Change Agents and Change Processes

All three theories emphasize the "invisible world": a world that can frustrate or help a change process. The first important implication for change agents is that this world deserves to be diagnosed, but that this need not necessarily be done in great detail: French and Bell (1984) demonstrate that the informal organization is difficult to recognize fully and that gaining knowledge of this world demands much more effort and perceptive ability than understanding its formal counterpart. The diagnosis must, however, be adequate enough to identify the major opposition and support mechanisms for the change involved. Concerning action theory, it is a question of identifying sources of power, formal and informal leadership, interests, and coalitions (see also 6.12). In the informal organization, the culture aspects as shown in 2.4.2 apply. With an economic exchange it is a matter of recognizing the unwritten rules of exchange that either strengthen or weaken the positions of the individuals in a group.

A second implication concerns the use of these insights during the change process. Change agents will have to use their insights concerning power relations and positions when assigning roles in the change process. If power plays a dominant role in the organization, they would do well to involve the most influential players in crucial decision-making processes, or to entice influential opponents into taking responsibility as champions of important parts of the change process or instead exclude them altogether from the process, and so on. The intention of the change agents in these kinds of organizations is to ensure that there is a sufficient power-base behind the intended change. If this is not the case, they had better pack it in right away.

Change agents can approach the informal organization in two ways. They can stimulate and even initiate informal activities in support of the formal process. A weekly office cocktail hour might serve to test new ideas or sow the seeds of controversial initiatives. A night with self-made sketches where colleagues poke harmless fun at the organization's sacred cows and each other's behavior can allow everyone to let off steam so that a fresher start can be made at the strategic conference the next morning. They can also try to open discussions about dysfunctional informal activities by highlighting the goings-on of the invisible world and challenging their legitimacy. This intervention can correspond to creating a tighter coupling of opinions and behavior (2.1.2): The tensions between the formal organization (intentions) and the informal real-life practice (behavior) are then exposed out in the open. These are serious interventions that become necessary if the two worlds have grown miles apart and the taboo about discussing it has corrupted the organization.

Two similar options are available to change agents when it comes to economic relationships in an organization. They can design a change process in such a way that everyone benefits in some way or another. They can include extra exchange mechanisms as motivating factors, while aligning these motivators with the organization's mores and thus reinforcing these mores. Here too, however, the mores can sometimes be a dysfunctional and destructive force. In that case, a change agent can decide to open discussions about existing mores and arrangements within the organization, specifically the unwanted side effects they have on the organization.

2.5 Four Clusters of Theories About Irrationalities

We consider the theories that we have outlined applicable and relevant irrespective of the nature of an organization or of the change process. The degree to which this is the case can of course vary considerably. In some situations you may encounter much pocket veto, or there may be a power struggle going on. The management may be extremely bureaucratic and have little respect for the workers; many garbage cans might be filled during meetings. The informal organization might be at odds with the formal organization, or, conversely, none of these situations needs to occur. What a change agent needs to do is to gain a good understanding of theories and images such as these and to make use of them when diagnosing and planning a suitable approach to change.

What the theories we have outlined have in common is that they demonstrate why change is complicated. They emphasize the irrationality of change processes or, put more precisely, they emphasize the existence of other sorts of rationality that we might not be aware of, or familiar with in organizational life. We find this function important. The theories make us think twice about the one-sidedness of how we talk with our colleagues and clients about change.

In our opinion, the dominant way of talking about change is captured in the terms *planning* and *contingency approaches*. Both assume the rationality of change processes as if new organizational states can be predictably "constructed." A stereotypical example is as follows: A change agent diagnoses the current situation (IST situation) in an organization and defines what it should become (SOLL situation). To do this, she often uses a checklist, for example, of organizational aspects: strategy, structure, systems, management style, culture, and personnel. The contingency approach appears in the principle that all these aspects are considered to be in a balanced and coherent relationship to one another depending on the kind of business and business environment the organization is in. Because of this, it is thought that in change processes you can't change one without the other: If one aspect needs to be changed, a change in the other aspects will be required. The planning approach comes in where a change process is considered to consist of placing on a time axis with neat decision moments all the activities that convert, step-by-step, at the same time, all the differences between the present (IST) and the future (SOLL).

This stereotype is tempting, partly due to its neatness and suggestion of the controllability and simplicity of change processes, a desire that we recognize in ourselves as well. The theories in this chapter can be regarded as falsifications or disruptions of this stereotype: explanations of why a predictable systematic route from present to future does not (always) work. A change agent or manager can read this as bad news: There are obstacles, there is resistance. It is as if dark powers are causing disarray from a shadowy, invisible world; as if weeds and roots are causing cracks to appear in the asphalt and making the road difficult to travel.

Still, this is but one side of the metaphor. In the same way that chaos is order which is not yet understood, and irrationality is a way of thinking that is not understood, each of the theories offered here also denotes positive forces; all is not negative. Resistance can also be the guardian of stability or an initiative for a different future. Ambiguities in organizations also create space for minority views and experiments. The pocket veto can help staff to survive bad management or even to achieve fantastic results in their own domain, individually or together with valued colleagues. Turning the metaphor around, it is not so much the weeds that attack the asphalt but the forces of nature that cannot be denied. Life always finds a way.

Figure 2.6 shows the four clusters of theories represented as four plant species interfering with the change process. These plants sprout through to the surface from the invisible world, spice up organizations, and make life interesting for change agents.

The theories give change agents food for thought and alternative viewpoints to observe and interpret organizations. The theories provide indications for how to adapt change processes to make them more effective. For instance, the very existence of loosely coupled systems implies the importance of transparency, providing feedback, and learning to understand one's own behavior in a group setting. Such adaptations breathe new life into the change. Managing autonomous staff implies, among other things, the importance of limiting domains and providing negotiation platforms where the struggle among professionals and their collective struggle with their managers to defend their own interests can be made productive. Chaos thinking implies, among other things, the importance of discovering the driving forces behind an organization and giving them meaning, creating space for emerging champions who have a commitment to one another and to the (controversial) changes and, by so doing, create a

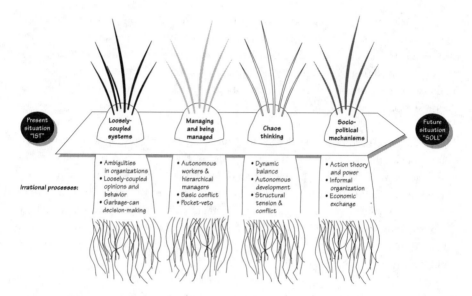

Figure 2.6 Four Clusters of Theories About Irrationalities

new order. Socio-political mechanisms imply, among other things, making good use of sources of power to organize informal activities and optimizing nonformalized barter.

We are of the opinion that contingency and planned approaches can work, but we feel just as strongly that the four clusters of theories indicate that, sometimes, it is necessary to plan and implement additional interventions. There are also situations where additions won't do and a totally different approach will be required. We have tried to find a spectrum of approaches that can stand up to the practice of changing organizations, views that do not nullify each other, but that can exist alongside one another. The following chapter contains explorations of these views.

3 Thinking About Change in Five Different Colors

The word *change* can be characterized as a container concept. A search for the underlying values of the word results in a whole range of meanings. For example, the word change is used to describe the desired outcome (the aim, product, result, effect): what is finished, what has been realized or achieved. This is seen in such phrases as: "This change is obvious," "The building is greatly changed," "Pete has changed a lot." But, the word change is also used for the process (plan of approach, working method, route, activities); the transition from one situation to another: the change process. This can be seen in such phrases as, "The change is still in progress," "We are in the process of changing the building," "Pete is changing."

The above distinction is generally common knowledge. We are used to distinguishing between the outcome and the process of change.

In addition, there is a world of difference between the underlying assumptions of the various strategies or approaches that are applied to change. As a result, the practical applications of these various strategies or approaches vary widely. Conceptual clarity therefore, is desired to better express the various meanings of the word change. There have been numerous attempts to do this (see section 3.1), but there is, in our opinion, room for improvement (see sections 3.2 and 3.3).

Such clarity is useful for the following reasons:

1. It facilitates clearer communication between the people involved. For example, communication between managers, between consultants, between academics, and across these groups. In particular, the returns are to be found at the level of common interpretations and meanings. It creates, as it were, a new shorthand language for a complex subject matter (see, among others, de Caluwé, 1997).

As change is generally a collective effort, this is a real necessity: Our professional language has become so "contaminated" that the same words are used to refer to very different concepts and meanings. *Projects, self-steering,* and *entrepreneurship* are but a few examples of words that are interpreted differently by different people (see Appendix 1).

2. It quickly makes clear for the people who are familiar with the concepts and terms what others' assumptions or paradigms are when they talk about desired changes or the change approach. Beyond that, it could be used to characterize dominant paradigms in groups or organizations as a whole. In short, it could serve as a diagnostic tool.

3. It provides situational characteristics for the selection and the application of a specific approach to change. In other words, given a certain situation, a more fitting and more considered approach to change can be designed and/or implemented.

4. It offers change agents a tool for reflection: What are your own assumptions? What is your (key) competence for bringing about change and what are your limits?

The chapter consists of the following parts:

In section 3.1, some known and accepted overviews of approaches to change are outlined. In section 3.2, we distinguish between five meanings of the word *change*. Colors are given to these meanings (yellow, blue, red, green, and white). Each meaning is coupled to five underlying views of change in terms of, "People/things change, if . . ."

In the following section (3.3), a link is made between each type of color-print thinking and existing literature and schools of thought.

In section 3.4, the colors are applied to some simple examples, and in section 3.5 the ideals and pitfalls for each color are summed up.

The possibilities of more colors and paradigms are discussed in section 3.6. In section 3.7, five different change approaches (one for each color) are given for the same real life case: Joseph and Joanne.

3.1 Change Strategies and Approaches

The best-known strategies are those of Bennis, Benne, and Chin (1979/1985). They distinguish three main strategies for change:

♦   Power-coercive strategies: Change is forced through from a (legitimate) position of power. Here, the change is generally enforced from the top down, and it is assumed that the presence of power and the threat of sanctions are necessary in order to assure the desired behavior.

♦   Empirical-rational strategies: Change is based on the assumption that employees are rational human beings and are guided by rational considerations and insights. Thus change is often based on expert analysis, rational planning, and factual communication.

♦   Normative-Reeducative strategies: These aim at supporting and stimulating people to generate change themselves. This is a more bottom-up approach. The belief is that people are intrinsically active and willing to learn.

Boonstra (1992, pp. 72-74) adds a fourth strategy that he takes from Mastenbroek (1986) and Zaltman (1987):

♦   Barter: People do their own cost-benefit analysis, work out how changes might hurt or serve them, and base their actions on that. When enough incentives are put into place, change will happen.

Marx (1994) distinguishes four approaches to change that correspond to some extent with the above:

♦   the deployment of expertise: in which knowledge is supplied by experts and acquired and applied by others
♦   the use of procedures: in which a change is set in motion by means of an agreed-upon set of rules (e.g., a working party prepares a proposal)
♦   the influencing of cultural elements in the organization: in which organizational development (OD) plays a central role
♦   the exercise of power: in which changes are enforced from the top down

Van der Zee (1995) also distinguishes four approaches that have a great deal in common with those mentioned above:

♦   The diffusion approach distinguishes between the development of the solution by a small (expert) group and making it available to a wide circle ("selling the idea")
♦   In the directive approach, the change agent defines a concrete end product and uses all means at his disposal to achieve it. Here, there is strict control on the basis of formal authority and power.
♦   The interactive approach has an open-ended character. Those involved give their own interpretation to change initiatives. Thus, there will be multiple solutions side by side. *Horizontal communication* and *mutual adaptation* are key words.
♦   The development-oriented approach is aimed at strengthening competencies. Change comes from within. People are assumed to be eager to tackle the problem themselves. It is focused on meta-cognitive qualities (learning to learn).

This section contains a modest literature overview. There are strong similarities and overlaps in the descriptions. For example, they differ in that one author places more emphasis on the underlying worldview of change strategies, while another describes the degree to which the change is "planned" or the role of the change agent. In this chapter we attempt to integrate these descriptions into five ways of thinking about change. This is explained using a couple of simple examples first.

3.2 Five Meanings of the Word *Change*

In just a couple of sentences, we want to make clear the five distinct meanings that the word *change* can have. The five ways of thinking differ in the assumptions that they make about why and how people or things change. This is illustrated and clarified in Table 3.1. Each way of thinking is labeled with a color. This simplifies the naming of the concept (which is further expanded on later). A certain degree of logic is attached to the choice of the colors, which is also indicated below.

a. "We are changing the policy"

   "Individual interests have been transformed into group interests."

   "The goal has been changed because of pressure from Pete."

Yellow-print thinking assumes that people change their standpoints only if their own interests are taken into account, or if you can compel them to accept certain ideas. Combining ideas or points of view and forming coalitions or power blocks are favored methods in this type of change process. Change is seen as a power game or negotiation exercise aimed at feasible solutions. This way of thinking fits smoothly into change processes where complex goals or effects must be achieved and in which many people or parties are involved in mutually interdependent ways.

We call this way of thinking "yellow-print thinking." Yellow is the color of power (e.g., symbols like the sun, fire) and of the type of process ("brooding and coalition formation around a fire").

b. "The building has been changed."

   "The production line has been changed to meet the specifications."

   "The information system has undergone radical change."

In blue-print thinking it is assumed that people or things will change if a clearly specified result is laid down beforehand. All steps are planned down to the last detail. Control over the result, as well as the path to be taken, is kept well under check. Project management is an example of this way of thinking. It is a favored approach in change processes where the result and the path can be well defined and predicted.

Change is considered to be a rational process aimed at the best possible solution.

We call this way of thinking "blue-print thinking." A blueprint is the (architectural) design or plan that is drawn up beforehand and guarantees the actual outcome.

c. "I change the organization."

"The stimuli for talent development have changed."

"We have changed our way of rewarding and disciplining personnel."

Change in this way of thinking is accomplished by stimulating people, by making things appealing to do. In this way of thinking, it is important to stimulate people and to inspire them, to seduce them into acting as desired. Red-print thinking assumes that people and organizations will change if the right HRM (Human Resource Management) tools are employed and used correctly. In other words, people change their behavior if they are rewarded (salary, promotion, bonus, a good evaluation) or "penalized" (demotion, poor evaluation).

Thus a key concept is barter: The organization hands out rewards and facilities in exchange for personnel taking on responsibilities and trying their best. On top of this, however, management's care and attention are also important. The aim is a good "fit" between what individuals want and what the organization needs.

The color chosen here refers to the color of human blood. The human being must be influenced, tempted, seduced, and stimulated.

d. "I am changing Pete."

"We have learned a lot, and as a result a lot has changed."

"Change equals learning."

In green-print thinking, the terms *change* and *learning* have very similar meanings. People change if they learn. People are motivated to discover the limits of their competences and to involve themselves in learning situations. They are provided with means of learning more effective ways of acting.

The aim is to strengthen the learning abilities of the individual and the learning within the organization. If people learn collectively, the organization learns and as a result change takes place.

The color green is chosen because the objective is to get people's ideas to work (with their motivation and learning capacity), giving them a "green light." But it also refers to "growth," as in nature.

e. "Pete is changing."

"This change is filled with meaning."

"Everything is continually changing."

In white-print thinking, the dominant image is that everything is changing autonomously, of its own accord. Panta rhei: Everything is in motion. Where there is energy, things change. When this is the case, "the time is ripe." Complexity is regarded as the enriching nature of things, not as disruptive chaos. Influencing the dynamics is a favorite approach. White-print thinking assumes that failure results where we think we can direct and manage change. It is more about understanding where opportunities lie and searching for the seeds of renewal and creativity. Sense-making plays an important role in this, as does removing obstacles and explicitly relying on the strength and soul of people. External stimuli are deemed of lesser importance.

The color white reflects all colors. But more important, white denotes openness: it allows room for self-organization and evolution. The outcome remains somewhat of a surprise.

The colors are basic colors plus their "sum": white.[1] The word *print* denotes the endeavors of change agents to work more or less according to some preconceived plan (compare "planned change"), even if they consciously allow everything to run its own course, so to speak. In a certain sense, you will want to be able to forecast something about how the change is going to work out. Change agents want to maintain a causal relationship between their actions and the outcomes of the change, however different the managing and planning might look in each of the colors. We examine this more thoroughly in the following sections.

3.3 Five Ways of Thinking About Change in More Detail

In this section, each way of thinking is elaborated. We try to describe its essence, referring to existing literature. The type of change process is also described. At the end of this section a diagram is presented (see Table 3.2) in which many aspects of the change process in relation to the colors are distinguished.

3.3.1 Yellow-Print Thinking

Yellow-print thinking is based on socio-political concepts about organizations in which interests, conflicts, and power play important roles (see, among others, Morgan, 1986; Greiner and Schein, 1988; Hanson, 1996; Pfeffer, 1981).

Yellow-print thinking assumes that getting everyone on the same wavelength is a change in itself. Policy making or producing a program for action requires getting the powers that be behind it, be it power based on formal position or on informal

	Things/People Will Change If You . . .
Yellow-print	— can unite the interests of the important players — can compel people to accept (common) points of view/opinions — can create win-win situations/can form coalitions — demonstrate the advantages of certain ideas (in terms of power, status, influence) — get everyone on the same wavelength — can bring people into a negotiating process
Blue-print	— formulate a clear result/goal beforehand — lay down a concrete plan with clear steps from A to B — monitor the steps well and adjust accordingly — keep everything as stable and controlled as possible — can reduce complexity as much as possible
Red-print	— stimulate people in the right way, for example, by inducements (or penalties) — employ advanced HRM tools for rewards, motivation, promotions, status — give people something in return for what they give the organization (barter) — manage expectations and create a good atmosphere — make things attractive for people
Green-print	— make people aware of new insights/own shortcomings — are able to motivate people to see new things/to learn/to be capable of . . . — are able to create suitable (collective) learning situations — allow the learning process to be owned by the people involved and geared toward their own learning goals
White-print	— start from people's drives, strengths, and "natural inclinations" — add meaning to what people are going through — are able to diagnose complexity and understand its dynamics — give free rein to people's energy and remove possible obstacles — make use of symbols and rituals

Table 3.1 Assumptions Underlying the Five Ways of Thinking

influence. It is thought that resistance and failure are inevitable if you do not get all or at least the most important players on board. This happens through the gathering of interests, creating a power base, and then solving contradictions or conflicts through negotiation.

Carrying out the policy or program to successful implementation demands the careful holding together of these interests by the change agent, maneuvering in a (possibly shifting) balance of power, resolving conflicts, and so on.

Setting goals, determining policies, and formulating programs is done by creating (political) support, by gathering together interests, by proposing win-win situations, and by political games, power plays, and negotiating tactics. Sticking to and realizing the outcome of these processes (in terms of goals, the policies, or programs) is a huge task because the socio-political context stays dynamic).

The "management" of the process of policy formation and of sustaining commitments demands certain political skills of the change agents as well as the ability to operate in a complex area of interests. Facilitating communication, lobbying, negotiating, and third-party conflict resolution are much-used interventions.

The change process can be employed within an organization or between organizations.

Type of change process

The result of change is difficult to predict because it depends on the distribution and shifts in standpoints and influence of the most important players. What is more, for a change agent the process is difficult to structure and plan. The creation of a "negotiating arena" in which the interested parties are represented is a means that is often used, as is an independent authority or body as facilitator. Specific rules of the game can be agreed on. Consulting with their power bases, the interests of all representatives need to be carefully built in during the negotiation process.

The foremost consideration of the yellow-print change agent is: Always bear in mind the conglomeration of interests, parties, and players.

3.3.2 Blue-Print Thinking

Blue-print thinking is based on the rational design and implementation of change (see, among others, Kluytmans, 1994; Hammer and Champy, 1993). Project-oriented working is a striking example of this (see, among others, Wijnen, 1988; Kor and Wijnen, 1999). Scientific Management (Taylor, 1913) is a classic example.

The theory behind blue-print thinking is to carefully describe and define the outcome or the result beforehand. The activities needed to achieve the result are planned according to rational arguments and expertise. There is continuous monitoring based on predetermined indicators to check whether the activities are leading to the desired result as planned. If not, adjustments are made to achieve that which has been agreed upon within the frameworks of time, money, quality, information, and organization.

The process and the result are, more or less, independent of people. Controlling (managing, planning, and monitoring progress) the change is considered feasible. Management is able to compel and effect the change.

Type of change process
The blue-print change process can be relatively short, at least in comparison with other ways of thinking.

It is feasible to determine rationally and ahead of time when the change will be completed. The subject of the change (the client or project leader) and its object (the ones who undergo the change) are often different people or entities. The approach is rational (planning) and empirical (indicators). Think first (define and design) and then do (implement) is the maxim. Thinking and doing are sequential.

The foremost considerations of the blue-print changer are these: Plan and organize first; use all possible expertise and don't let people's individual ideas and preferences interfere; and never lose sight of the intended result.

3.3.3 Red-Print Thinking

Red-print thinking has its roots in the classic Hawthorn experiments (see Mayo, 1933; Roethlisberger, 1941). McGregor (1960) developed the tradition further. In recent years, Human Resources Management (HRM) has been a much-discussed subject (see, among others, Paauwe, 1995; Fruytier and Paauwe, 1996; Schoemaker, 1994).

The intention of the red-print changer is to change the soft aspects of an organization, such as management style, competencies, cooperation.

The red-print school of thought contends that people change as a result of the deployment and adequate use of a set of HRM tools such as rewards, appraisals, career paths, structures, assessments, recruitments, out-placements, and promotions. It has to do with the development of competencies, of talents, and of getting the best out of people—an optimal synergy between the organization and its employees. People will do something or change if they get something back (the "barter" principle).

The outcome of the change (the result) can, according to red-print thinking, be thought out beforehand, but it cannot be fully guaranteed because it is dependent on the response of the "victims"; the desired outcome might change somewhat as a result. Monitoring takes place, but, for both ethical and political reasons, there is a limit to how forcefully it can be adjusted along the way. Compelling change is possible to only a limited extent for the same reasons.

Type of change process

The red-print change process takes time. The subjects, the change agents, and the objects, those who are supposed to change, are different people but they do frequently interact. On the basis of intermediate results, the change agent can adjust the desired result. Management motivates and puts forward arguments for the change. They get up on a soapbox, give speeches, and seduce people into embarking on a change made attractive. The HRM instruments try to make concrete what the desired behavior is thought to be and add incentives and penalties to entice people to act accordingly.

The foremost consideration of the red-print change agent: The human factor plays an important role. People make changes happen if you guide them in the right direction and reward them for changing.

3.3.4 Green-Print Thinking

Green-print thinking has its roots in action-learning theories (see, among others, Kolb, Rubbin, & Osland, 1991; Argyris & Schön, 1978). It has been expanded enormously in the more recent thinking on "learning organizations" (Senge, 1990; Swieringa & Wierdsma, 1990). Changing and learning are conceptually closely linked (see, among others, de Caluwé, 1997).

The outcome of green-print change is difficult to predict in this way of thinking because it depends, to a large degree, on the extent and the nature of what people learn, and this, in turn, depends on both their learning ability and the effectiveness of the learning environment itself. The process is characterized by setting up learning situations—preferably collective ones as these allow people to give and receive feedback as well as to experiment with more effective ways of acting. Change takes place as a result of people and organizations learning continuously. Monitoring is not meant to adjust the change in the direction of some predetermined outcome, but just for planning a follow-up that is in line with what the people involved regard as the most relevant learning goals. Compelling change is deemed counterproductive; green-print thinking is much more concerned with allowing and supporting people to take ownership of their learning.

Type of change process

The change process takes time: you can't force learning. It is a fluctuating process of learning and unlearning, trial and error. Subject (change agent) and object (change victims) can be different people, but there is a great deal of interaction between them. They can even switch roles; the change agent is also always learning.

The management of the change is very limited in a directive sense. Motivating, facilitating feedback, supporting experimenting with new behavior, structuring communication, setting up interactions, giving meaning, and learning, in the broadest sense of the word, are much-used interventions. Thinking and doing are tightly coupled, not sequential (as it is in blue-print thinking).

The foremost consideration of the change agent is this: Motivate people to learn with each other and from each other in order to establish continuous learning in collective settings.

3.3.5 White-Print Thinking

White-print thinking arose as a reaction to the deterministic, mechanistic, and linear worldview derived from Newton and Descartes. It is nourished by chaos thinking, network theory, and complexity theory (see section 2.3), all of which are based on living and complex systems with limited predictability (see, among others, Capra, 1996; Bateson, 1984). Self-organization is a core concept. Stacey (1996) defines self-organization as, "The process by which people interact with one another within a system, according to their own codes of behavior, without there being an overall picture that makes clear what has to be done or how it is to be done." The self-organization process encompasses the emergence of new structures and behavioral patterns through developmental, learning, and evolutionary processes. The system finds its own optimal dynamic balance (see, among others, Bicker Caarten, 1998).

In the white-print way of thinking, change is autonomous. "Panta rhei: everything is in motion"; "The route is the refuge"; and Morgan's flux metaphor (1986) are all expressions of this view. People and organizations are in a constant state of change. The inner desires and strengths of people, both individually and as groups, are the decisive factors. Outside influence, whether from a change agent or a manager, can be of only limited effect and then only if the ones who are changing welcome it.

Type of change process

The concept of planned change is somewhat at odds with white-print thinking; planning, controlling, and managing the change are, to a great extent, irrelevant notions. Resistance is also an irrelevant concept.

Aspects of the Change Process / Prints	Yellow Print	Blue Print
Firmness of result/outcome	Describing and defining outcomes is a complicated game of power politics. So is achieving them. Outcomes can be adjusted during the process.	The result is determined beforehand. It is carefully defined and achieving it can be guaranteed.
Result/outcome is dependent on . . .	Developments in the environment, changing opinions and positions of the players and of the progress and agreements made so far.	Proper and integrated phasing, managing, and decision making. Responsibilities are clearly defined.
The results/outcome can be measured by. . .	The convergence of positions. The creation of and support for overarching goals. Maintaining support for the goals and the investments in achieving them.	The output in terms of concrete results. The management aspects (time, money, quality, organization, information).
How to achieve the change/What approach to take	Intuition as well as rationality are used. Discrepancies between what people desire and the status quo lead them to take particular stances and utilize their power. Combining positions creates sufficient force to fuel activities and affect something. Power politics play an important role.	It is a rational approach. Results (with margins) are deduced from goals. The expertise of the project team creates progress. Decision moments are crucial in keeping things on track.

Table 3.2 The Five Colors and Aspects of the Change Process

Red Print	Green Print	White Print
It can be premeditated but cannot be guaranteed, because people have to (be enticed to) join the effort.	It can be premeditated but cannot be guaranteed. The outcomes can be defined clearer as people gain insights.	It is almost impossible and not deemed relevant to forecast. The purpose resides in the process itself.
The fit between the goals of the organization and the goals of the people. People's (extrinsic) motivation for the change effort plays an important role.	The learning ability of individuals and (possibly large) groups. People's motivation to learn and the degree of openness between them.	What people truly want and long for, their creativity and their degree of self-organization. Taking coincidence seriously: "fate" and "luck" frequently lend a hand.
Changes in behavior, in the atmosphere, in the organization's climate, and in people's loyalty and pride. The degree of job satisfaction and the sense of well-being.	Changes in behavior, especially changes in the learning capacity of individuals and the organization. The motivation to learn and the speed of development.	Evolution. The emergence of other ways of working and understanding. The ability to handle paradoxes and to adapt. The forming of (personal) networks.
Rational process, but intuition may also play a role. A good choice of (HRM-)tools is essential. The attention and carefulness with which these tools are used is what makes them truly effective.	Both a rational and an intuitive process. Methods and settings for organization development and for learning are selected, especially on a group level. Facilitating a feeling of ownership among the people involved is a crucial aspect.	Rationality supports intuition. The dynamics within the organization and in context of its environment are studied and made sense of. This should lead to the discernment of underlying patterns. Subsequently, influencing these patterns is attempted to get things moving and to remove obstacles.

Prints Aspects of the Change Process	Yellow Print	Blue Print	
Typical approach (examples)	(Re-)negotiating, creating win-win situations. Forcing people to reconsider their opinions. Involving the context. For example: – conclave methods – political arenas – forming coalitions	Using research and creating detailed plans. Using benchmarks. Monitoring any progress with the aid of preset standards and systematically making the adjustments required. For example: – analysis, e.g., of markets, strategy, or systems – project management – (re)design of structures or business processes	
Manageability of the process	Moderate. It can be improved by adjusting goals or increasing efforts. The context must also often be managed.	Extensive. It is possible to adjust either the management aspects or the result (within the agreed-upon margins).	
Typical players/actors	There is often a complex field of interests. Usually one party/player takes the initiative. There can be different units or layers in the organization playing a role, but the environment (market forces, interest groups, academia, media, etc.) may exert influence too.	Manager or management team is the initiating party. There is a project leader and a project team.	

Table 3.2 (continued)

Red Print	Green Print	White Print
Developing and using HRM methods. Employing talent management (job redesign, staffing, rewards, careers, recognition, etc.). Furthering a motivating and careful management style. Talent management style. For example: – appraisal, rewards, recognition – workforce diversity, career paths – job design, task enrichment – social activities, soapbox speeches	Creation of learning situations, feedback, and facilitating learning cycle (preferably double-loop learning). Making people conscious of their incompetencies. For example: – organization development methods – gaming, team building, clinics – participative planning, quality circles – coaching, intervision	Create space, catalyze, autopoeisis, feed-forward, pattern recognition. For example: – self-steering teams, network organizations – search conferences, open-space meetings – personal growth, empowerment
Moderate. Other HRM tools can be selected or more carefully employed. Also the human resources themselves can be replaced or supplemented.	Moderate. Other learning methods can be chosen or the current ones intensified or made to enforce each other. Also, other target groups can be included.	Minimal, only by facilitating the process differently. Different perspectives can be shown, confrontations can be arranged, "feed forward" used.
Manager or management team takes the initiative. There are champions, implementers, trendsetters, change "objects" (sometimes also "victims").	Manager or management team sponsors the initiative. They often also take the initiative but this need not be the case. There are facilitators, organizers, participants (also "change objects").	All those who want to. Initiative can come from different sources, as can sponsoring and champions. It is generally not clear who all these people are. Subject and object often coincide.

Aspects of the Change Process \ Prints	Yellow Print	Blue Print	
Characteristics of working domain	Often shapes policies in companies or politics. It can also enforce or execute policies when the context is very dynamic. Complex, sensitive to new events or sudden developments, difficult to structure	Focus is on concrete implementation. Well demarcated and concrete subjects that can easily be controlled. Flexibility decreases as the change progresses. Risks can be reasonably analyzed in advance.	
How can progress be safeguarded? How is the change anchored in the organization? (examples)	Policy documents. (New) balance of power.	ISO-like systems. Decision documents.	
Guiding notion for the change agent	– mobilize sponsorship/support – exchange opinions and interests – agree on rules of the game and players	– clear assignment, clear tasks – achieve results within the planning – control relevant parameters	

Table 3.2 (continued)

It is assumed that no one can stop change from happening; it can only be aided or hindered. The opportunities to exert influence lie mainly in helping to clear obstacles and in challenging people, calling on their strengths and self-confidence. These opportunities in the relationship between the change agent and others are often spotted by these others rather than constructed by the change agent. They can request help, support, or coaching from the change agent and from each other. In a way, white-print change agents catalyze the emergence of more white-print change agents.

The foremost consideration of the white-print change agent is: Observe what is making things happen and change; supply meanings and perspectives, remove

Red Print	Green Print	White Print
Strongly focused on implementation through people. It aims at measures that allow for optimal job satisfaction and performance. Difficult to control because it depends on the ability to motivate people.	Focuses strongly on implementation with people. It concerns learning as vehicle for change. Learning goals may vary among people, and goals may change as a result of learning. The process is difficult to control as it depends on individual and collective learning capabilities.	Focus is on complex, often nonlinear, situations, where there seems to be a low system rationality. Multi- and meta-paradigmatic approaches that show order in/next to chaos. It is hard to control, as it seeks out experiments, creative ways, dynamics. Taoistic.
HRM systems and their adequate use.	Permanently learning organization.	Self-organization. Self-management.
– seduce and motivate people – appeal to people and reward their contributions – offer a good work atmosphere	– facilitate learning and communication – closely link actions and thoughts – develop and grow	– release and let go – remove obstacles – discover meanings

obstacles, get initiatives and explorations going, and empower people while giving them sufficient free rein. The belief that "crisis provides opportunity" applies here.

(Note: The above does NOT equal doing nothing or laissez faire. On the contrary; it demands in-depth observation, analysis of underlying drivers, and often confronting interventions. Change agents must be capable of making sense out of complexity, often looking at historical patterns and psychological mechanisms. They will require quite a few theories about irrationalities in organizations and strong powers of observation to allow them to do so).

3.4 Some Examples

A couple of simple examples will serve to illustrate how the colors can be applied. With these examples we try to show just how relevant it can be to understand the underlying concepts and ideas—the colors—behind someone's words in order to better understand each other and better design change processes together.

The example in Table 3.3 shows how someone (like a change agent) would be inclined to deal with the furniture setting in a room and what his motive would be. Many examples could be added to these; we mention just a few in Table 3.4.

These examples indicate, even though they are just simple exercises, how great the differences can be between the colors when it comes to aim/outcome, the change process, and the tools used. The role and the actions of the change agent are likewise different (see also Chapter 8).

3.5 Ideals and Pitfalls

Each color has its own ideals; that is, what change agents dream of for the long run. But each color also has its pitfalls: situations or conditions when the approach is no longer effective or even becomes counterproductive.

In yellow-print thinking, the *ideal* is that people focus on common interests and strive toward collective goals. The ideal is that people want and are able to weigh different interests and achieve common ground. In a way it is a very democratic ideal. *Pitfalls* include lose-lose situations like destructive power struggles. Building castles in the air (allowing a "false" consensus) is another pitfall, severing the link between the goals, means, and efforts.

The *ideal* in blue-print thinking is that the future is in our hands and we can construct it. Everything is possible and controllable and can be achieved by rational planning. The *pitfall* is to steamroller over people and their feelings and thus create resistance rather than commitment. This can be aggravated by the inclination to pay insufficient attention to "irrational" aspects. Impatience is another pitfall: not granting others sufficient time to come on board.

The *ideal* in red-print thinking is searching for the optimal "fit" between people and "hardware," between the goals of the organization and those of the individual. It strives to make organizations "more beautiful" and to inspire and care for those who work there. The *pitfall can* lie in the lack of concrete outcomes by "sparing the rod" and avoiding conflicts. Red-print thinkers can be addicted to maintaining a good atmosphere. Also, HR systems can smother brilliant staff members, as these never fit

	By buying (certain) tables and placing them in a specific way, the aim is to . . .

Yellow-print thinking	Only one round table
	    – so people can sit around it together
	    – talk with each other on equal footing and negotiate
	    – reach joint policy decisions and agree to carry
	      them out
	NOTE: Many management boards and political bodies have such round tables (e.g., the UN).

Blue-print thinking	Several tables
	    – arranged so that people can work undisturbed
	    – constructed of simple materials, easy to clean
	    – to enable people to work efficiently (good surface,
	      correct height)
	    – arranged so activities can best be passed from one table
	      to the next
	NOTE: The layout of a fast food restaurant or a printing office.

Red-print thinking	A variety of tables
	    – constructed of pleasant, attractive, and warm materials
	    – arranged so people can create their own comfortable
	      environment
	    – that help and motivate people to perform well
	NOTE: Some concepts of the "office of the future" (a sympathetic, pleasant environment) have these characteristics

Green-print thinking	Tables arranged to enhance open communication
	    between people
	    – so you can effectively exchange ideas and offer help
	    – to allow learning from one another in different ways
	NOTE: A groupware-setting, is one example. A U-shaped table for the whole group with presentation materials (flip-chart, overhead projector, etc.) and adjacent meeting spaces for small groups is another.

White-print thinking	Tables turned upside-down
	    – to enable something creative and unexpected to happen
	    – you certainly can't sit comfortably
	    – a lot of room is left for . . .
	NOTE: Multifunctional office layouts or office landscaping can have these characteristics.

Table 3.3 The "Table" Example

	Setting up a Workshop in Order to . . .	Formulating a Mission To	Introducing Knowledge Management By . . .
Yellow-print thinking	– reach agreement with one another about aims or policy	– lay out the results of negotiations	– forming heterogeneous assignment-teams – organizing across-disciplines
Blue-print thinking	– have a plan of approach on paper as a result of the workshop	– have the best strategy clearly defined (to be used in external marketing or internal monitoring)	– writing handbooks – developing information systems – doing research
Red-print thinking	– create more involvement – have a good time together	– getting everyone on the same wavelength – give words to what brings us together/create a "family" feeling	– introducing job rotation and sabbaticals – management development programs
Green-print thinking	– learn from one another – exchange viewpoints	– enable a useful exchange of views – explore different possibilities together	– bringing people together in such a way that they learn from one another – intervision and coaching
White-print thinking	– expand our thinking – arouse creative energy – stimulate creative ideas	– to bring about an evolutionary leap – transcend apparent contradictions	– taking on challenges – making new things possible – catalyzing new communities and networks

Table 3.4 The Example of a Workshop, a Mission, and Knowledge Management

the neat competence profiles of a red-print thinker. It also ignores power in organizations, top-down as well as bottom-up.

The *ideal* of green-print thinking is a learning organization where learning is consciously and continuously applied. Everybody learns what they need to learn and comes up with their own solutions to their own problems. The *pitfall* is that green-print thinkers can ignore the fact that not everybody is always willing or capable of learning. For instance, in situations that lack safety, like power struggles or conflicts, people are not keen to participate. Also there can be a lack of "hard" outcomes: an overabundance of reflection can breed a lack of decisiveness and action.

In white-print thinking, the *ideal* lies in spontaneous evolution, in "lucky" coincidences, and in people taking responsibility for their own lives and learning. What is more, there is a positive attitude toward conflict and crisis. The *pitfall* lies in the idealization of everything magically taking care of itself. This leads to injudicious acceptance of problems. Another pitfall is fashionably using "white" ideas without grasping white thinking's essence: for example, managers using the concept of self-steering teams to abdicate their own responsibilities. A last pitfall is having insufficient insight into the underlying patterns of an organization to confidently know what might bring life (back) into it.

3.6 New Colors and "Meta Paradigms"

Clearly, each color has its strong and weak points. The circumstances (context), the outcome, the kind of organization, the kind of resistance, the principal actors, and the change agent are all factors that strongly influence what change strategy, in terms of color, might make a difference. Some kind of combination of the colors will often be used during a change process, but preferably one color will always be dominant at a given time. Given the great differences between the colors in terms of their assumptions, approaches, interventions, role of the change agent, key success factors, and so on, a mix of colors in a change approach will certainly have many internal contradictions and will increase the chances of failure. Which color to choose in what kind of situation and the (im)possibility of combining colors is discussed in section 5.2.2.

Is this a complete overview? The colors do seem to cover most of the steady stream of experience, research, and publications that we are aware of. Nevertheless, the list is probably not complete. Recalling genocides in the Second World War, or in Rwanda or Kosovo, we realize that violence and repression are also strategies; ones of manipulating and threatening people, of infusing hate and fear. We call this type of thinking about change "steel-print." It characterizes methods employed in organizations as well, and that it is effective is obviously still believed by quite a few people.

Besides steel-print, there might be still another way of thinking about change. Living, traveling, and working in India, we observed that people were more inclined than we were to say "yes" to change while also leaving action more up to circumstances like the weather, people they met, the hand of God. If God wants it, the change will happen.

People work hard, but rational planning is taken much less seriously than we are accustomed to. A person is considered only a small part in the timeless game (*maya*) of life. This might be a way of thinking about change that is little influenced by Western beliefs in progress, and it also appears to be effective: India, the largest democracy in the world, operates under its assumptions. We think that silver may be a fitting color for this way of thinking.

In most of our consultancy work, we do not engage in steel or silver paradigms. These are not generally considered part of the professional repertoire.

In section 3.1 we described a number of accepted descriptions of change strategies as found in the literature. It will be obvious that there are partial similarities between these strategies and one or more of the colors described. Thus the normative reeducative strategy (Bennis et al., 1985) has a strong affinity with green-print thinking, and the directive approach (Van der Zee, 1995) has much in common with blue-print thinking. There are many more affinities. Nevertheless, we feel that this colored classification of five approaches is more complete, distinguishes in a clear conceptual way between the different approaches, and allows for detailing in a comparable fashion. Further development of the colors is possible, and in the next chapters the colors will return and be further detailed and applied: in how to choose a change approach, how to categorize interventions, how change agents develop, what expressions to use, and so on.

There is also a (meta)paradigm behind the five-color classification described here. The undoubtedly useful distinction between the five ways of thinking emerges from a meta-paradigm that posits a need for analysis and order. An additional (meta)paradigm arises from the need for wholeness, intuition, and continuity that searches more for a way to combine all the insights instead of separating them into five categories. We will leave this second (meta)paradigm alone for much of the book, as it is beyond our scope to describe or to conceptualize it at this time.

3.7 Working With Colors: The Joseph and Johanna Case

We use a case to help clarify thinking in colors. The same case is then dealt with in five different ways, each time illustrating one of the five colors as the change strategy.

> The case involves two health care institutions: a nursing home and a rest home. They are discussing the possibility of collaborating closely or even merging. There are a number of relevant factors in relation to the environment:
>
> ♦ The market for intramural geriatric care is shrinking, and this is leading to competitors scaling-up all around the country.

- A merger could give the new institution a stronger negotiating position with insurers and other care providers.
- A merger would give the new institution a stronger position in the labor market.
- There is increasing competition from other large institutions that are capitalizing on the care needs of the elderly.

But there are also relevant developments within the institutions themselves:

- Intensive cooperation can create a residence-care-continuum in terms of services possibly spread over a number of locations. One of the institutions is better equipped to provide the residential element, and the other can better provide the care element. Combining these two core competencies can result in improved and modernized care provision.
- Scaling-up can give greater impetus and allow for more means for continuing education for personnel.
- The elderly demand more privacy; this necessitates renovating the facilities, reviewing the type of help, and so on.
- Efficiency can be increased by combining general and technical services, research facilities and laboratories, for example.

The two institutions are different in many ways. One has a Supervisory Board, an Executive Board, and a division model, whereas the other has a Board overseeing one single director as chair of the Management Team, and has a functional structure. The latter organization is spread out over five locations in the city, while the other has only one location.

Furthermore, a limited culture survey has revealed a number of other differences. The ethos of one institute is "residents come first." Here, the staff is given a great deal of responsibility for decentralized planning and budgeting, while workers are pragmatic and solution oriented. The other institution also considers its patients to be its reason for being, but here its management has a no-nonsense approach, and careful, proven, and stylish working methods are deemed essential. Fewer administrative tasks are delegated to the staff; however, management does involve them, together with the residents, in planning processes. Professional care and maintaining high professional standards are considered important.

Five change agents familiarize themselves with the situation, carry out supplementary diagnostic activities, and come up with the following (unicolor) ideas.

Number 1

This change agent places the emphasis on what the two institutions wish to achieve jointly, each from its own position. She proposes setting up a joint work group to formulate a common care vision. The work group must be broadly based with representatives from the Board, the management, and the workers' council, but also include several professionals from both institutes. The initial task of the work group will be to make an inventory of the most important points concerning the care vision and then to discuss them.

If the members of the work group can reach agreement, they will then bring out a care vision document that will be comprehensively discussed in both institutions before being finalized in a carefully worded decision-making document. The workers' council will also be closely involved in this process. Only then will new work groups be formed to discuss four specific (and often sensitive) topics: the organization structure, the new name and identity, the financial and personnel aspects, and the composition of the new top structure. After these work groups have reported their findings and decision making has taken place through the usual and proper channels, the agreements will be signed and the subsequent steps undertaken.

The change agent regards the search for joint interests and goals as an advantage: the important players are given the opportunity to get to know each other and respect each other's opinions. This will probably prevent resistance down the road, as support can gradually be built up. The disadvantages are the slow pace, the high cost, and the fact that the results remain uncertain until the end of the change process.

The change agent feels that it is important to involve the board and the management during the whole process, to clearly distinguish decision-making moments and to carefully record decisions. An independent outsider, like herself, can be of enormous help in bringing the parties closer together.

The new organization must have leaders who will be able to work successfully with and within the new power balance. They must also be able to discern the (shifting) composition of dominant coalitions.

Number 2

This change agent has a completely different plan in mind. In his opinion, the first thing to determine is whether cooperation or a merger would provide economies of scale, improved market position, or more efficiency. If not, then the whole idea is rather pointless. A study would be conducted by outside experts who have in their possession relevant benchmarks from comparable institutions and joint ventures. Their task is to determine the advantages and disadvantages of any possible form of cooperation or merger. Market trends must also be examined in order to be able to assess ways to capitalize on them.

This outside agency must then make a number of recommendations to the authoritative bodies of both institutions, and a copy of the report containing these recommendations should be given to the workers' council. These recommendations will set out which strategy should be followed and how the top structure needs to be adjusted to fit this strategy (because "structure follows strategy"). Through a careful selection procedure, the new members of the Board are appointed.

When the decision has been made either to cooperate or to merge, a project organization will be set up in which the new Board has the principal role and is supported by a sounding-board group from the workers' council. An external expert would become the project leader and direct five task-oriented groups: care functions, personnel and organization, purchasing and procurement, computerization, and finance. The groups are made up of internal experts. The groups will report back to the project leader at a previously determined time, and he will then present a final report to the Board and the sounding-board group.

According to the change agent, the main advantages of this approach are the demarcated time frame with clear decision-moments, the transparency of the decision-making process, and the rationality and matter-of-factness of the decisions themselves. It should be very clear what could be gained by merging before embarking on it, and there is no time to lose in establishing that. This strategy might encounter sporadic resistance, but this is normal and to be expected. Do some people think the whole process is going too fast?

The leadership of the new institute has the exact competence required to implement all aspects of the new strategy. Does our marketing, especially, have to be improved? Then marketing experts will be part of the board. Does the organization have to be slimmed down? Then that expertise will be introduced into the board. Specialized external consultants are welcome only if they provide clear-cut added value.

Number 3

This change agent assumes that mergers will always create initial hesitation from those concerned: Will I be any better off for it? She feels that a great deal of time and effort must be given to wooing and winning over the staff so they will work together.

She will preach the advantages of the merger for the staff and the organization with unbridled enthusiasm and will continue to emphasize them during the course of the change. She will organize social events and parties to reduce tension and emphasize the brighter side and new possibilities of what is happening. More important is her wish to reward cooperation from the outset. Individuals and groups seeking synergy can be certain of receiving attention and being provided with the facilities they need. She will draw up norms for cooperation between the two institutions and concentrate on the design of the "soft" side of the organization at an early stage. The staffing of the new organization must be approached with the utmost care. After giving staff the opportunity to apply for the various positions, an objective process of selection will take place. Those who are selected will be dealt with just as carefully as those who are not. The latter group will be offered alternatives and, as a last resort, will leave the organization with generous financial help.

In the new organization, advanced tools for staff development will be sought, such as a Management Development process, multiple career ladders, and integrating personnel management into general management tasks. Special emphasis will be placed on a review system that takes cooperative behavior into consideration, with incentives for collaborative efforts and the like. A system of performance-related bonuses will be introduced, as well as combined child care facilities.

The change agent sees enormous advantages in this approach. If the joint organization offers its staff a range of advantages and incentives, they will be quick to integrate and to cooperate. If the new situation proves to be significantly better than the old one, the change could be very rapid. It is a case of making the new organization attractive, convincing people of its worth, and encouraging the desired behavior.

One possible disadvantage is the emphasis on personnel management and its possible high cost. Where do individuals' intrinsic motives really lie in this approach? And how does this approach take advantage of market opportunities?

The leaders must be able to instill enthusiasm and be well versed in the use of personnel tools. They must be able to get along with people and know how to motivate individuals. They must have a variety of styles and exercise care in their dealings with people. Outside help may be necessary to build up the HRM systems and to train the managers in their use.

Number 4

The fourth change agent has a completely different plan. He has observed that the two institutions have different cultures and practices. He has observed subtle differences in the ways in which employees regard their work as well as differences in their competencies. The change agent realizes that both differences could lead to misunderstandings, irritation, and long-term problems if nothing is done about them. However, he also thinks that these differences can be turned into something productive and pins his faith on forming groups across the two institutions that can learn from one another. After all, it is the very differences between these institutions that make learning possible. His plan is based on bringing the staffs of the two institutions together to enable them to learn from each other's strong points, thus improving the skills of both parties, which will be reflected in a more skilled and integral approach to their patients and residents. They can, of course, also learn a lot from the patients and residents themselves, whose opinions can be sought with regard to positive and negative changes they experience in the way employees treat them.

The change agent creates learning situations and forms mixed learning groups. During intervision sessions, they exchange information on working methods and jointly think up new and more integral approaches to the work. If there is a danger of communication breaking down within the groups, he will supply a facilitator to help them out. He will also have a list of training needs drawn up and offer groups the opportunity to gain new knowledge and skills jointly. In addition to their learning together, the change agent will also seek opportunities to allow people to work together. He will introduce work placement, offering employees the opportunity of working in another department for a certain period to learn other working methods. He will initiate joint experiments, too, in which new innovations are tested within the workplace.

The main advantages of this approach are that you can learn a lot from one another and strengthen cooperation at the same time. Also, if things go less well, you can slow the process down a bit or take it in a slightly different direction (incremental strategy). You do not have to be ahead of yourself, nor do you have to wait "until things get better": no matter what happens, the institutions gain by transferring knowledge to one another and checking and exploiting possibilities for synergy. This teaches people a lot, and when people learn, organizations prosper and they, in turn, also learn. There is scope for innovation and the new working methods are, from the outset, the psychological property of the employees themselves. This means there will be minimal resistance.

This cooperation will take substantial time and energy, especially from those on the work floor. It is self-evident that it is difficult to place this process within a framework of time spans and milestones. A great deal of attention will have to be given to communicating good examples and successes. Verbal communication and information are vital, particularly when it comes to sharing experiences. All this takes time. Perhaps not everyone is able to learn? How do we measure our achievements? These might be real problems.

The organization's new leadership must be able to orchestrate learning and to provide a role model in terms of reflective practicing. They must be self-assured, empathic, good communicators, and they must be especially able to facilitate good communication among employees. The institute should involve people who can design and facilitate learning situations and bring in coaches to teach the managers how to develop a learning organization; perhaps they might occasionally use a simulation or a management game?

Number 5

This change agent believes that cooperation or a merger will come to nothing if it fails to recognize the energy and motives of those it affects. She assumes that the majority of the staff, residents, and patients are full of ideas about how things could be improved and that they are intrinsically motivated to express them. After all, a nurse does not enter the profession just for the money. The change agent thinks that there may be reasons that frustrate employees' attempts to express themselves in this way. These are her basic assumptions.

She is very keen to organize a vision conference as soon as possible that can be voluntarily attended by those concerned and where the "ideal future" for residents, patients, and staff can be jointly worked out. She realizes producing a vision from the "top" would only encourage a passive attitude. During the meeting a great deal of time will be devoted to exchanging views, making people aware of the possibilities, and making sense and adding meaning to the process those concerned are part of. What could cooperation bring us? Which new horizons may it open? Will this assist us in achieving what we desire? Who is eager to experiment? How can we level the barriers that are inhibiting our further development? How can we get back to what made us join this profession, to raise the quality of care? Where are all those interesting pilot projects taking place? Should we look outside these walls too? And how do we learn from the histories of both our institutions and use our proven strengths for this process?

The vision conference marks only the start of a series of developments. The change agent stimulates a culture of openness conducive to intrapreneurship, one in which people create personal networks, bond over new ideas, and seek or create new role models. Various groups try out new things, not because they were talked into it by management but because they want to and no one is stopping them. Successful changes become new symbols that the change agent will help to highlight and celebrate. Change agents breed more change agents. And the successful ones become the new heroes who will be given room to dive into new ventures, but, more important, to encourage and coach others to take responsibility for both their own professional and private lives. Coaching will be stimulated and personal growth facilitated. It demands a great deal of skill to be able to understand what is happening, where it all came from, and where it is all leading. This should become clearer all the time; if not, people can be inhibited or confined in a straightjacket of existing norms. The change agent sticks her neck out by challenging such straightjackets, and where necessary, deconstructing sacred cows in the process. Failure to do so could result in stagnation. If the renewal is successful, the old institutions will make way for a brand new one.

The advantages are clear. The people themselves provide the energy and ideas for the change. "We are the mission and strategy." People form closer ties, are more adaptable, and have greater strength and more freedom than they would have had if the change had been centrally directed. If the development can evolve from the inside out, using people's strength, the new will be rock solid and the old will perish on its own. A process will have been set in motion in which all have their hands on the wheel, and because of this, it is an adventure.

There is concern about who and how many will take part and if they have enough energy to pull it off. Are enough people able to search out their rightful place in this organization? Moreover, because there are so many people involved, the process will be a long one and the ultimate outcome unpredictable. There are no guarantees, and during the change it will often look like you as change agent have relinquished your influence. Will you be able to get it back if the need arises? Is there a way back, and at what cost?

Who the leaders are will become self-evident. Their qualities make them emerge from the fray and because of this, they are, by definition, accepted. Outside help is occasionally needed to assist people to recognize patterns and to expand awareness.

With which change agent or with which approach do you feel most at home?

Note

1.   De Bono (1985) uses six colors for his so-called Thinking Hats, the five colors used here plus black. In his approach, ways of thinking are unraveled in order to use just one method or to enable a group to exercise the different approaches. In our description of the colors, any relationship to De Bono's Thinking Hats is expressly avoided. There is, in other words, no connection between these two concepts.

4 The Main Elements of Planned Change

In the previous chapter, we examined the various meanings that people attach to the concept of change. We emphasized the diversity in these meanings in terms of five different colors, and we explored how the five different ways of thinking, along with their ideals and pitfalls, are revealed in the assumptions and approaches of change agents. In a way, we explored the psyche of professional change agents: What do they believe in? What makes them act the way they do?

Discussions with colleagues and clients and a close examination of the literature also reveal a large number of similarities across the diversity of change processes, not just differences. Certain elements appear to be present in successful change processes irrespective of which color mind-set a change agent might have. These recurring elements, of which there appear to be six, can be regarded as a general method of planned change. We describe these elements in this chapter.

We consider it essential to bring clarity to a common method for two reasons:

- Seen as a whole, the elements offer a reasonably comprehensive framework within which to describe and to communicate about change processes.
- Together, the elements form a "road map" that helps change agents shape change processes and increases their awareness of their own blind spots.

In the first section, we explore the concept of planned change and name the elements. We then describe each of the six elements in sections 4.2 through 4.7.

4.1 Elements of the Method

Heraclitus (circa 500 BC) wrote that change is the only constant in the universe. Change occurs consciously and subconsciously, at any time and anywhere, thanks to

69

and despite the people affected by it. Trying to direct all that change would appear to be a hopeless task. Feltman (1993) even characterized such a pursuit as a typical male neurosis: the urge to guarantee happiness by possession and control, by definition and order, and by planning and evaluation. We feel that a certain degree of humility would not be out of place here, so we limit our method to only a fraction of all change processes: those change processes that can "rightfully" be characterized as "planned change." These are the changes that you do not leave up to chance and fate, but to which you are able, willing, and committed to give some degree of direction.

What are the elements of planned change? The literature is full of all sorts of definitions of planned change, change management, and organizational change. These definitions reflect what each of the authors considers to be inextricable elements. Table 4.1 lists several such definitions.

The definitions show different nuances. Kanter's interpretation of planned changed is tinged with yellow: the most influential actors determine the direction. In contrast, French, Bell, and Zawacki turn it into a growth-oriented definition, which almost seems to imply that the purpose resides in the process. A green approach? Or white maybe?

The similarities are just as striking as the differences, however, and that is what interests us in this chapter. We express these similarities as the presence of the following six elements (see Figure 4.1, Elements of Planned Change):

♦ outcome (also known as goals, results, direction, improvement, renewal)
♦ history (also referred to as cause, need, motive, context)
♦ actors (also referred to as roles, parties, the social dimension)
♦ phases (also referred to as steps, sequence, order, activities, technical aspects)
♦ communication (also referred to as interaction, cultural aspects, sense-making)
♦ steering (also referred to as monitoring, directing, orchestrating, guiding, managing, keeping in one's awareness)

The six elements are in may ways similar to the distinction of five dimensions in change processes made by Vinkenburg (1995), namely, the content dimension, the social dimension, the structuring dimension, the sense-making dimension, and the conditional dimension (see Table 4.2). Each of these elements or dimensions appears to be equally relevant to all change processes, be they multi-year organizational transformations or single, one-hour consultations.

The six main elements of planned change complement each other. Together they form our comprehensive definition of planned change. Planned change is

(Continued, p. 73)

Bennis, Benne, and Chin (1985)	Planned change is a conscious, deliberate, and collaborative effort to improve the operation of a system—whether it be a self-system, a social system, or a cultural system—through the utilization of scientific knowledge.
Lippit, Watson, and Westley (1958)	Planned change is a purposeful decision to effect improvements in a personality system or a social system that is achieved with help of professional guidance.
Van der Vlist (1993)	Organizational change consists of goal-oriented and, to a degree, preplanned actions, the final result of which can be, more or less, clearly formulated in advance.
Tichy (1980)	Management of change is predicting, channeling, guiding, and altering the three organizational cycles: the political cycle, the technical cycle, and the cultural cycle.
Kanter (1992)	Change involves the crystallization of new action possibilities (new policies, new behaviors, new patterns, new methodologies, new products, or new market ideas) based on reconceptualized patterns in the organization. The architecture of change, the design and construction of new patterns, or the reconceptualization of old ones, to make new, and hopefully more productive, actions possible.
French and Bell (1984)	Organizational development is a top management-supported, long-range effort to improve an organization's problem-solving and renewal process, particularly through a more effective and collaborative diagnosis and management of organization culture—with special emphasis on formal work team, temporary team, and intergroup culture, with the assistance of a consultant-facilitator and the use of theory and technology of applied behavioral science, including action research.

Table 4.1 Planned Change Is . . .

Dimension	Related Questions
1. Content (what should improve? what can improve?)	— What ideas already exist and are communicated about the change's direction and goals? — In what (vague or detailed) terms do people refer to the changes? — What do the change agents regard as possible and impossible to change in the foreseeable future? — To what extent and how can the changes be made visible and measurable?
2. Structuring (approach; in what sequence? by what rules?)	— What are the change agent's visions on and approaches to change? — To what extent are these visions made explicit, shared, and recognized? — To what degree is/are the most dominant vision(s) operationalized? — To what extent is the progress of the change monitored and adjusted?
3. Social (who are involved? how do they interact?)	— Who are actively involved in the change and who turn their backs on it? — What positions do leaders take with regard to the change? — What impression does the change agent's communication leave on others? — To what extent are the change agent's roles and authority recognized by others?
4. Sense-making (meaning, importance, weight accorded by individuals and by the organization)	— What are the natures of change triggers and where do they originate? — Whose interests are served by the change and whose are clearly not? — To what extent do those involved hold each other accountable for their contributions to the change? — To what extent do the various parties feel a degree of solidarity with regard to the change? — How strong and visible is the relationship between the organization's policies and the change at hand?
5. Conditional (is it feasible?; does it receive sufficient attention?)	— How much attention does this change effort receive in comparison to other (competing) changes? — What perspectives does the change hold for those involved? — To what extent does the general situation allow the intended result to be realized? — To what degree is the change agent's behavior congruent with interaction characteristics fitting the intended change outcomes?

Table 4.2 The Five Dimensions of Change Processes (Vinkenburg, 1995)

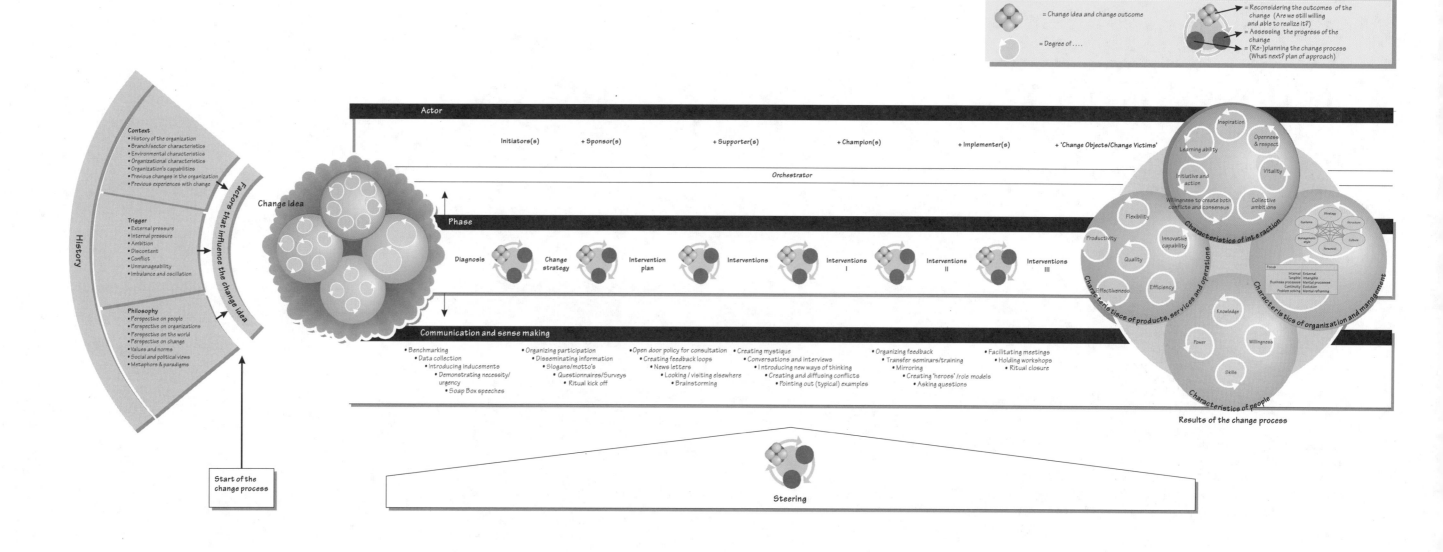

Legend

= Change idea and change outcome

= Degree of . . . .

= Reconsidering the outcomes of the change (Are we still willing and able to realize it?)

= Assessing the progress of the change

= (Re-)planning the change process (What next? plan of approach)

Context
• History of the organization
• Branch/sector characteristics
• Environmental characteristics
• Organizational characteristics
• Organization's capabilities
• Previous changes in the organization
• Previous experiences with change

Trigger
• External pressure
• Internal pressure
• Ambition
• Discontent
• Conflict
• Unmanageability
• Imbalance and oscillation

Philosophy
• Perspective on people
• Perspective on organizations
• Perspective on the world
• Perspective on change
• Values and norms
• Social and political views
• Metaphors & paradigms

History

Factors that influence the change idea

Change idea

Start of the change process

Actor

Initiators(s)   + Sponsor(s)   + Supporter(s)   + Champion(s)   + Implementer(s)   + 'Change Objects/Change Victims'

Orchestrator

Phase

Diagnosis   Change strategy   Intervention plan   Interventions   Interventions I   Interventions II   Interventions III

Communication and sense making

• Benchmarking
• Data collection
• Introducing inducements
• Demonstrating necessity/ urgency
• Soap Box speeches

• Organizing participation
• Disseminating information
• Slogans/motto's
• Questionnaires/Surveys
• Ritual kick off

• Open door policy for consultation
• Creating feedback loops
• News letters
• Looking / visiting elsewhere
• Brainstorming

• Creating mystique
• Conversations and interviews
• Introducing new ways of thinking
• Creating and diffusing conflicts
• Pointing out (typical) examples

• Organizing feedback
• Transfer seminars/training
• Mirroring
• Creating 'heroes'/role models
• Asking questions

• Facilitating meetings
• Holding workshops
• Ritual closure

Steering

Results of the change process

Figure 4.1 Elements of Planned Change

- ◆ realizing intended outcomes
- ◆ while recognizing and building on the historical context
- ◆ by actors who influence each other
- ◆ by going through a sequence of phases or steps
- ◆ by communication and sense-making
- ◆ while the change process is monitored and guided by change agents

We further examine each of the elements in the following sections. However, three observations must be made here:

◆ Each element seems patently obvious. At the same time, we think that in most change processes one or more elements are neglected, with all the risks and consequences that this entails. Consequently, we present a model/checklist in each section to assist change agents in minimizing these risks, hoping to ensure that the obvious may indeed remain obvious.

◆ Depending on his own paradigms, each change agent colors the elements differently. Take the element "actors," for example. Red-print thinkers readily think of employees who need to be seduced and tempted by motivating bosses; yellow-print thinkers speak of the dominant coalition; and blue-print thinkers talk about a clear division of roles and demarcation of tasks. We have no wish to repeat the different paradigms on change that were covered in Chapter 3. This would lead to five different renderings of the method of planned change, each a "color tainted" version of the one we outline in this chapter. We shall, however, pay some attention to the colored nuances of each of the elements in the next sections.

◆ The most important observation concerns the way in which we illustrate the method in Figure 4.1. Its shape has been criticized for favoring the blue approach to change because of its orderly rectangular outlines. We share this criticism; we too think that the figure is too linear and too static to accurately represent the spectrum of planned change. Ideally, there would be five different figures, one for each color. Perhaps this will happen one day. Nevertheless, we feel that a common picture has a certain charm, and after many attempts to amend it we have decided to keep the current format, with the reservations we mentioned.

4.2 The Preceding Change Idea and the Actual Change Outcomes

Change can be regarded as the realization or facilitation of (intended) outcomes. At the start of the process, initiators have some idea of what these outcomes should be. This is not necessarily predefined and predicted in detail. Zuijderhoudt (1992), for example, posits that organizational changes are not, as such, consciously sought but emerge more from the dynamics of chaos and self-regulation. He dismisses the notion that "we are masters of our universe": Life evades our true control, as do organizations. But even he admits that it is possible to actively influence the direction of the

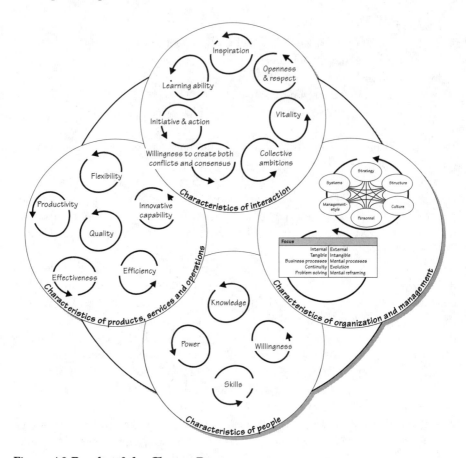

Figure 4.2 Results of the Change Process

change by deliberate interventions. We are not condemned to the (laissez faire) attitude of "we will know where we were going when we get there." There can be a specific change idea at the start to point you in the right direction, an idea that resembles the actual outcome right from the start, that takes more shape as time progresses and grows into the outcome by the time the change process is complete.

Figure 4.2 shows a general model for naming desired outcomes. The model has proved to be workable when applied to change processes as diverse as infrastructural projects, organizing a front office, participative strategy development, human talent assessment, and many others. The model consists of four separate sets of characteristics, namely

- ♦ characteristics of products, services, and operations
- ♦ characteristics of organization and management

♦ characteristics of interaction
♦ characteristics of people

The characteristics can be of quite different class, and they can overlap, but we believe that, together, they provide a good general checklist. Definitions of all the characteristics are set out in Table 4.3.

How can this model be used? We see three applications:

1. The model can be used as a tool for brainstorming about intended outcomes. It also provides language for describing outcomes.

2. The model can help reduce the bias of change agents. It provides a means for reflection and reframing. This is much desired, given that where business economists are inclined to focus on business performance, organization developers are biased toward interpersonal processes, and chaos thinkers are inclined to strive for dynamic balance.

3. The model can help to explore and safeguard interconnectedness between characteristics. It aids discussion about what should be regarded as means and what as ends. It facilitates prioritization of various possible outcomes.

In short, the model helps to clarify and detail outcomes. This is an important step in the change process, because different change ideas require different designs of the change process. Careful delineation of outcomes can prevent a whole range of problems. For example, in a particular nonprofit organization wishing to make the changeover to self-steering teams, a network organization, and knowledge management, there was a tendency to talk about the change idea in terms of improving business operations and restructuring the organization (i.e., delayering). After all, this was how they had been accustomed to talk and think about change in the past. The model helped initiate discussions about the validity of this tendency. Other possible outcomes were explored, such as empowerment and entrepreneurial spirit on the shop floor, sharing knowledge across different layers and offices of the organization, an attitude of asking for support from colleagues, and, more important, one of willingly giving it as well. These discussions led those involved to conclude that these other characteristics should be regarded as the more important ones. Operations and structures still needed to change, but they were considered as means and no longer as ends in themselves. In truth, nobody was attached to any particular characteristic of the structures or systems of the organization as long as they did not thwart empowerment, knowledge sharing, and the like. One was willing to experiment with whatever structure might offer more support. The model thus assisted quite a shift in the intended outcomes (and the associated design of the change process).

Strategy	the means by which previously determined goals are achieved
Management style	the characteristic behavior patterns of management within the organization
Systems	the rules and procedures used to steer day-to-day functioning
Personnel	the characteristics and competences of the staff as a whole
Culture	the common values and norms of a group of people and the associated behavior
Structure	the division of tasks, responsibilities, and authority and how these are compensated
Focus	the degree of either one-sided or synergistic attention to "opposites"
Knowledge	all the information, experience, and awareness that someone possesses and the level to which these are integrated
Power	the degree of autonomy someone realizes based on his or her self-confidence, entrepreneurial spirit, strength, and perseverance
Willingness	how open people are to change—ranging from active resistance to active leadership
Skills	people's capabilities, in terms of competences, attitudes, and talents
Efficiency	the degree to which all activities (goal setting, organizing, and realizing) are carried out with a minimum of resources
Effectiveness	the degree to which an organization's goals are realized
Quality	the degree to which an organization is willing and able to fulfill a client's wishes
Innovative capability	the degree to which people are able to bring about internal or external renewal

Table 4.3 Definitions of the Terms Used in Figure 4.2

Flexibility	the ability to react swiftly and adequately to unforeseen internal and external circumstances
Productivity	the degree to which profits are offset by investments
Willingness to create conflict and consensus	the degree to which the staff are willing to engage in debates, discussions, and dialogue
Collective ambition	the degree to which the goals of the employees overlap
Vitality	the degree of enthusiasm and energy shown by people for getting a job done or for working together
Openness and respect	the degree to which people communicate without fear and in accordance with feedback rules
Inspiration	the degree to which people within an organization can arouse and/or strengthen each other's enthusiasm
Learning ability	the degree to which the members of an organization are capable of increasing each other's knowledge and skills
Initiative and action	the drive that a group of people has and the extent to which they are allowed to take change of their situation

The designation of outcomes depends upon an individual's philosophy and, just as important, upon the management philosophy most in fashion within the sector within which the individual works. The outcome-model discussed here is reasonably general and "uncolored" but by no means written in stone. There are many good alternatives to be found in the literature, especially if you wish to focus on specific characteristics or have already decided on a specific colored change strategy.

Cummings and Worley (1993) describe four separate subsets of outcomes that match their backgrounds as green/red organization development practitioners:

♦ Development of human process issues, like: How to communicate? How to solve problems? And how to provide leadership?
♦ Development of human resource issues, such as: How to attract competent people? How to set goals and reward people? And how to plan and develop people's careers?

♦ Development of strategic issues, like: What functions, products, services, markets? How to gain competitive advantage? And what values should guide organizational functioning?

♦ Development of technology/structure issues, such as: How to divide labor and coordinate departments? How to design work? And how to produce products or services?

Conversely, Kanter (1992) uses three subsets of outcomes that reflect her viewpoint as a consultant who is often closely involved with major transformations or turnarounds in organizations:

♦ change of identity, in which the boundaries and relationships with the environment are fundamentally altered

♦ change of culture and structure, in which the size, shape, and/or customs and values are fundamentally altered

♦ change in control and power, in which ownership and/or governance structure is/are fundamentally altered.

Loman (1998) often describes outcomes in terms of the dynamic (im)balance between classic opposites. However, in his view these opposites do not intrinsically contradict each other, they only seem to. They are, as it were, two sides of one and the same coin. His description fits with his mind-set as a white "chaos thinker":

♦ internal versus external orientation, whereby balance ensures both internal stability and anticipation of external influences, while imbalance causes either internal navel-gazing or overheating

♦ tangible versus intangible orientation, whereby balance ensures both a sense of reality and experimentation, while imbalance causes either fire fighting or pie-in-the-sky ideas

♦ business processes versus mental processes, whereby balance ensures both efficiency and innovation, while imbalance causes people to become either too set in their ways or too relativistic and unpredictable

♦ continuity versus evolution, whereby balance ensures both harmony and an optimal conflict level (see section 6.10), while imbalance creates either clinging to the status quo or a disposition to disintegration

♦ problem solving versus mental reframing, whereby balance ensures both targeted action and learning, whereas imbalance creates either reactive behavior (flight or fight) or too much lethargy to complete a task.

Wijnen, Weggeman, and Kor (1999) refer to common criteria for an organization's general performance as ways to describe intended outcomes:

♦ effectiveness as a measure of client orientation
♦ creativity and flexibility as a measure of people orientation
♦ efficiency as a measure of action orientation

Finally, Kaplan and Norton (1996) show how outcomes can be defined in a so-called Balanced Scorecard, which is described as a diagnostic tool in section 6.3.

4.3 History: Driving Factors Behind the Change Idea

Planned change does not come out of the blue. It has a history, an engine or source that brings forth the necessity or desirability of the change. What causes change is embedded in the organization's history up to the present. But what exactly is this source? Why do organizations seek change? Van de Ven and Poole (1995) outline four theories that shed light on this mystery:

♦   Evolution theory looks for the source of change in "the survival of the fittest." The theory maintains that the organization that is best able to adapt to its environment is better equipped to attract scarce resources such as clients, finances, raw materials, and personnel. This enables it to survive, while those less adaptive languish.

♦   Life-cycle theory regards organizations as organisms that undergo a kind of "natural development." An organization is born, grows, harvests, and dies. However, it can also renew itself in the final stage. An organization develops primarily by being in touch with its roots, being aware of its identity, and realizing its intrinsic possibilities.

♦   Teleological theory regards organizations as auto-creative entities. The source of the change lies hidden in the dissatisfaction or aspiration of those involved, causing them to set goals and expend their energy to achieve them. The future is consciously and specifically created by the organization itself, from the inside out.

♦   Dialectic theory, in conclusion, regards change as the result of the introduction of new concepts that call existing concepts into question. The struggle between the two brings renewal. From thesis and antithesis arises a synthesis that opens new possibilities and futures for the organization.

The four theories are not incompatible. We feel that they offer a good overview of the various engines that can lurk behind one and the same change. Figure 4.3 shows a working model that brings together a range of factors that we regard as fuel for these engines. They are split into three categories: context, triggers, and philosophy.

Context can be regarded as the "factual" environmental and historical characteristics that contribute to the emergence of a change idea. These characteristics are part of the evolution and life-cycle theories:

♦ characteristics and changes in the social environment
♦ characteristics and changes in the competitive environment
♦ characteristics and changes within the organization
♦ experiences with previous changes within the organization (process and outcome)

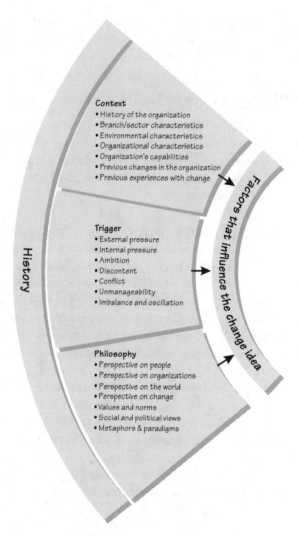

Figure 4.3 Driving Factors Behind the Change Idea

The *triggers* can be regarded as the "emotional" characteristics that contribute to the emergence of a change idea. These characteristics find their origins in the teleological theory. The argument is that all the facts that make up the context are not in themselves enough to put change on the agenda. Doing so seems also to require the involvement of initiators who, within a given context, find a number of characteristics within the organization unacceptable, or realize that they are longing for something different or better. This realization is sometimes little more than intuition, sometimes it can already be spelled out. Either way, initiators are aware of it because they are triggered on a personal level: It is close to their hearts, it matters to them. The triggers can come from inside as well as outside the organization and can be either reactive or creative in nature.

Reactive factors could be

♦ dissatisfaction, complaints, conflicts, problems
♦ unmanageability, imbalance, threats
♦ external pressure

Creative factors could be

♦ ambition, desires, goals
♦ invitations, possibilities, opportunities
♦ role models, heroes

The *philosophies* of those involved can be seen as the characteristics that make sense, that give meaning to a change idea. The source of these characteristics can partly be traced back to the dialectic theory. This theory implies that no context leads to triggering a change idea unless the initiator attaches a certain meaning to this context. What that meaning is depends on the paradigms or philosophy of the person in question. What one person regards as a problem is seen as business as usual by another. One person's dream is another person's nightmare. Relevant characteristics are, for example,

♦ one's perception of people, organizations and the world (think, e.g., of "images of organizations" as described by Morgan, 1986)
♦ one's perception of change (see the colors in Chapter 3)
♦ social, political, and religious beliefs
♦ values and norms
♦ use of language, metaphors, and symbols

The model of driving factors has a number of applications:

♦   It helps you to gain insight into the logic behind change initiatives. If the whole sector is in the process of merging to lower production costs (context), it explains a similar intention in your organization and perhaps even its inevitability.

♦   The model also serves as a checklist to recognize if there are (sufficient) people within the organization to whom the change idea is important. And whether they are sufficiently triggered. We once helped an organization to draw up a really nice environmental strategy. No one in the organization was against it, but neither did many lose any sleep over the absence of such a strategy. There had been little motivation from the very start, and as a result the strategy never came to life. We figure that if no one owns a problem, it will endure and that this is something that is best found out at the outset. You won't climb a mountain unless you have some longing for the peak.

◆   Finally, the model is designed to track down prevailing convictions or mind-sets, especially to assess whether these are dysfunctional. Sometimes the problem is more in the mind (philosophy) of the initiator than in the organization itself. If this is the case, the change agent would be well advised to recognize this and focus his attention on the mental processes of the initiator instead of wasting his efforts on organizational processes.

In short, the model helps the change agent not to jump blindly into a change process, but to look before leaping; to think twice about it.

A nice example of the effect that someone's philosophy can have on a change idea is illustrated by the discussions that took place in a postgraduate course between change agents who work mostly for the public sector and change agents who work mostly for the private sectors. When a case study from the public sector was discussed (especially its political processes), the private sector change agents were quick to suggest measures to improve efficiency. Delivery time had to be cut and cost-effectiveness improved. Some proposed that "business process redesign" would provide the solution. Their view was based on a "machine metaphor" for organizations. They were convinced that by tuning the "organizational machine," more reliable and inexpensive products could be delivered—a noble ambition for any organization. This metaphor, and the associated solutions, horrified the public sector change agents. They believed that the most important characteristics of political processes in the public sector are such things as political legitimacy and administrative scrupulousness. This implies extensive debate and weighing up the pros and cons. In other words, acting with deliberate slowness and designed inefficiency to achieve "higher values." A consultant from the private sector who attempts to streamline a public sector organization as a result of lacking insight into his own philosophies, is likely to make matters worse. He would do well to mistrust his reflexes and assess the usefulness of his convictions and philosophies.

Another example: We observe that managers with a background in more bureaucratic (industrial or government) organizations often have dysfunctional beliefs and perceptions about management when they end up in professional organizations later in their careers. Armed with the experience that stability and control, and peace and quiet, are keys to productivity within a bureaucracy, they mistakenly assume that this will also hold true for their new working environment. But nothing could be farther from the truth: Professional organizations need a certain amount of conflict. Professionals have strong views and a high level of autonomy. A peaceful organization usually means that the professionals are avoiding one another and that the organization has become fragmented. There needs to be constructive friction among the self-willed professionals to promote cohesiveness and innovation within an organization. Vanderdriessche talks of an "optimal level of conflict" that allows creativity to blossom; too much conflict and the organization blows itself up, too little and lethargy sets in (see section 6.10).

Models other than Figure 4.3 are readily available, some of which fit well with certain color-print thinking. Blue-print thinkers find "SWOT" analyses very helpful:

charting the Strengths and Weaknesses within an organization in relation to the Opportunities and Threats from the environment. The combined factual information gained from such an analysis provides an almost mechanistic exercise to define the desired change. The same subject of how an organization relates to its environment is discussed in Porter's models of the competitive structure (see section 6.4), but the language is different. It talks of market forces and of parties fighting for market shares. Information is gathered about negotiating power, coalitions, and entry barriers for new competitors. This is a good alternative for yellow-print thinkers when they deal with the same subject matter. Green-print thinkers on the other hand will probably be more interested in the development and evolution of the organization up to the present time, wondering, "How did it grow to this?" They might, for example, embrace Greiner's (1972) life-phase model, as described in section 2.3.2. This model sketches the various types of crises that organizations (need to) encounter and overcome as they grow and develop. Each phase in the organization's life cycle implies certain types of crises, all of which must be completed if the organization is to blossom (in season).

History greatly influences the change idea. This change idea is the actual starting point of any planned change. This planned change process tries to turn the intended outcomes into real ones. The path of planned change is made up of three elements: actors, phases, and communication. We discuss these elements in the next three sections.

4.4 Actors

In the 15th century, Machiavelli wrote,

> Nothing is more difficult to take on, more precarious to lead, or less certain of success than introducing new things, because the person introducing them makes an enemy of those who fared well under the old situation and those that might fare well under the new situation do not (yet) defend it zealously.

He regarded a change process as a political arena for interested parties. Morgan (1986) speaks here of the political metaphor of organizations: a place where interests, power, and conflicts play dominant roles. People with this metaphor in mind tend to recognize insiders versus outsiders, to distinguish measures of power and types of interests, to characterize the ties between important players, and to gauge attitudes toward the intended change. The political dimension does not always need to play a major role, but if the dimension is less strictly defined in terms of power play, the "actor" perspective remains relevant in just about every change process. This perspective could be defined as "the necessary roles in a change process." Distinguishing various actors, each with a different role, would appear to be an undisputed element of change processes.

Our general model, illustrated in Figure 4.4, shows seven roles that can be distinguished during the course of a change process. Typically, the change starts when

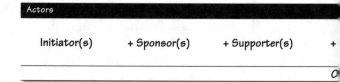

Figure 4.4 Actors Involved in Change

initiators have a "change idea." They put the change idea on the "agenda." Initiators look for sponsors who will use their formal and informal powers to help legitimize the intended change or at least ensure that it is tolerated. They will search for orchestrators, assuming it is not straightforward who that needs to be. Orchestrators do not necessarily have to come from within the organization. They might be regarded as a "professional conscience" who have the primary responsibility for safeguarding progress toward the planned ambitions. Orchestrators set up the change, stimulate its implementation, and monitor its progress (often all the way from start to finish). They share their responsibility at the earliest possible opportunity with supporters and, as soon as the approach can be defined clearly enough, with "champions." The difference between these two roles lies in their degree of responsibility. Supporters have no formal responsibility and give their informal support because, for any variety of reasons, they find the change desirable. Conversely, a champion shares the formal responsibility for drawing up and coordinating the intervention plan. Together, they gradually involve a larger number of people in the change: implementers, who realize (parts of) the interventions and "change subjects who realize the change" on the shop floor (or "change victims" who just undergo these changes). Categorizing the roles in this way puts them into a certain sequence and illustrates that the number of people involved generally grows as the change progresses.

This categorization of roles is a useful tool

♦   for naming and organizing essential contributions in the process: an initiating contribution at the outset, supporting contributions early on, followed by planning contributions, and so on. We have seen enough projects come to grief because the realization of "support from the top" or "support from the grass roots" was not woven into the process. Also, we have observed a lack of continuity when there was no orchestrator to keep an eye on the big picture.

♦   for avoiding the mixing and blurring of roles where this is undesirable. In project management, for example, the principal should never take on the dual roles of principal and project manager. This would compromise her objectivity; she would interfere too much with the implementation, which could even result in her redefining the results during the course of the project for her own ends.

A good example of an avoidable problem is the powerlessness of middle managers in some bureaucratic organizations. At an insurance company we noticed great

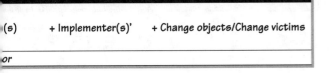

reluctance among middle management to voice good ideas—which they did have—and we wondered why. It turned out they were afraid of automatically being made responsible for implementing improvements they might suggest, which indeed turned out to be a common occurrence. They had realized that such responsibility got them into trouble as they often did not have sufficient time, resources, or influence to bring those "good ideas" about by themselves. This was especially the case for all the ideas that transcended the boundaries of their own departments and addressed interdepartmental synergy. The actor model helped the middle managers to realize that they, as initiators, should not feel obliged to take on any of the subsequent roles. Those roles might be necessary, but they can also be filled by others, often with better results. Role demarcation gives breathing space. Their main (and sometimes only) task was to find sponsors. Nothing more.

We regard this normative role demarcation as an ideal to strive for, but not one to be restricted by in the real world. Some elements will, for instance, be iterative: When a new stage of the change process is started, new sponsors, supporters, champions, and so on will often have to be found. Furthermore, some roles can and should sometimes be taken on by one and the same person, while other roles might at times be of minor importance. This is all tightly linked to the colors.

In the white-print processes, for example, there is no "change subject," and the "initiator" is also the "implementer." There are predominantly self-directed leaders and network partners. The emphasis in blue-print processes is largely on implementation roles; the roles of sponsor and supporter are not made explicit. There are change subjects (even victims), but you do not, by definition, have to take them into account. Typically the result comes first, people last. Zaltman and Duncan (1977), for example, use two roles for these kinds of changes: the "change agents" and the "change targets." Wijnen, Weggeman, and Kor (1999) use three: the "principal," the "change manager," and the "target group." In their views, these roles can and must be kept strictly separate, because, for example, a principal who is also in a target group will quickly internalize and express the resistance common to target groups. A yellow-print thinker, on the other hand, always recognizes the role of sponsor. Nadler (1981) says,

> for a change to occur successfully, a critical mass of power groups needs to be assembled and mobilized in support of the change. Those groups that may oppose the change have to in some way be compensated for or have their effects neutralized.

Figure 4.5 Phases in a Change Process

In addition, Mintzberg (1983) offers a list of possible internal and external coalition partners. As external partners, he mentions owners, associates, employee associations, and publics that must be considered and managed during a change process. Red-print thinkers pay special attention to staff involvement: They strive to reduce the number of change subjects to a minimum by involving them in the implementation. Selznick (1949) wrote, "Others will have to be included in the planning of the change so that their participation will motivate them, or co-opt them."

4.5 The Change Phases

In addition to the game of influence played by actors, there is also the content of the change: activities as constituent parts of the process between history and outcomes. These activities are not a homogenous, continuous stream. There are always various phases that can be distinguished in retrospect (descriptive), but our main concern is being able to distinguish these various phases in advance (prescriptive). Doing so improves the chance of a successful change. We have opted for a simple four-way split that appears to be equally applicable to all colors of change (Figure 4.5). The division is: diagnosing, finding a change strategy, drawing up an intervention plan, and, finally, carrying out interventions (possibly in multiple successive phases).

The division into phases is useful for creating visible steps within major change processes such as a three-year merger process. You could, for example, carry out a three-month diagnosis of the partners to be merged and then, together with them, draw up a strategy and an intervention plan during the next two months, followed by a number of major implementation steps in the subsequent two years. This implementation could entail the formation of a new top structure followed by policy formation, restructuring, staffing, training, and then finishing the whole thing off with a celebration. The three-year period would furthermore be interspersed with interim evaluations or monitoring, and replanning of the change process. But this division in four phases is just as useful for the "invisible" maneuverings of a change agent in, for instance, his single first meeting with an initiator. In the course of such a meeting, the change agent could be diagnosing what is being said and making strategic choices for certain interventions (e.g., a confronting question or an empathic rephrasing) within this selfsame meeting. In this sense there is talk of a Mamouschka-effect, like nested Russian dolls, one inside the other, inside the other, inside the other . . . Within the

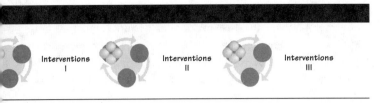

Interventions
I

Interventions
II

Interventions
III

phased three-year merger process, there could well be a phased period of training the staff and within that period several vital meetings, again with phases. Such divisions into phases or steps take place at many levels concurrently.

What, then, is the use of such a division? We can see at least two reasons:

♦   increasing the transparency and structuring of change processes by splitting up and sequencing the activities. Moreover, it allows you to incrementally focus the change process. One can tailor each new phase while rounding off the previous one.

♦   increasing the effectiveness of the change process by allowing time for reflection. Change is not a trick, it's a competence. Each step should include a deliberate design and replanning of the next one based on insight into the effectiveness of the change process thus far and the circumstances that are helping or hindering it. This increases the coherence between steps and the feasibility of the next one.

We look at the various phases in more depth in Chapter 5. Suffice it to say here that each of the phases helps to avoid specific problems in the process as a whole:

♦   The diagnostic phase helps to clarify what is at the heart of the matter. A hastily drawn-up plan of approach and too little diagnosis is an occupational hazard for change agents, partly because clients or principals are often perceived to demand answers and solutions. Coming up with quick fixes might look sharp, but jumping to conclusions has severe drawbacks. More often than not, change agents realize down the line that these quick fixes do not deliver what they promise, for example, because the necessary conditions are not checked in advance. For instance, they might find out later that there never was enough time for their approach (5-min-utes-to-12 situations; see section 6.11) or that the root of the problem lay somewhere else, like a squabbling management team and not, as they might have thought, a messy organizational structure.

♦   The change strategy phase helps to clarify what the lever for change must be. Determining a change strategy is possibly the most neglected of the phases. We recently came across a good example of such neglect. During the diagnostic phase, the change agents had carefully worked out the IST (present) and SOLL (desired) situations, but then immediately went on to draw up a nine-month plan of approach into which they crammed all the differences between IST and SOLL. The psychology of the change was severely flawed as a result. New positions were set up and staff members selected (red) while new training was offered (green) concurrently even though such actions are generally not compatible—the first raises anxiety and competitiveness, whereas the latter requires a safe environment to be effective. Furthermore, such cramming is overkill, like using a cannon to kill a mosquito. Trying to implement a multitude of interventions is usually far less effective than tackling a couple of key interventions seriously.

♦   Drawing up an intervention plan helps implementation: In which order should the interventions be carried out, and which will reinforce others? In short: How do we segment and phase the interventions into a consistent and feasible package? If one fails to segment and phase, complex changes will rest on the shoulders of only a few because the activities cannot be divided up among a number of champions. Clear hand-over moments cease to exist. If the intervention phases are not clearly separated and sequenced in advance, then necessary conditions for change can easily be compromised. We witnessed, for example, an insurance company cutting its "culture change" short after a six-month period because the board started to feel an urge to restructure the firm. This despite the obvious need for a sustained multiyear effort and for the absence of competing changes to allow any organizational culture to shift.

♦   Interventions are implemented in accordance with an intervention plan. Because things hardly ever go as planned, it is quite usual for a plan to be reviewed and adjusted after the completion of a number of interventions. Activities might be slowed down or perhaps speeded up. Such decisions might require the drawing up of a new series of interventions, possibly after making a supplementary diagnosis and agreeing on amendments to the change strategy.

The degree to which division into steps or phases is possible depends to a large extent on the change agent's view of change. Moreover, this view also affects the naming of the phases, and rightly so: Phasing can be adjusted to each specific color-print strategy, even while still based on the same general considerations as outlined above.

For the sake of convenience, Senior (1997) divides the world of change into two halves: a "hard systems model of change" and a "soft systems model of change." She regards the first model to be primarily suitable for simple systems, clear power structures, and well-defined relationships, while she recommends that the second model be used in more complex situations with multiple power bases and network structures.

The roots of the hard systems model of change bring Senior into the realm of systems engineering, operational research, and project management. This model consists of three main phases. In the description phase, goals for change are systematically determined on the basis of a diagnosis. The options phase is used to think up alternative scenarios and select one of them. Finally, in the implementation phase, the plans are put into practice and the results monitored. Thus you can also recognize our suggested four way-split: diagnosis, change strategy, intervention plan, and interventions. A more elaborate division of phases within the same hard systems realm can be

Model	Process		
Lewin (1947)	Unfreezing	Changing	Refreezing
Beckhard and Harris (1977)	Present State	Transition State	Future State
Beer (1980)	Dissatisfaction	Process	Model
Kanter (1983)	Departures from tradition and crises	Strategic decisions and prime movers	Action vehicles and institutionalization
Tichy and Devanna (1985)	Awakening	Mobilizing	Reinforcing
Nadler and Tushman (1989)	Energizing	Envisioning	Enabling

Table 4.4 Phases in a Change Process (Kanter, 1992)

found in the concepts of project-based working. Wijnen and Kor distinguish six phases, namely, the initiation, definition, design, preparatory, realization, and postdelivery phases. This division has many merits, including its versatility to allow for choices during the process at an increasingly detailed level within the framework laid down in the previous phase. It allows for very efficient change processes. You will undoubtedly have already noticed the similarities between the hard systems model and the blue-print approach, but it is also suitable for relatively simple red processes.

The roots of the soft systems model of change brings Senior into the tradition of organization development. Among others, she refers to Lewin's triple-phase model in which actual changes are preceded by "unfreezing" and followed by "re-freezing." With the passage of time, many organization development practitioners have thought up variations to this model, as illustrated in Table 4.4.

Common questions raised in the field of Organization Development pertain to the psychology of change processes: How do you deal with resistance? How do you get people to support change? How can people be made to feel comfortable with the change? How can they internalize the change? These are chiefly "red" questions. Cummings and Worley (1993) employ a more detailed division in five phases that fits within this tradition: "motivating change, creating a vision, developing political support, managing the transition and sustaining momentum." In their view you must first state why the change is necessary before coming up with a vision. They also feel that a vision can win people over and be instrumental in gaining sufficiently powerful backing for the change in the political arena. The political support element in their phases also introduces yellow-print thinking into the equation. Their five-phase division is just as convincing as

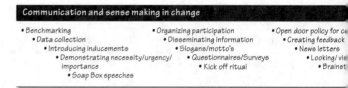

Communication and sense making in change

- Benchmarking
  - Data collection
    - Introducing inducements
      - Demonstrating necessity/urgency/ importance
        - Soap Box speeches

- Organizing participation
  - Disseminating information
    - Slogans/motto's
      - Questionnaires/Surveys
        - Kick off ritual

- Open door policy for c
  - Creating feedback
    - News letters
      - Looking/vie
        - Brainst

Figure 4.6 Communication and Sense-Making

the project-based one, but for different reasons. They are not primarily concerned with the content of the change, but more so with the process by which it takes place.

4.6 Communication and Sense-Making

In addition to actors and phases, the third element that connects history to outcomes is communication. Change processes are perhaps more than anything else a dialogue between those involved: a process whereby people collectively create a new reality through language. This new reality then expresses itself in new ways of thinking and acting, in people's minds and hands.

There is a "narrow" and a "broad" approach to this way of thinking. The narrow approach focuses on communication *about* the change process. Kotter (1990), for example, regards change as a problem that can be solved by helping people to understand the change and the new roles that will be expected of them. Beckhard and Pritchard (1992) emphasize the use of communication to announce and explain the change and to manage positive and negative expectations. Kotter and Schlesinger (1979) see it as a means of addressing resistance and increasing commitment. Beer (1980) states that communication is a critical factor in enabling people to experience psychological ownership of the change at hand. All these perspectives emphasize communication as a tool that must be deployed alongside the actual change process to increase its feasibility.

In their article, "The Role of Conversations in Producing Intentional Change in Organizations," Ford and Ford (1995) present a broader approach to communication. They argue that change is a part of communication and not the other way around: "Change is a process that is created, produced and maintained by and within communication." No change without communication. Communication is seen as the mechanism that people use to create the reality in which they live (Giddens, 1984). Such conversations are not to be taken lightly. "The art of conversation is the feast of reason and the flow of soul." Change sprouts from conversations and is carried by them: Communication takes place between those involved within every phase of the change process; during the diagnosis, the interventions, in determining the outcomes, in expressing the innovator's world vision, and more.

In the checklist that we have created (Figure 4.6), you will find both approaches: communication about the change and communication within the change process itself.

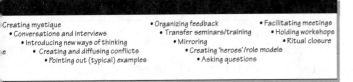

Creating mystique
 • Conversations and interviews
  • Introducing new ways of thinking
   • Creating and diffusing conflicts
    • Pointing out (typical) examples

• Organizing feedback
 • Transfer seminars/training
  • Mirroring
   • Creating 'heroes'/role models
    • Asking questions

• Facilitating meetings
 • Holding workshops
  • Ritual closure

This checklist supplies communication channels and resources that can often be used for both purposes. These channels and resources are not randomly listed, but are partly phase linked. It is obvious that a start-up ritual (a manager on a soap box, for example) and a ritual ending, in the form of a concluding celebration, will necessarily take place toward the beginning and the end of the process, respectively.

This checklist's value is that it

♦ reminds us to give attention to organizing communication *about* change, the aim of which is to inform those involved, to address resistance, to create involvement and to supply meaning to the change

♦ reminds us to give attention to facilitating communication *within* the change, the aim of which is to enable collective efforts. There are thousands more possibilities for people to misunderstand one another than there are to get each other's point. This frustrates collective efforts more than anything else. Only by reducing miscommunication will those involved be able to jointly realize the change

♦ offers an overview of channels and resources that offer ideas on how to orchestrate communication a little more creatively and a little more in depth.

Communication *about* a change process can do wonders. We once helped a school racked by conflict, with the principal on one side and a group of teachers and pupils who did not shy away from using banners, publicity, and strikes to further their cause, on the other side. The arrival of an external consultant soon became the talk of the school. Whose side would she take? Everyone had his or her own suspicions. As consultants, we were asked to diagnose the source of the conflict through interviews and roundtable discussions, but no one was prepared to wait six weeks for the result, or to accept the result if there was any doubt as to our impartiality, the meticulousness of our approach, exactly what our approach consisted of, and so on. With whom would we be talking? Would the discussions be confidential? What was to be our reporting protocol? Would we be making recommendations? And would these be binding? Communicating about the nature of our assignment and the procedures and protocols we were intent on following defused the situation. It bought us the necessary time to diagnose the conflict and postponed further strikes, as it later turned out, indefinitely. This was perhaps a more important intervention than the diagnosis itself.

Partly because you cannot *not* communicate, conscious communication is vital from the beginning to the end of a change process. Otherwise a multitude of different interpretations will emerge among those involved, thereby fueling further miscommunication.

Dimension	Choices
Style	formal versus informal confidential versus open informative versus persuasive or directive
Focus	directed toward knowledge, attitude, or behavior directed toward exchange of information or learning
Participation	horizontal, vertical, or diagonal involvement involvement of clients, actors in the production chain, or even external networks
Contribution	involved in decisions, discussions, implemention , or just being informed
Level	aimed at content, procedure, interaction, or feelings aimed at perceptions (physical, emotional, etc.), at meanings (mental models, mystique, symbols, heroes, images), or at resolutions (intentions, plans, commitments)

Table 4.5 Choices for Organizing Communication

For this reason, we feel that communication needs to be an integral part of every intervention plan, and should be consciously managed even before the intervention plan is drawn up. A tool to help achieve this is a planned approach, in which systematic choices are made about message, resources, style, timing, and so on (see Koeleman, 1992). There are a great many choices to make (see Table 4.5) and, as yet, there are few hard and fast rules on the subject. The only thing that can be said is that good communication about change should not be unnecessarily one-sided (therefore appropriately alternating between formal and informal, between content and emotion, etc.), should be based on conscious choices (with regard to who may/must take part in the change, for example), and should be given constant attention.

With regard to communication *within* a change process, Ford and Ford (1995) make a distinction between four types of conversations that are more or less consecutive in the change process. The first of these are the "initiative conversations" that try to focus people's attention on what could or should be done. This takes the shape of directions, proposals, declarations, promises, and the like. It is the call to action. "We must do something about the high staff turnover," or "We must reduce the budget deficit by one quarter." If these types of conversations do not take place, you are left with inconsequential small talk. The initiative conversations are followed by "conversations for understanding" where information, arguments, and opinions are exchanged. The aim is to increase participation and create transparency concerning feasibility. This is also the time to make choices. Should these types of conversations not take place, common insights and a common language will fail to develop. Initiators will remain a lone voice crying in the wilderness, insisting they are not understood by those around them. The third type of conversation is "conversations for performance"; these initiate concrete action. They mark a period full of requests, promises, negotiations, and agreements. Results, tasks, and time limits are specified. The end of the change process is marked by "conversations for closure." Those involved realize and proclaim that it is over. They look back on their efforts, recapture what has been achieved, and speculate on the future. It is a time to bask in contentment or come to terms with disappointment. Because these conversations for closure are seldom held, the majority of change processes just peter out. And that is a pity. It leaves a feeling of nothing ever being completed and of lessons never learned.

Obviously, the emphasis, target group, and content of all this communication differs for each color. In yellow processes, for example, there is relatively little communication *about* the change to the organization as a whole; most of it is being confined to group settings where the change is being negotiated. There, communication focuses on roles and ground rules for the negotiation and the need and criteria for possible outcomes. In contrast, poor communication about change in red processes is a capital offense— here it is essential to motivate others for one's plans. The content focuses on "what is expected of you" and "what is in it for you." In blue processes most of the talk is about the details of the content and work plan of the change at hand, while in white processes people skip over that to talk about the significance and meaning of the whole thing.

Also the resources or instruments for communication will differ between colors, although some instruments can be used for different means. Typical red instruments include the soap box, keeping people informed, office hours for consultation, and news letters, while the green approach uses feedback loops, brainstorming, mirroring, and introducing new ways of thinking. White-print thinkers prefer to optimize conflicts, create mystique and heroes, increase diversity by pointing to alternatives, and arrange a virtual closure. The blue approach uses reviews, audits, memos, benchmarking, and clear hand-over periods, whereas yellow thinkers lobby, leak information to the press, carry out surveys among the members of the organization, and set up heterogeneous work groups to determine their common position.

4.7 Steering

Planned change presupposes a belief in causality: that interventions can be consciously designed and carried out, making desired outcomes a fact or at least a probability. The word *consciously* is pivotal; progress is closely monitored and adjustments are made on the basis of new insights. From start to finish, especially during

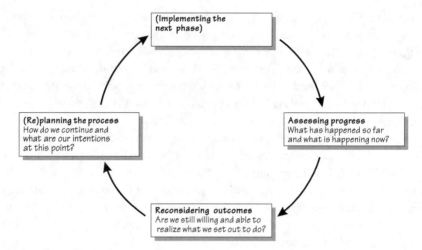

Figure 4.7 Steering Cycle

less-predictable processes, there is someone who is constantly reviewing the sense and effectiveness of the interactions, the activities, and the aims of those involved. If there is no steering, a change process is like a runaway train thundering past without a driver. This final element, steering, is, as it were, the glue holding the other elements together. It enables the whole thing to work.

Steering can take place on many levels at the same time. It can be directed at the change process as a whole, but just as easily at certain parts of the process, carried out by specific groups or individual champions within the organization. It plays a part in the head of individual change agents when they think about their day-to-day activities. We would like to remind you of the Mamouschka doll metaphor that we used earlier to illustrate the simultaneous applicability of phases for change agents' small "invisible" discussions and the larger "visible" three-year merger processes (see section 4.5). Here, similarly, there is talk of steering within steering within steering.

Figure 4.7 shows a general model. The essence of steering is the installation of feedback and feed-forward cycles with both long and short time horizons. It comes as no surprise, therefore, that our model is circular. Three questions must be answered in the steering cycle before beginning the next phase in a change process:

- ◆ Determining the change's progress: What has happened so far, and what is happening now?
- ◆ Reconsidering the change's outcomes: Do our goals still stand, and are they still feasible?
- ◆ Replanning the change process: How do we continue? What's next?

What use is this model? We see three possible applications:

◆ Designing the nature and frequency of the monitoring beforehand. What has to be measured, what needs specific attention? When will these measurements take place?

◆ Delegating the steering to various actors and to various organizational levels in advance. Who plans, who monitors, who reviews and reconsiders, and who replans? Is this done by different people, and are there enough of them? Are they competent enough?

◆ Determining ahead of time how these actors communicate with each other. What means are used for reporting? Is it written down or does it suffice when it remains in the heads of those involved?

The model helps to remedy the problem of change processes going off course. This applies equally to each color. Green management development processes soon fizzle out if the program does not play into the participants' changing learning ambitions. The risk is just as great for seemingly rational projects. We observed how a major blue construction project was at the risk of experiencing numerous delays and budget overruns as the result of local elections. New political parties taking office might think differently about the construction project. The change agents involved anticipated this and were quick to have crucial decisions signed and sealed just before the handing over of power. They also involved the new actors in advance, even if informally, in the planning of the subsequent steps—a bit of yellow adjustment to the blue approach, as it were.

Another problem that concerns us is the difficulty of proving or demonstrating the effect of most of the change processes in organizations. In many cases measuring and reviewing progress is rare, with the exception of the more rational and power-oriented approaches. Here, at least, there is "a building," "a new structure," or a "policy" at the end of it all: There is something concrete to show as an outcome of all the effort. But in learning processes, culture change, or when self-steering teams are introduced, the result can be somewhat hazy. Particularly for green and white processes, the literature is full of inspiring formulae but short on empirical data. Do these fashionable concepts really work? Or is it a question of faith? We think that it is in the interest of our profession as change agents to diagnose the relevance of our actions: Designing a monitoring and steering process in advance is one way of doing this.

Obviously the color of the change influences the nature of the steering. On the blue side of the spectrum steering can be quite cut and dried, partly because the results have been so well defined beforehand. This side of the spectrum uses a control cycle, essentially a variation of our model. Here, assessing progress is called measuring and is carried out on the basis of empirical data at previously determined decision points.

In project management (Wijnen, 1984) there is a set number of aspects that must be included in the decision documents; namely, time (when?), money (how profitable?), quality (how good?), information (on what basis?), and organization (for/by whom?). Reconsidering outcomes is defined as the comparison between the measurements and the previously determined norms and margins. These are sometimes even determined on the basis of (external) benchmarks. The responsibility for the steering is also unambiguous: There is one project leader who draws up the decision document, and one principal (or steering committee) who is responsible for making the necessary decisions. The roles are clear.

The steering on the white side of the spectrum is more a function of the sensitivity of change agents than the hard data of measurements. Here, the object and subject of the change are identical: The change agent is also the "change victim." Moreover, the purpose resides in the process. In these cases, "old fashioned control" will just not do it, and certainly not from one central point within the organization. This does not imply the absence of steering, however; white-print processes need not be unprofessional or laissez faire. As the change is self-directed, the steering lies more in a fundamental variation of the learning cycle (based on Kolb, 1991; Argyris, 1978; and Schön, 1983). Here assessing progress is called observation and reconsidering outcomes is known as sense-making, while replanning is more like committing one's self. Schön (1983) calls this "reflective practitioning," a term we return to in Chapter 8. Such reflection is not restricted to previously determined indicators, but might take any emerging relevant indicator into account. It resembles a kind of openness and perceptiveness of what is happening in the environment and in the (private) world of the person concerned. Awareness is the watchword here. Making sense of something is the creative process of seeing the interconnectedness among all kinds of (conflicting) information and turning this into a personal concept of, for example, the organization, the change process, or the person himself. It goes a step farther than comparison with a previously determined norm. Weick (1995) cites many examples of this kind of sense-making. It sometimes has people completely reverse their opinions half way down the line when dealing with concrete matters as a new structure, a merger, or the choice of one's intervention style. However, when it comes to the overarching less tangible outcome that the white-print thinker was striving for (be it increasing intrepreneurship or creating a dialogue, for example), the white-print thinker holds his course; steering toward the outcome is his motto, not paying attention to today's hype.

We have sketched the nature and method of monitoring and steering for each individual color in Table 3.2 of Chapter 3. The two extremes we described above are illustrated in Figure 4.8, which depicts both the blue control cycle and the white/green learning cycle. Yellow steering is similar to blue steering when it comes to formal lines of reporting at previously determined decision moments and determining clear

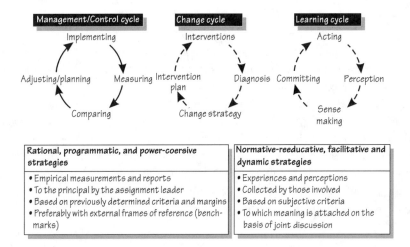

Figure 4.8 Three Cycles

authority boundaries for project managers. But previously determined norms and margins for (interim) results are less clear in yellow changes and there is no sign of benchmarking. Red steering covers the middle ground. It does collect experiences and perceptions of change subjects and takes them as seriously as green/white steering, but there will always be reporting to a higher level. Figure 4.8 also shows the change cycle; the phases in change processes can be regarded to be essentially the same as in both other cycles. Diagnosis is a form of measuring/assessing progress, strategy development a form of reconsidering outcomes and approach, and so on. We look more closely at this change cycle in Chapter 5.

4.8 Playing With the Elements: A Case Illustration

Every change agent can use the method described in this chapter as a tool to develop change processes ("Have I forgotten anything?") and to describe them. To illustrate how you can typify a change process in terms of how the six main elements play a role, we examine a randomly chosen consulting assignment (in which some details have been changed to ensure anonymity). The assignment in question took place in South-East Asia and was commissioned by a Western development organization. The assignment consisted of a definition phase lasting three to four months, and an implementation phase lasting about three years. To keep our description short we concentrate solely on the definition phase. Because we describe it for illustrative purposes only, the description is not complete, numerous details have been left out, and we keep as closely as possible to the terminology introduced in this chapter.

Change Idea

The desired outcome of the definition phase was to produce a document based on a thorough investigation that sets out how a cluster of approximately 1,200 small textile factories that seriously pollute the environment could be persuaded to take measures to reduce the damage they are causing (with the help of development aid). This was the change idea as presented by the development organization, the initiator as the first actor. The change idea was primarily expressed in terms of characteristics of operational management (see Figure 4.2): in this case feasible projects to unburden the environment effectively and efficiently. Neither the necessary preconditions nor the necessary changes for other characteristics (organization and management, interaction, people) were previously determined.

History

The "objective context" was that the change idea should involve a complete town containing approximately 1,200 small textile factories and 100,000 inhabitants. The factories produced about 2,000 kilometers of textiles in a day and more than 30,000 liters of heavily polluted industrial effluent. Some of this effluent was used to irrigate the land (desert region), but sooner or later most of it found its way into one river. This caused serious public health problems in towns and villages even hundreds of kilometers downstream, especially during the monsoon. The town's standard of living was low. Environmental issues were low on everyone's agenda as well, except on that of the authorities. The industry had installed a wastewater treatment plant some ten years ago, but this plant was always breaking down and hardly ever in operation.

The industry was financially reasonably healthy. This fact emerged from an earlier investigation of all of the textile manufacturing regions in the country. That investigation also showed that the environmental pollution in this town was no exception to the rule. It was, however, an exceptionally serious case. The trigger for the assignment was the recommendation from the previously mentioned investigation to invest development aid in this town. But the assignment was also triggered by the increasing pressure on the textile industry from the state authorities and the surrounding towns.

The "philosophies" were, as is usually the case, peculiar to each particular actor. The initiator was convinced that environmental degradation in general is one of the most important issues of our time, but also that little (sustainable) improvement can be expected if the nontechnical aspects are excluded from the change effort, such as economic, socio-cultural, and legal aspects. This was especially true because environmental issues ranked much lower on town people's scale of priorities than that of the initiator's. The town people's mind-sets differed in that sense. The initiator was convinced that cooperation with the textile factories would be decisive to reduce pollution. Somehow a bridge between the two mind-sets needed to be forged.

Actors

The actors involved in the process were as follows. First, there was the "initiator," who was part of the development organization. Second, there was us, whom we regarded as the process's "orchestrators." Who were the "sponsors"? Financial sponsoring came from the development organization's decision makers and political sponsoring from the national and regional authorities in South-East Asia. The textile industry was considered to be potential a "supporter" from the outset. The formal representatives from the coordinating industrial association and a number of prominent factory owners were approached as soon as sponsoring was secured. The "champion" roles were assigned to a team consisting of a number of local consultants with experience of similar change processes and who also had a certain amount of status in that part of the country, and the directors of a textile research institute who had had links with the industry for years. Staff from the institute would also take responsibility for most of the activities of this phase in collaboration with the industry. This setup allowed us to assess whether the institute's staff had the skills necessary to carry out the subsequent "implementation." The "change subjects" (or change "victims," if you will) were the 1,200 factories and the 100,000 inhabitants of the town, most of whom derived their livelihood from these factories and all of whom were subject to the resulting environmental and health threats. And, of course, the natural environment was a major change victim.

Phases

Based on first impressions, the team decided from the outset to spread the mission (at no extra cost) over a period of three months with three or four visits of one week instead of the six continuous weeks proposed by the initiator. The reason for this lay in the nature of the assignment: the team estimated that the projects would have an effect on the interests of a large number of people and that time would be needed to find a means of gaining political legitimacy and support.

The "diagnosis" consisted of interviews with the main parties involved, first in the Netherlands and then in a round of interviews lasting one week in the country itself. They included local, state, and national authorities; local consultants; research bodies; and industry representatives. The diagnosis also included a quick study of the literature available on characteristics of the country's textile industry, environmental legislation, economic development, earlier change efforts and their subsequent success or failure, and so on. All this took about a month. The main point of discussion was under which conditions the definition phase and the subsequent implementation might be successful.

The "change strategy" could be summed up in two complimentary approaches. On the one hand, it was thought that permanent solutions could be achieved only with the help of a great deal of factual analysis: Just how extensive is the environmental damage, just how much money does the industry make, what kind of institutions and procedures play a role in decision-making processes,, and what is the potential for possible technical and organizational interventions? It soon became clear that everyone had their own answers to these types of questions, but a foundation in fact for these answers was scarce or nonexistent. To get these facts on the table, the chosen approach was primarily blue.

On the other hand, it was felt that the team would succeed in gaining access to this information only if the industry thought it to be in its own interests, a win-win situation, and that possible subsequent implementation would stand or fall with their willing cooperation. In addition, it appeared necessary to convince the authorities to give the industry sufficient time and lenience to work on real improvements instead of offering cosmetic, bogus solutions to relieve the political pressure. This led us to a complementary yellow approach.

In this case, the "intervention plan" (for this definition phase) was made up of a combination of ultra-systematic planning and outright improvisation. The systematic planning, complete with mega-diagrams outlining activities, deadlines, and decision documents and such, was designed to help the champions and implementers collect reliable and complete information. It touched on a wide range of technical, commercial, cultural, and political aspects. The improvisation aspect was necessary to manage the political arena incrementally. For instance, not one of the three consecutive visits went as planned. On one occasion there was talk of litigation, which immediately caused panic within the industry, and on another occasion we were confronted by researchers who wanted to cancel meetings or steer the mission in a completely different direction. We had expected this sort of gamesmanship and the extra room for improvisation proved to be badly needed. A great deal of time was spent on the following activities: aligning the views of champions and implementers, involving the industry and securing its commitment, reassuring the authorities, and testing and adjusting implementation plans with all parties involved.

Communication and Sense-Making

The four types of "conversations" distinguished by Ford and Ford (see 4.6) were fairly recognizable in this project. The "initiative conversations" were aimed at getting to know one another, inviting people to participate, and gauging expectations. This meant many meetings in secluded locations. With champions and implementers these meetings were largely informal, but, in contrast, the talks with the industry and the authorities were sometimes accompanied by a great deal of fuss and ceremony. These talks were followed by "conversations for understanding." During these talks much information was brought to the surface and exchanged. The subsequent "conversations for performance" were designed to spur people into action using such means as requests, negotiations, and promises. They often took place in other locations. In the town itself, the industry organized a number of large meetings that were more like political gatherings. Together with the Indian consultants and researchers, this was our chance to explain our intentions and how the town could profit from our efforts and the possible future support of the development organization. Leading members from the industry spelled out why they were working with us and called upon others to join them. Toward the end of the definition phase "conversations for closure" took place in which we presented our findings and proposals for the implementation phase (previously checked by various key players) to the industry and the authorities. We talked of the future and of the commitments that those involved needed to make; tentative agreements were forged and steering committees formed, a newsletter was written, representatives from the development organizations were introduced, future workshops were agreed on, and much more.

Steering

The steering was extremely rational with regard to the ("blue") content: Decision documents were assessed at previously determined times in accordance with previously agreed checklists and tables of contents, for example. Steering the (yellow) interactions and negotiations was quite different: It consisted mainly of the orchestrator's observations and frequently gauging the experiences of those involved. We then retired to our hotel for the evening, with a glass of whisky in one hand and a cigarette in the other, talking until deep in the night about how the next day's program would have to be altered, who would have to be approached, and how to encourage people to remain committed to the project. The champions, the Indian consultants and the management of the research institute, played an important role in this as sounding board.

Outcomes

The actual outcomes of the definition phase included the previously determined change idea. One result was a bulky document, based on extensive investigation, that proposed an implementation program (made up of ten interlinked projects over a period of two to three years) to help the textile factories limit their damage to the environment. Moreover, the whole document had a solid analytical foundation. It also gave an insight into subcultures, generational problems, sensitivities, and power balances that had to be taken into account in the implementation phase.

A start was also made on organizing and staffing the subsequent phase. The competence of the research institute was increased by some training and coaching (though not yet to the level needed for successful completion of the next phase).

The most important additional outcomes (beyond what was part of the original change idea) concerned characteristics of interaction: A network of relationships had been created that had reached consensus on the change program and felt that it could bring about something positive.

Postscript

As in every development aid project, the subsequent implementation phase did not follow the implementation program to the letter (nor should it!): Deadlines were postponed, people changed office, priorities changed, and so on. We remained involved as "coaches" of those who were in charge of the implementation program. Our involvement ended after another two years during which we saw the textile factories' operational management improving considerably, resulting in decreased environmental damage. There were disappointments as well. There is certainly no guarantee of sustainability, but, fortunately, those involved at the local level are still keeping things going. There has been considerable change, but the change is far from complete.

5 From Idea to Outcome

In Chapter 3 we discussed paradigms concerning change: What exactly does the concept of change mean to an individual (which color?), and is this meaning experienced consciously or subconsciously? In Chapter 4 we looked at a method for change: Which main elements seem to be constant irrespective of how people view change? What does a road map for change processes look like? In this chapter we will delve yet a little deeper: What exactly do you, as a change agent, do in each specific phase of a change process? How do you steer through the four phases from idea to outcome?

This chapter probably offers the change agent in the field the most practical advice. During external and in-house courses in change management we have noticed that most change agents wrestle with the question of how to structure each phase (Figure 5.1). How do you find answers to questions such as the following:

♦ What exactly is the problem? How do I uncover that? Why are things the way they are? How do I make sense of what I see? These questions lie at the heart of the diagnosis, and we deal with them in section 5.1.

♦ Where can you find a driving force for change? How do you achieve leverage: maximum effect through minimal effort? On what do you base your approach and what do/should you call it? These are questions related to change strategy. We address them in section 5.2.

♦ What constitutes an integral, consistent, and feasible plan? How can you have activities building on each other rather than interfering with each other? How do you compartmentalize and phase all the activities, and how do you keep track of them? Questions concerned with the intervention plan (5.3).

♦ How do we implement such a plan? Which tools are available, and how do we structure our interventions? Questions to do with interventions are examined in section 5.4.

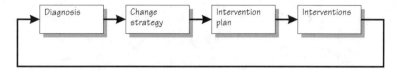

Figure 5.1 The Four Phases

The contents of this chapter offer a deeper insight into the phases (4.5) and the steering cycle (4.7). You can observe the four phases in a change process of, say, two years. But you can also go through miniature versions of these phases when you reflect for half an hour on a certain situation: When you assess progress, you are in effect diagnosing, and when you reconsider outcomes and re-plan you are in a way crafting a change strategy and intervention plan.

5.1 Diagnosis

Diagnosis has two aspects: the process by which you try to find out what is going on, and the information that is gathered as a result. Both are discussed in the following pages.

5.1.1 Diagnostic Process

Research approach or action approach?
Block (1981) argues that the diagnosing can basically be done in two contrasting fashions; namely, by using either a research approach or an action approach. The research approach looks more "scientific." Its aim is to bring together as many relevant factors as possible, as it is vital to form a complete picture. Researchers attempt to be objective, and for this reason prefer quantitative over qualitative analysis. They strive to maintain a neutral stance. Researchers regard the action approach as being rather imprecise, because in that approach completeness is not deemed as important. The action approach focuses on factors that the organization can influence and may exclude others. In this approach, people are part of the diagnostic process and importance is attached to subjective information such as feelings and intuition. Change agents do not remain passive on the sidelines, but seek to associate themselves with those involved and, where necessary, take a stand. Block feels that the research approach is inappropriate for consultants because their most important goal should be change, not knowledge. We suspect that he would reach the same conclusion with regard to change agents in general, be they consultants or not.

We are not convinced that a "scientific approach" is always wrong. For example, if an organization finds itself no longer viable, we can certainly imagine that many staff members would be neither willing nor able to take part in the diagnostic process.

Moreover, an objective collection of data can help provide warring parties like unions and shareholders with a common point of departure. In our opinion, however, Block's remarks emphasize one crucial point: The process of diagnosis is never value-free, it always has direct consequences in or for the organization. The diagnosis in itself is an intervention.

If a neutral expert makes an objective diagnosis of what is going on with the intention of convincing those involved that she is right, her assessment, no matter how brilliant, could be rejected because it was invented elsewhere. Her role makes the diagnosis ineffective. The change agent can lower resistance by opting for a participative role within which she facilitates a joint diagnosis with people working in the organization. Because increased amounts of information and viewpoints can be considered, this approach can also improve the quality of the diagnosis. Sometimes a situation can be so critical (e.g., when the organization's survival is at stake) that there is just no time for a research approach, and sometimes employees are just not able to deliver quality or are not willing to remain honest when there is bad news on the horizon.

We feel the most important lesson this teaches us is that we must design or choose our process of diagnosis consciously. It should at the very least reflect both what is appropriate for the changing organization and the approach the change agent prefers and can believably do. Until ten or twenty years ago, organization developers who followed Block's ideas tended to use action research (a participative diagnosis method), always and in every situation. They made lavish use of diagnostic models that characterized cooperative processes and focused on qualitative and subjective information (see, e.g., Cummings and Worley, 1993; French and Bell, 1984). Business consultants had an almost innate reflexive preference for the expert-sounding research approach. They in turn used quantitative and descriptive models for strategy, structure, and operational processes and padded these out with such things as benchmarks, concentrating on quantitative data, and objectivity (e.g., Porter, 1979; Andrews, 1991). Management consultants usually took the middle road, carrying out research while also keeping an eye on human factors and the legitimacy of their results for the target group. They made use of contingency models for the structuring of organizations and for human resources management, which was largely qualitative, but certainly not completely subjectively determined (e.g., Mintzberg, 1983; Peters and Waterman, 1982).

These are, of course, stereotypes, because recent publications from all those involved show an increasing tendency to trespass into each other's territory. Currently we are more likely to come across analytical models on strategy and operations in publications from organization developers and chapters in business science books dealing with resistance to change. This broadening of subjects in each of these schools of thought confirms, in our opinion, that the design of diagnostic processes should be eclectic and tailor made.

Unconflicted adherence:	problems are not recognized or taken seriously
Unconflicted change:	the tendency to believe that "more of the same" will suffice to tackle the problem
Defensive avoidance:	no one really trusts that solutions can be found; as a result, those concerned "stick their heads in the sand"
Hyper-vigilance:	the belief that things are so serious and urgent that there is no time for reflection

Table 5.1 Dysfunctional Diagnostic Patterns

Diagnostic steps

Authors from various schools also recognize common steps in the process of diagnosis. Whether this concerns an action or a research approach, both usually comprise a preliminary and a realization phase. The preliminary phase is designed to ensure that the initiator is willing to support the diagnostic process, and also to accept its results. Block (1981) is of the opinion that you are too late if you start paying attention to these matters during the process itself or, even worse, when feeding back the results to the client. One of the standard steps of the preliminary process is to define the scope of the problem and, in many cases, also to redefine it, because the original definition can often mask the real, underlying problem by excluding relevant factors, and thus lead to an inaccurate diagnosis—something that is difficult to rectify later on. Doppler and Lautenburg (1996) agree with this: They regard the fact that "privileged members of the organization already have a clear and firm opinion about what works and what does not, why it is not working and what needs to be changed" as being the greatest obstacle to a good diagnosis. In this context, Tichy (1983) refers to the necessity of creating psychological, organizational, and management conditions within which a meaningful diagnosis can be carried out, and names four possible dysfunctional patterns that the change agent must deal with before starting his diagnosis (Table 5.1).

The essence of the preliminary phase is to find agreement about the goal, the working methods, and the conditions of the actual diagnosis. This is not reserved to agreement about practicalities only, but also about things like trust and openness, which are needed to acquire relevant information.

Regarding the realization phase, Nadler (1977) distinguishes five steps: "planning to collect data, collecting data, analyzing data, feeding back data, following up." Tichy (1983) talks about "decision as to type of diagnosis, developing diagnostic plan, analysis of components of the organization, analysis of alignments between these components,

Step		Aim
1.	Identifying the presenting problem	What is the reason for the diagnosis?
	Making the decision to proceed	Check if there is a desire to make improvements in the organization, not just a desire to do research
2.	Selecting the dimension. Deciding who will be involved. Deciding the data collection method.	Define the subjects to be investigated. How far do we extend our study within and outside the organization? Which methods (interviews, questionnaires, observations, workshops, etc.) are suitable and complementary?
3.	Collecting and funneling the data.	Ensure that the information is just sufficiently complete, profound, and reliable to draw conclusions.
4.	Summarizing the data. Analyzing the data.	Find a format (presentation, report, memo, graphics) to report the data. Give meaning to the information.
5.	Giving feedback and making recommendations.	How will we feed back our results; to whom, when, how, and in what order?
6.	Making a decision and implementing it.	Ensure that the findings do not end up collecting dust somewhere .

Table 5.2 Steps in the Realization Phase of a Diagnosis

and developing change strategy," in that order. Block (1981) even succeeds in distinguishing thirteen different steps. Because his steps work out in detail what his colleagues suggest in general, we reproduce them in Table 5.2. We cluster his steps only for the sake of convenience and emphasize that the clusters are equally suited to a diagnostic afternoon discussion as for setting up a two-month process of diagnosis, although the time span and the intensity will, of course, differ.

5.1.2 Diagnostic Content

Even when the diagnostic approach—whether it is research or action oriented—and the steps are clear, change agents still have to make a number of decisions. Will they use analytical or phenomenological observation? Will they employ one integral model or make use of many different one-sided "snapshots" of the situation? What (camera) "angles" or viewpoints are available? And how will they turn all of their observations into a narrative that makes sense of it all? We deal with these questions next.

Analytical or phenomenological?

The content of a diagnosis is supplied by observations, sorting these out, and giving meaning to it all. With regard to observation, there are two main methods: the analytical and the phenomenological.

In the analytical approach, one model or several models are employed to look at the phenomena. It is a reductionist activity. Information is collected to fill in the models, and then sorted and condensed by such means as meta-plan-boards, groupware, and statistical analysis. In contrast, the phenomenological approach allows the phenomena to speak for themselves: Their meanings are not provided by models but must be searched for, making it a more open process. The phenomena are open to a wider range of interpretations and meanings. It is also a more integral approach, examining the whole as opposed to focusing on a pre-set and limited number of aspects derived from one or more models. Tools used to structure information in the phenomenological method include mind mapping, association, and the use of metaphors. Tools used in both approaches are sparring and writing or just allowing time to do its work. It is always necessary to take the time to stand back before reevaluating the whole process again. A good night's sleep can do wonders in terms of developing more powerful perspectives.

Diagnostic models are important tools for gathering data. There is a tendency in the analytical approach to opt for certain models *beforehand*. Conversely, in the phenomenological approach, models serve more to aid interpretation, in which case they are kept at the back of the observer's mind *during* his observations and come into play only where or when appropriate. The choice of a model is just as directional as the design of the diagnostic process. If an organization is viewed as a money-making machine, both problems and solutions will often be sought in the area of strategic choices or process improvements to enhance profits. If, on the other hand, the organization is regarded as a meaning making machine, the problems and solutions are likely to fit organization developers. Anyone with a hammer tends to see nails, a process that Perrow (1970) referred to as "pigeon-holing." In this context, Feltmann (1993) emphasizes that change agents must learn to recognize when prevailing mind-sets or mental frames are part of the problem. Change agents are advised to conduct at least a quick, informal, unsolicited, and open-scoped diagnosis. This allows them fresh viewpoints and might prevent them from inadvertently reinforcing prevailing biases.

An integral model or a hundred pairs of glasses?

One way to counter one-sided diagnoses is to use integral diagnostic models. Camp (1996) provides an integral matrix as an aid for, among other things, organizational research, decision making, and project management (Figure 5.2). Tichy (1983) also presents a matrix covering different systems on one axis (technical, political, and cultural systems), with the other axis covering change triggers (changes in the environment, in technology, in agreement over goals, in agreement over working methods, and in people). Cummings and Worley (1993) present an even more detailed model (see Figure 5.2) that targets input, design, and output within an organization at three levels: individual level, group level, and organizational level. Each of the models claims to be all-embracing and to protect the change agent from being one-sided. In our view, all the models can indeed broaden the horizons of inexperienced change agents. The claim of being all-embracing is comforting and the models have a certain allure. At the same time, a great disadvantage of these models is their sheer comprehensiveness, and using them in change processes can be classed as a bit of overkill. Not all organizational problems are by definition complex, extensive, and multifaceted. Besides, the level of abstraction has to be relatively high if the model is to remain even slightly manageable. In our opinion, however, the biggest disadvantage is to be found in the underlying premise that you can capture reality with one model—that reality can be unambiguous and knowable. You can look at the world through any model or any pair of glasses, but whichever pair you choose, even an "integral" pair, it lets you see only a certain cross-section. Because any model draws your attention toward specific aspects, it is best used selectively for problems that are related to those aspects.

The use of multiple contrasting models makes for richer diagnoses. Therefore, we advise change agents not to stick to any single model; we would not know which one to recommend anyway. As for the analytical approach, we regard it as unprofessional if the change agent is not aware which (one-sided) "pair of glasses" she is using. To avoid missing vital information, we feel that change agents should use at least ten contrasting analytical viewpoints. Our point is well illustrated by Godfrey Saxe's poem (see p. 111) about the "Industani" blind men who went to see an elephant. The first blind man felt a wall (the flanks), the second a spear (the tusk), the third a snake (the trunk), the fourth a tree (the knee), the fifth a fan (the ear), and the sixth a rope (the tail). The poem speaks of the blind men squabbling among themselves to no avail. Their views are complementary, however, and together they provide a fair picture of what a peculiar animal the elephant is. So too, can the complementary information of contrasting diagnostic models reveal the workings of that strangest of animals, called organization.

In the phenomenological approach, there is much less risk of change agents getting stuck in one particular model or view. However, we still would urge change agents to continually enrich their "cognitive library" to at least a hundred different pairs of glasses or models. Having such richness in the back of their minds not only fuels their own professional development, but also increases their perceptual skills and allows them to make out strange (new) animals at least as well as their analytical counterparts do.

Figure 5.2 Three Integrated Diagnostic Models

	Policy	Organization	Personnel
Technical	**Goals and methods** 1 2 3 4 5 • Amount of detail required • Presence of a policy framework • Clarity of quality standards and control • System of financing • Financial framework	**Tasks and responsibilities** 1 2 3 4 5 • Role of the Board • Leadership • Geographical coverage • Linking various tasks • Coherence between disciplines and services • Christmas tree structure?	**Expertise** 1 2 3 4 5 • System of training • Quality and contribution of staff • Continuous education • Social policies dealing with sick leave, layoffs, etc.
Political	**Influential actors** 1 2 3 4 5 • Communication and contacts with clients • Clients' participation in policy making • Influence of board members • Influence of other interested parties	**Decision-making** 1 2 3 4 5 • Diversity of contributions • Distrust • Hidden agendas • Inadequate response • Impasse • Making it personal vs. keeping it business like • Familiarity with the shop floor	**Autonomy** 1 2 3 4 5 • Job satisfaction • Career policy • Job Description • Attention and care of staff • Compensation • Room to maneuver • Status • Work pressure
Cultural	**Organizational climate** 1 2 3 4 5 • History of the organization, including unresolved issues • Staff involvement in policy making • Staff involvement with each other • Work climate • Culture of 'political games'	**Cooperation** 1 2 3 4 5 • Frequency of meetings • Meeting protocols • Putting interests of own department first • Supporting staff • Staff interaction • Pooling of knowledge and experience • Creation of interdependencies • Informal co-operation • Negative effects on new staff	**Attitude** 1 2 3 4 5 • Personal dedication • Creativity • Passing the buck • Willingness to take risks • Transparencies and accountability • Motivation • Management style

(Camp, 1996)

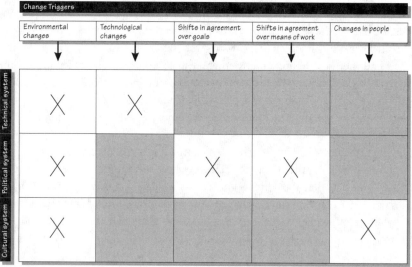

Triggers for change (Tichy, 1983)

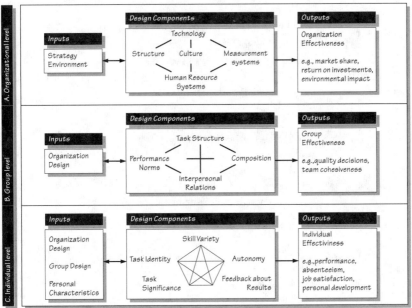

Organizational diagnosis (Cummings & Worley, 1993)

The Blind Men and the Elephant

It was six men of Indostan
To learning much inclined,
Who went to see the Elephant
(Though all of them were blind)
That each by observation
Might satisfy the Mind.

The First approached the Elephant,
And happening to fall
Against his broad and sturdy side
At once began to brawl:
"God bless me but the Elephant
Is very like a wall!"

The Second, feeling of the tusk,
Cried, "Ho! What have we here
So very round and smooth and sharp?
To me 'tis mighty clear
This wonder of an Elephant
Is very like a spear!"

The Third approached the animal,
And happening to take
The squirming trunk within his hands,
Thus boldly up and spake:
"I see," quoth he, "The Elephant
Is very like a snake!"

The Fourth reached out an eager hand,
And felt around the knee,
"What most this wondrous beast is like
Is mighty plain," quoth he:
"'tis clear enough the Elephant
Is very like a tree!"

The Fifth who chanced to touch the ear,
Said: "E'en the blindest man
Can tell what this resembled most;
Deny the fact who can,
This marvel of an Elephant
Is very like a fan!"

The Sixth no sooner had begun
About the beast to grope,
Than seizing on the swinging tail
That fell within his scope,
"I see," quoth he, "the Elephant
Is very like a rope!"

And so these men of Indostan
Disputed loud and long
Each of his own opinion
Exceeding stiff and strong,
Though each was partly in the right,
And all were in the wrong!

Moral

So oft in theologic wars
The Disputants, I ween,
Rail on in utter ignorance
Of what each other mean,
And prate about an Elephant
Not one of them has seen!

—*John Godfrey Saxe (1816-1887)*

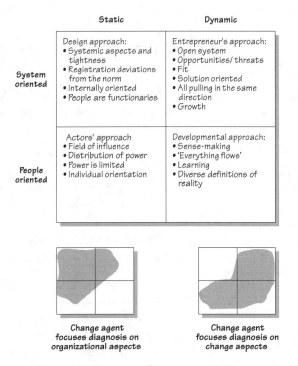

	Static	Dynamic
System oriented	Design approach: • Systemic aspects and tightness • Registration deviations from the norm • Internally oriented • People are functionaries	Entrepreneur's approach: • Open system • Opportunities/ threats • Fit • Solution oriented • All pulling in the same direction • Growth
People oriented	Actors' approach • Field of influence • Distribution of power • Power is limited • Individual orientation	Developmental approach: • Sense-making • 'Everything flows' • Learning • Diverse definitions of reality

Change agent focuses diagnosis on organizational aspects

Change agent focuses diagnosis on change aspects

Figure 5.3 Static vs. Dynamic Diagnosis (Luscuere, freely translated)

Types of models

If change agents use models as suggested, they need to be familiar with a broad range of models based on widely divergent understandings of the world, of organizations, or of mankind. Elaborating on Cummings and Worley's integral model (see Figure 5.2), this implies models dealing not only with the organization level, but also with groups and individuals. We are inclined to add the organization's environment to this as well. Cummings and Worley's model reminds us to look at the design aspects of the organization, as well as its operational and output aspects. Camp, in his model, adds the political dimension as a necessary viewpoint, examining how the organization deals with issues of power and influence. Luscuere categorizes diagnostic models on a double axis (Figure 5.3). Cummings and Worley's and Camp's approaches fall mainly into Luscuere's "static" dimension: describing characteristics of systems and people. What might be overlooked as a result is the "dynamic" dimension that would have allowed for describing relationships and forces that develop over time. Tichy's model, however, makes reference to this when he questions which forces trigger change. The attraction of Luscuere's model is that it makes clear that a purely

	Business Aspects	
Individual	– What do I have planned for Monday morning? – How do I prioritize my work? – Has this employee reached her target?	
Group	– What % of costs does R&D take up? – What is that group's performance in the quality audit? – What % of their turnover is from external clients versus internal clients?	
Organization	– What products does this company make? – What is its core technology? – What is the market share of its Product XX and is this increasing? – What system do they use for resource planning?	
Environment	– Have any new competitors come on the scene? – Can the labor market provide the kind of people you need? – What might the consequences be of this new legislation?	

Table 5.3 Diagnostic Matrix With Sample Questions

Organization Aspects	Change Aspects
– What are this employee's main competencies? – What is this employee's profile? – Is she good at her job?	– How long has she held this position? – What are her ambitions? – What's preventing her from taking this step? – Does she always deal with people in this way?
– How are the roles divided within the team? – What is the staff turnover in this unit? – What kind of autonomy is this business unit allowed in the holding?	– Is the group focused more on cooperation or on achieving results? – How conscious are they of their lack of competence? – Have meetings become simply a ritual here?
– Is the structure based on markets or on geographies? – How would you define the management style? – What stories are told to new staff members to illustrate "how things really work around here"?	– Is there a crisis (11:55) situation? – Have the same dilemmas kept on reappearing over the past 3 years? – What is causing resistance to our expansion plan?
– How is cooperation organized between business partners in the production chain? – How are freelancers deployed? – Are environmental groups involved in the decision making concerning the factory's expansion?	– How does the present situation compare with the stock market crash 20 years ago? – What is making this merger so difficult? – What perception does this governmental department have of your school?

	Business Aspects	
Individual	— Eisenhower Principle — Curriculum vitae — Time sheets	
Group	— Profitability formula for professional firms — Fishbone diagram — Task division scheme	
Organization	— Balanced scorecard — Portfolio analysis — Activity-based costing	
Environment	— Competitive structure — Environment analysis — Experience curves	

Table 5.4 Matrix With Diagnostic Models

static diagnosis can offer a great deal of information about what elements work or do not work in an organization, but it does not address what drives or moves it.

The contributions made by Weick (1995), Feltmann (1984), and Kanter (1992), among others, to all these diagnostic viewpoints, is the importance of continuous self-reflection by the change agent as an additional source of information. Here, questions are raised such as, Why am I selected for this change effort? Which role would fit this change effort? And: Am I capable enough and brave enough to fulfill this role?

We know from our own experience and from our observations how tempting it can be at the end of a diagnostic phase to just sum up all that is presently (in a static sense) wrong and to sketch how, ideally, it should be different. It would be even harder to avoid the next pitfall of setting up an improvement plan aimed at tackling all these problems at the same time, following an ambitiously tight time schedule. It might, of course, work, but then again, it might not. Without diagnosing the dynamic aspects there is no way to judge its effectiveness in advance: The diagnosis is too blue to be true. Embarking on such an improvement plan remains a highly speculative and therefore unprofessional endeavor.

To facilitate a comprehensive diagnosis, we often use a 4 × 3 grid (Table 5.3). This grid encompasses all relevant dimensions mentioned thus far. To illustrate this grid, we

Organization Aspects	Change Aspects
– Core qualities – I/R professionals – Competencies	– Biographical fit – Power sources – Levels of learning
– Team roles – Team conditions for success – Roles for staff units	– Optimal conflict level – Learning curve – Process/Result orientation
– Culture types – Organizational configurations – Organizational Iceberg	– The clock – Passage of resistance – Two forces for change
– Network organization – Public/private cooperation – Industrial ecology	– Field of influence – Megatrends – National cultures

have added a number of typical questions to each cell. The idea behind the grid is to encourage change agents to come up with more questions for each cell during their diagnostic activities. Sometimes the diagnosis will focus on a specific aspect of the organization. In such cases only the appropriate cells are relevant; the environment might be an irrelevant factor, for example. In other cases a general survey is needed. When questions from some cells bring up little relevant information, this signifies attention needs to be focused elsewhere. When we diagnose cases in course programs, we find that most people tend to come up with questions related to business and organizational aspects and to focus on the organizational level. The grid is designed to suggest a broader range of aspects and levels to look at, and to come up with questions and models revealing these additional viewpoints.

The grid can also be used to arrange your own favorite diagnostic models. You might want to add models to those cells that are newest to you by browsing through the literature or surveying fellow change agents. The limitations of this book prevent us from sharing our personal one hundred favorite models. To give you some idea, however, we have included a number of models in each cell in Table 5.4. We have deliberately chosen some well-known "classics" that you should have no trouble finding in the literature. Moreover, we have selected one less well-known model for each cell. The models in this grid are described in more detail in Chapter 6.

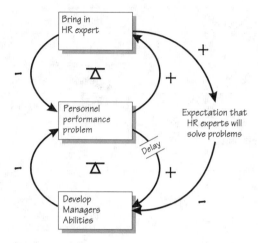

Figure 5.4 System Archetype "Shifting the Burden"

Sense-Making

As already mentioned, an analyst chooses a number of diagnostic models *beforehand*, whereas the phenomenologist has a great many in the back of his mind *during* his observations. *Afterwards*, however, both must be capable of sorting out their observations, often through both reason and intuition, and be able to communicate them to others. It is rather like making a film from a stack of photos, or in other words, piecing together a meaningful story from a large amount of impressions. This process of sense-making is a creative process. Observations are given meaning: "Here's the underlying pattern," "The real point is this," "This is what it's all about." Some change agents will do this by (subconsciously) brooding on it for a couple of days until the pieces of the puzzle fall into place. Others make it a more analytical endeavor by drawing mental maps, by brain-writing, or by making diagrams or tables.

An extremely effective way of methodically coming to grips with complex situations is to use causal loop diagrams. Basically this involves selecting the thirty or forty most dominant factors from your data and then determining the relationships among them: Which factors enhance each other and which weaken each other? By arranging and rearranging these factors, causal patterns emerge that appear to provide an insight into the working of that part of the organization that is being diagnosed. There are often gaps in these patterns, factors that were overlooked in the first instance but that are vital to completing the picture. These gaps become obvious during this process and can be filled in. Causal diagrams resemble a series of interlinked feedback loops. A simple example of this is illustrated in Figure 5.4. This figure represents one problem: mediocre staff performance (Senge, 1990). It concerns an example of an organization with busy line managers who spend too little time addressing this mediocrity. A human resources specialist is brought in. This helps to a certain extent, but it is impossible for one extra pair of hands to accomplish what it would take a whole group of managers to do, given their history and proximity to their staff members. This symbolic solution actually prevents managers from doing what they should have done in the first place, namely, spending more time and effort taking care of their staff. Because of this, the symbolic solution can even make matters worse in the long run. Managers' development erodes as they keep turning to HR experts who "fixed it last time." Overhead costs rise while managers' stand-ings fall. These types of counterintuitive effects, not uncommon but hard to spot in dynamic and complex situations, are especially well suited for illustrating with causal loop diagrams. The methodology of causal diagrams is extensive (e.g., Loman, 1998), but in keeping with the general character of this book, we will not go into further detail.

The process of sense-making is especially relevant where problems are multifaceted, persistent, and affect large organizations. In those cases a good diagnosis brings up so much information that without sense-making, a change agent drowns in it. Reducing this magnitude while capturing its complexity is what it is all about. A good "story" or "causal loop" will have the effect of different people all recognizing their part of the story in it, whereas they might previously have fought among each other over whose side of the story was most true. In that sense this exercise is different from prioritizing problems or viewpoints. Instead, it looks for an underlying or overarching one.

5.2 Change Strategy

Isolated attempts to bring about permanent change are probably doomed to failure because of the (stabilizing) resistance of dominant existing systems. After all, every change threatens day-to-day operations, thus both evoking some resistance and requir-ing some support. We do not know exactly how fundamental and radical the changes that one may bring about can be, but the more all-embracing they are, the more insight is needed into where "driving forces" for change are to be found and how to mobilize them. No change agent can focus on all relevant aspects by himself, let alone implement everything by himself. To a large degree, the same is true for organizations, especially when it comes to tough persistent problems in organizations, such as mak-ing an IT organization more client centered or encouraging professors to focus their efforts on supporting student learning, and the like. Such problems have more often than not plagued an organization for five or ten years or more. We see many change efforts that want "too much too soon" and as a result lack the focus, depth, and stamina that might make a difference. The idea is to look for leverage and to concen-trate on the "seeds" from which change will grow.

This underlines the importance of finding "a cohesive set of basic principles" to structure the change—the change strategy, or "the critical path," as Beer (1988) calls it. Cozijnsen and Vrakking (1995) refer to change strategy as a targeted and purposeful consideration to implement a desired change in an organization with optimal effect and with the least possible resistance. Kanter (1994) talks of the vision and a way to realize the vision from the grassroots level in the face of uncertainty and chaos. No matter how it is defined, change strategy is the link between understanding what is going on, arrived at by diagnosis, and the impulse for action, specifically through planning of interventions. So there is no talk yet of concrete interventions, timing, or tasks in a change strategy. That comes later. The change strategy builds upon the diagnosis. It offers the ideal opportunity to prevent the change agent from acting like the man with a hammer who sees nails everywhere. It asks him to refrain from standard recipes, cherished schools of thought, or popular dogmas, all of which might suggest too specific interventions.

We distinguish two parts in crafting a change strategy: first, the analysis of all the diagnostic material by means of six basic questions, and second, choosing a change strategy based on the answers to these questions. This is set out in the following sections.

5.2.1 The Six Basic Questions

A number of matters will be clear at the end of the diagnostic phase. The first basic question concerns the outcome of the change: What should it bring about? The actual outcome might be well defined, though it sometimes remains rather vague or ambiguous. In both cases the change idea (or desired outcome) can and should be clear enough. Sometimes various actors come up with a diversity of outcomes. Perhaps these outcomes contradict each other. If so, some steps will need to be taken before progressing farther.

The second basic question requires a characterization of the present situation: What is the organization's current state and what created it? This covers static aspects (the extent or weight of the problem or goal) as well as dynamic aspects (the degree of perceived urgency; the interactions fueling the problem or the change; the history that has led up to this). In a way, these first two questions summarize the starting position. The remaining four questions look farther into the future.

The third basic question is: Just how substantial and fundamental is the difference between what we want and what we already have? Do we want a complete transformation or just to adjust the organization's structure? Do we want to train our managers or realize a culture change for everyone in the organization?

1. The outcome: what has to change?
2. The diagnosis: what is the present situation?
3. How large is the difference between the desired and the present situation?
4. Is there resistance and opposition or is there motivation and energy?
5. Is this what the change agents want and are capable of?
6. Is it feasible? Can it be realized?

Table 5.5 Six Basic Questions That Precede the Choice of a Change Strategy

The fourth basic question addresses resistance to or energy for the desired change. Mild or fierce resistance and opposition can come from individuals, groups, or, indeed, the whole organization. It can have its roots in earlier (unsuccessful) changes, in bad experiences, and so on. If resistance is fierce, a blue-print strategy would quickly aggravate the situation and prove to be the wrong approach. But you might just as easily be faced with (groups of) individuals who long for the change to happen and have the energy to realize it. This would be a positive force that can support the change or even bring it about.

The fifth basic question concerns the change agents themselves, the key figures who play a role in the process at this given moment. Change relies on us as individuals, too! Do the change agents want this: Do they/we consider a certain change strategy workable and are they/we willing to try? And can the change agents do this: Do they/we have the skills and competencies required for a specific change strategy?

The final basic question has to do with the sum of all the answers provided by the previous questions. Do they add up? Can we really make this change happen? Is it feasible? Are we able to do this? Given the desired outcome, given the present situation, and given the characteristics of management (as change agents), there are situations where it must be concluded that a particular change cannot be realized. A negative answer to this last question should, in theory, halt or cause a review of the change process. Unfortunately, there are still many "missions impossible," that should be recognized as such.

The answers to these six questions (Table 5.5) support us in determining a change strategy, which at this stage is still nonexistent. Tichy (1983) illustrates with medical analogies how such determinations can take place. The starting position can be summarized by at least the first two basic questions. For example, it might be clear

♦ that the patient is dying as a result of a heart condition (static diagnosis)
♦ that the patient recognized his problem just in time (dynamic diagnosis)

Wijnen, Weggeman, Kor (1999)	Improvement		Renewal	
Kloosterboer (1993)	Continuous learning and improvement (step-wise)		Abrupt changes (leap-wise)	
Sprenger (1995)	Perfecting the status quo		Changing underlying beliefs	
Buijs (1988)	Learning by developing		Learning by leaps and bounds	
Blanchard, Waghorn (1997)	Improvement		Creation/innovation	
Watzlawick (1974)	First-order changes		Second-order changes	
Argyris & Schön (1978)	Single-loop learning		Double-loop learning	
Bekman (1998)	Maintenance issues	Problem-solving issues	Renewal issues	
Ackerman (1986)	Developmental change		Transitional change	Tranformational change

Table 5.6 Depth/Scope of Change Processes

♦ what must be resolved if he is to be cured (intended outcome)
♦ how the patient feels about this (he wants to change)

Tichy emphasizes here that nothing has yet been decided regarding the kind of treatment strategy to be employed. Of course, putting the patient's leg in a cast is not the first thing that springs to mind. This limits the choices somewhat, but there are still enough options left to choose from. Should he be treated with diet pills, with psychotherapy, with open-heart surgery, or would it suffice to lay down the truth? Or are all these options to be pursued, be it concurrently or consecutively? Additional information from the other basic questions will help make such choices. Suppose:

Improvement	Renewal
– Maintenance, problem solving	– Innovation, creation
– Promotion of synergy	– Transition, transformation
– Step-by-step, incremental, evolution	– By leaps and bounds, revolution
– Constant, everywhere, everyone	– Brief, localized, few
– First-order solutions	– Second-order solutions
– More of the same	– Not better, but different
– There is always room for improvement	– It can't go on like this; this might also be possible
– Often preventative	– Often curative
– Often slow	– Often swift

Table 5.7 Improvement and Renewal

♦ the patient has an aversion to psychologists (he is not willing or capable of being a good patient)
♦ his health is extremely poor (major gap between present and desired situation)
♦ his wife has had bad experiences with prescription drugs (resistance)

Knowing all this, the doctor is likely to recommend surgery as a healing strategy. At least, if she is somewhat client-centered rather than enamored with any one medical technology.

The literature contains a number of models to help change agents categorize their answers to the six basic questions. We discussed the first basic question (intended outcomes) in section 4.2, and addressed basic Question 2 in the previous section, 5.1, on diagnosis.

We now look at Questions 3, 4, 5, and 6.

The difference between present and desired situations (basic question 3)
Many authors make a distinction between the depth or the scope of changes. What is the difference between present and desired situations? Such distinctions usually involve the recognition of a dichotomy (Table 5.6).

What makes up this dichotomy? How do you distinguish between the approaches? Wijnen, Weggeman, and Kor advise us to distinguish the degree of order versus the degree of chaos. In times of relative order, one attempts to compensate the entropy

Level of Resistance	Individual
Symptoms: A number of examples	– Fear of the unknown – Lack of trust in others – A need for security – A desire to maintain the status quo – Cynicism, negative attitude – Resistance as a strategy

Table 5.8 Resistance on Different Levels

for as long as possible: that implies improvement strategies. But in times of chaos, change is accomplished by tackling regression and disintegration more drastically: through renewal strategies. Blanchard and Waghorn support this distinction. Sprenger expresses that the more radical the change is, the more it will need to focus on mental processes rather than material ones. You perfect the status quo in down-to-earth approaches. For bigger changes you will have to tinker with mental models, beliefs, and convictions. Others, like Kloosterboer and Buijs, illustrate their distinction entirely on the depth and speed of learning. Argyris, Schön, and Watzlawick also follow this line of thought. Watzlawick maintains that first-order changes take place within existing strategies, cultures, norms, and mind-sets. Argyris and Schön refer to this as "doing the same thing better and better." Watzlawick further argues that second-order changes break through mind-sets and open them up to discussion. It's all about "doing things entirely differently." All these distinctions can be regarded as variations of one and the same dichotomy, as summarized in Table 5.7.

It is, of course, always possible to make an even more detailed distinction. Bekman (1998), for example, sketches three types of questions; maintenance issues, problem-solving issues, and renewal issues. He defines maintenance as the continuous and incremental improvement of such elements as procedures, facilities, or cooperation, and defines problem solving as single concerted actions that significantly improve deadlocked situations. Renewal, on the other hand, implies, in his view, redefining the business an organization is in, both internally and externally, with all the associated changes in identity, structuring, and such. Essentially, Bekman thus makes a further distinction in the "improvement" category. Ackerman (1986) also uses a three-pronged approach. He uses "development change" to describe renewal through improving what already exists. "Transitional change" is renewal toward a previously determined desired situation, and "transformational change" is concerned with renewal through turning a chaotic situation into one with an unknown future. In fact, he subdivides the category "renewal."

Group	Organization
– Poor decision making	– Collective selective perception
– One part of a team not knowing what the other part is doing	– Conflicting values and norms
– No benchmark for quality	– Reminiscing about the "good old days"
– Accepting the obvious	– Strong pressure to conform
– Lack of loyalty	– Defending balances of status/power
– Uncertainty reduction	– Competition for limited resources
	– Mutual overdependence

The importance of the difference between improvement and renewal lies in the fact that it has implications for the choice of change strategy. You do not wish to upset things more than necessary. Conversely, you would not choose to launch a revolution in tiny steps. The case of Kodak illustrates this well. Some time ago Kodak stated that the future of photography lies in photo CDs, and was therefore reducing its investment in photochemistry. Photochemistry is an example of a branch of the industry that can still invest a lot in improving its quality, process, or product, but despite this, will lose in the long run in the competition with photo CDs. First, because it will always create more environmental damage than the photo CD, but more so because the IT revolution brings both rapid quality improvements and price reductions of photo CDs. The Kodak people realized they were faced with a problem of renewal, not one of improvement. Consequently, their strategy has not focused on quality circles or product expansion, but rather on the development of new technologies, such as digital imaging, which require forming alliances with IT companies and taking on new staff.

Resistance, opposition, and energy (basic question 4)

As we have already mentioned, attempting to bring about permanent change often evokes resistance. This appears to be just as true for positively as for negatively rated change. Watson (1969) regards resistance as: all the forces that contribute to a stable personality or social system. Thus defined, it is a normal and valuable reaction that probably protects us from chaos. More often, and especially in change agents, the word *resistance* evokes a less desired image: that of thwarting management's or change agents' good efforts. Where the ability to change overshadows the ability to resist, chaos is evoked. Where the ability to resist overshadows the ability to change, organizations stagnate. In that sense, resistance is an integral part of change processes, neither entirely good nor entirely bad.

Resistance can be the result of an accumulation of past events, in existence long before the new change came on the scene. Sometimes resistance can also be regarded as energy that goes in a different direction. Resistance movements often illustrate this point. Conversely, some changes are met with a great deal of energy and enthusiasm rather than with resistance and opposition: these responses can be the seeds and experimental plots for renewal. Not recognizing this kind of energy is just as undesired as failing to understand resistance, although the latter has been far better documented and debated in management literature. To do justice to the latter, we devote the next few pages to the phenomenon of resistance.

Various forms of resistance will have been tracked down and localized during the diagnostic process. At this stage it is important to gauge what it adds up to and what the implications are. What actually prevents the organization from changing or, phrased differently, gives it the strength to resist? Where does resistance against certain views or people come from? Were earlier experiences negative? Did resistance arise only because the change was rigidly enforced, and would people be more amenable to an interactive approach? What kind of resistance can we expect at the kick-off stage?

Resistance and energy are present at three levels: individual, group, and organizational. Each level can be relevant. In the literature we often read descriptions of symptoms that accompany this phenomenon. More important than this is the description of the processes that individuals, groups, and organizations go through when they experience resistance. Insight into exactly where people are in this process offers a clue for strategy planning. We take a look at resistance at each of the three levels in the following section. Table 5.8 offers an overview.

Individual level

In this context, Cozijnsen and Vrakking (1995) speak of psychological barriers: fear of the unknown, low levels of appreciation, disinterest on the part of the manager, lack of trust in others, the need to feel secure, and the wish to maintain the status quo. Dealing with these psychological barriers involves emotional healing and grieving.

Kübler Ross (1981) mentions that grieving processes have a number of phases that you should be aware of as change agent: First, when people are confronted with an undesired change in their lives, there is disbelief and denial. Next is a period of anger and conflict, followed by resignation and grief, and finally acceptance and renewed courage. According to Kübler Ross, it thwarts this healing process when you confront people who find themselves at the beginning of a grieving process with enthusiastic tales about how marvelous things are going to be in the future. This denies the person concerned the chance to first come to terms with the situation. Forced jollity just fosters resistance, sending it underground only to erupt in the form of pocket vetoes and cynicism down the line. Looking at change from this angle, change agents do well in the beginning to stick to informing people. Involve them and clarify why the proposed change is thought desirable, but do not move beyond that. During the anger stage, confrontation with reality by change agents and setting limits makes sense. The time ripe to start asking for commitment only after acceptance has set in. From there on, change agents can offer support and explore new perspectives with the people involved.

Group level

Here we look at group dynamics. Vroemen (1995) lists aspects of resistance including being unaware of what other team members are doing, having no benchmark for quality, poor decision making, accepting the obvious, lack of loyalty, and a drive for uncertainty reduction.

Kuyper (1986) distinguishes consecutive phases in group development. When a group gets (temporarily) stuck in its development, it is rendered incapable of functioning effectively or of learning how to function. These phases are

♦ the orientation phase (Who may be part of this group? What should your attitude be as a group member? What is the reason for being in this group?)
♦ the influence phase (Who determines what? To what degree do we have to conform? How can each individual take responsibility?)
♦ the affection phase (How much do we let our guard down and remove our masks? How much do we want to mean to each other? How do we wish to communicate with one another?)
♦ the separation phase (When do we call it a day? What use have we been to one another? What have we learned and how will each of us go on from here?).

The change strategy that you choose will sometimes have to take into consideration the phase that a group is in. If the group members have worked together for some time but have lost the will to take part in constructive conflicts, then they have become bogged down early in the affection phase. In this case there is little point in asking them to reflect on their goals (first-phase issue) or their roles (second-phase issue); what is required is a way of improving communication between them.

Organizational level

Tichy (1983) mentions how some symptoms of resistance are based in the company culture: collective selective perception, conflicting values and standards, harking back to "the good old days," strong pressure to conform, and convictions that the change is not necessary, desired, or feasible. He also refers to symptoms of a political nature: threats to existing power balances, the fight for scarce resources, the conscious manipulation of information to avoid loss of face, an affinity for power and status, or mutual over-dependence.

Not every change incites the same degree of resistance. We often look at four factors as indicators for organizational resistance. These can be charted in advance.

First, the distribution of power: The more power is shared, the stronger resistance might be, because in these cases it is almost impossible to force through and legitimize change. Such power can be both formal, with strongly decentralized authorities, and informal. Organizations with professionals, for instance, have workers with both kinds of power: often these are "flat" organizations with lots of formal autonomy on the shop floor. But professionals also have considerable informal power that they have acquired on the basis of their knowledge, connections, or personality. In these organizations resistance can make a manager's life hard.

A second factor is absence of a clear need or desire for change. The more this is absent, the higher resistance may be. A need for change is not an objective given, but rather a sense of urgency perceived by those involved. Time pressure (a threat to survival, for instance) will strengthen this feeling, but even when things are critical, resistance is sometimes lowered only temporarily. Under pressure, people will often accept a step forward, but when the crisis is resolved, motivation often ebbs away, just like dieters whose self-discipline evaporates like snow in summer when they have lost a few pounds. A desire for change, often in the shape of a vision, is more enduring (see the theory on structural conflicts in sections 2.3.3. and 8.4.3.). If there is no vision to be found, the writing is on the wall.

A third factor is the scope and complexity of the change. The bigger the change, the greater the resistance is likely to be. This much is obvious. But sometimes just the implication of a larger scope can arouse resistance. For example, changing a technical detail or doing an experiment in one part of the organization can sometimes produce a domino effect that will have consequences for other aspects or units, and this provokes resistance to change. A good example of this is the introduction of self-steering teams. Van Amelsvoort (1994) concludes that most pilot projects fail because they continually have to fight against the established order that feels threatened by the implications of the possible success of the pilot. This is a war of attrition and the experiment is doomed to failure. He finds that when self-steering teams are introduced throughout the organization and resistance is also addressed and facilitated, the chances of success are greatly improved.

A fourth and final factor is how emotionally charged the change issue is. Otto (1994) points out that feelings run highest when questions of identity are at issue, followed by ideology, policies, and working methods, in that order. Normally, no one will loose any sleep over a change in a minor administrative system (working method). But changes to product development policy, for example, could cause the odd sleepless night. Ideology issues sometimes attach themselves to, for example, discussions on social guidelines during restructuring of a company, and questions of identity can be found in situations of employee appraisal or in situations of conflict. It is a safe bet that questions of identity and ideology will always create a great deal of unrest.

Knowing the nature of the resistance is vital to the formation of a change strategy. Is there resistance because the proposed change affects the identity of the firm? Or because various aspects of the organization are reinforcing each other to maintain a dysfunctional status quo? In the first instance, the change agent's initial reaction will be to organize participation, to plan communication, to take a step-by-step approach, and so on. In the second instance, his strategy would probably be to attempt to mobilize formal power in favor of a top-down management decision to separate the organizational aspects and change them concurrently in order to break the reinforcing mechanism.

Is this what the change agents want, and are they capable of achieving it? (basic question 5)

The one who takes the initiative and the one who orchestrates the process are the key figures at the time when the change strategy is actually determined. They can each have very different ideas about how far-reaching or dynamic the change should actually be. This is strongly influenced by their assumptions and ideas about organizations and change.

Certainly when both of them work in the same organization there will be (usually implicit) mutual expectations with regard to the other's role based on what has gone before. This can cause an initiator to assume that power interventions fall within his area and not in the area of the orchestrator. Frank discussion of each other's vision and expectations is therefore vital. Even if they reach communality, the question still remains how each of them will assess his own ambition, courage, influence, and competence to further shape the change and the change process. Put more simply: What does each want? How far is each prepared to go? How capable is each of them?

These factors play a role in determining which strategy they will ultimately choose. Both players will be inclined to suggest change strategies that they have come to believe in and depend on, that will not create a role conflict between the both of them, or with the rest of the organization, and that they feel suits them.

This is an appropriate place to refer to the diversity in change agents' competencies, skills, attitudes, charisma, and personality. These aspects are more closely examined in

Chapter 8, but we feel that we need to make a comment on this here as well. Someone with a dominantly blue mental model cannot (with any degree of credibility) initiate a strategy of another color. Another example: Implementing a white change strategy demands an exceptionally well-developed ability to see patterns and mechanisms, a high acceptance of uncertainty, and considerable practical experience. If such capability and seniority are not present, the white strategy is doomed.

A change strategy is difficult to execute if the main players are not prepared or able to focus their intentions and actions in the same direction. . In other words, they have to (want to) think in the same kind of "color." If they do not, or if it remains implicit, it is likely to lead to tension and conflicts.

Is it feasible? Can it be realized? (basic question 6)

When all the other basic questions have been answered and the picture is reasonably complete, there is time for a final call to judgment: Is the change really feasible?

For instance, can we introduce self-steering teams (intended outcome) into a hierarchical organization (present situation)? Would the difference between present and desired outcome not be too great? If a previous change led to employees having major reservations (resistance), and if one key figure is opposed to the idea, is such an attempt at renewal not simply a bridge too far? If you have carefully charted the answers to the previous five questions, your only conclusion in this example can be that it is. Such a change does not seem feasible.

You could, of course, appease the opposing key figure by adjusting the intended outcome, for example, by creating departments "with limited autonomy." Or, alternatively, have that key figure leave the organization.

You can also take interim steps that will set the stage for an easier implementation at a later date. For example, you might train managers in coaching skills as a means of softening their hierarchic reflexes. Or take steps to reduce staff resistance by bringing them in contact with their peers in other organizations where such changes have made a positive difference. You could do this by organizing a company outing to these organizations or bring the peers to an internal seminar on "New Images of Organizations."

5.2.2 Choosing a Change Strategy

Choosing a strategy brings us to the central idea behind an intervention plan. Such an idea can be expressed in terms of color-print thinking as highlighted in Chapter 3,

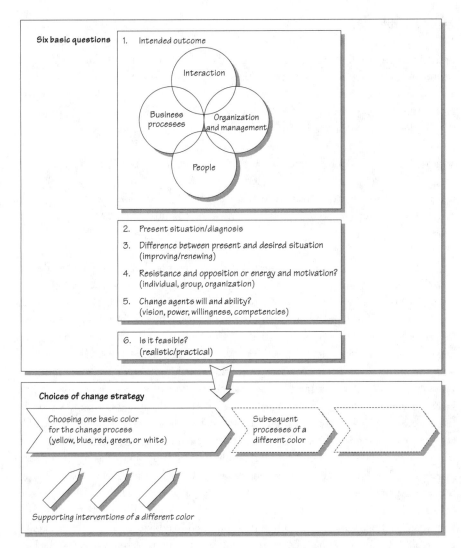

Figure 5.5 From Six Basic Questions to the Choice of a Strategy

as a starting point. In that chapter we discussed the colors as the often subconscious meanings that those involved in change processes give to change. We emphasized that change agents can become aware of their own paradigms, can recognize those of others, and can make communication about change clearer and more manageable. In this section, we approach thinking in colors in a slightly different way. Imagine it as a palette of five colors from which the change agent can make a choice based on the basic information (see section 5.2.1) that she has collected. Here, color-print thinking is not so much a tool for personal awareness, but more a tool for crafting a change strategy.

One basic color print

Because the underlying principles of the various color prints show such contrast, we believe that workable strategies must be based on the dominance of one leading color print: the basic color. A learning situation (green) will for instance be limited in its success when issues relating to power and interests (yellow) come into play. The principles and the characteristics of each color (results, process, roles, etc.) are explained in Chapter 3. We will not go into them again here.

The dominance of one leading color may be limited in time (e.g., restricted to a certain phase) and space (e.g., restricted to certain parts of the organization). After all, each color has its strengths and weaknesses given both the kind of change and the system that is being changed. However, we do advise against mixing colors in the same time and space.

The intended outcome, the present situation, the gap between present and desired situation, the existence of either energy or resistance, and the individual styles of the change agents are five factors that can strongly influence the choice of the basic color (see Figure 5.5). We regard these factors as the building blocks for a situational model for strategy design. It is obvious that if all the factors are of the same color as the chosen change strategy, life would be very simple for the orchestrator. His relationship with the initiator would be cordial because they would both have the same mind-set. Even though this cozy alignment of factors does not mean success is guaranteed, there is reason to believe life gets more difficult when such an alignment is absent. Color differences do create tension, and what remains to be determined is whether this can be constructively channeled, and if so, how. Is it possible to execute a blue-print strategy in a yellow-print environment? And is this still the case if the intended result concerns learning and when the key figures believe that learning is the viable road to change ($2 \times$ green-print thinking)? What would such an endeavor result in? Which color combinations lend themselves to constructive friction and which inevitably produce conflicting impossibilities? A little arithmetic shows that five factors can produce a couple thousand different combinations. We have not worked all these out, nor do we feel this to be desirable. We do, however, want to start the ball rolling by describing how the five factors codetermine change strategy.

Factor 1: Outcomes

The intended outcomes make some strategies less suitable than others. As in Tichy's earlier example, the doctor will not put a heart patient in a plaster cast. As a rule, a new head office will not be constructed with the help of a self-steering approach (white), and HRM tools (red) will be of little use in questions of power politics . But there is still enough left to choose from. What helps when choosing a strategy is to remember that the intended outcome and the strategy should preferably enhance each other: "Practice what you preach." It would be difficult to create empowerment and self-steering (white) as outcomes by using a strategy based on powerful coalitions (yellow).

Factor 2: The present state of affairs

In a blue engineering firm, a blue approach will seem familiar, while in a yellow action group, the formation of coalitions will be considered normal. It illustrates how the internal functioning of organizations is often tainted by the character of their primary process. In these settings, we find that applying a change strategy that is perceived as "normal" is often effective: people know how to deal with it, understand how to make it work, expect it, etc. Even if it takes a slight detour to reach its goal compared to another color strategy, a familiar approach can often be at least as successful.

However, this is not always possible or appropriate: Sometimes the need for change has even arisen out of the suffocating effect of a dominant color in the organization. In the (blue) engineering firm the problem might be bad internal communication and an inability to learn from one another (needs more green), while the (yellow) action group perhaps might have developed inefficient operational processes and slow decision-making procedures (needs more blue). The sense making exercise at the end of the diagnostic process often reveals what the root causes of the problem are and its color label implies a preferred strategy.

Factor 3: The difference between present and desired

We have spoken about the difference between improvement and renewal. We think that step-by-step, continuous processes generally require a good "color match": for example, an (improved) blue-print approach in a blue-print environment, or a better HRM approach in a people-oriented organization. The idea is that you make use of what works best in that organization as long as the the organization still functions adequately. Renewal, and taking a leap forward, demands different colors, introducing another way of thinking with different words and meanings. And thus adding a new color.

Factor 4: Resistance and energy

We have described resistance at the individual, group, and organizational levels. In general you could say that the greater the resistance, the more well-considered and impactful the interventions must be and the more careful the process orchestration. The emotions inherent in questions of identity are badly served by a blue-print approach. But a white-print approach will be equally useless if all sorts of power factions have developed in the meantime: the effect of increased self steering and autonomy (white) is to fuel fighting among themselves. If in addition, there were no sense of urgency then there would be little to stand in the way of severe fragmentation of the organization. Consequently, the nature and scope of resistance provides indications for the choice of strategy. The presence of energy provides pointers that are just as important. For example, if a number of people demonstrate "resistance" as a strategy, there would appear to be space for entrepreneurship and alternatives (on the periphery of the organization).

Factor 5: Personal style

Are there change agents who can both understand all the color approaches conceptually and implement them as acting interventionists? It might not be impossible, but would definitely be a tall order. If we look at ourselves or at our colleagues, we see in most of us a strong affinity for one or two approaches or styles. On the one hand, they denote your strengths and on the other hand show what you believe in. Behaving in accordance with these colors would encourage successful change as the change agent uses his strongest competences and is believable in so doing.

In addition, the question arises how, for example, can the orchestrator deal with differences in dominant color thinking (in terms of colors) among himself, the initiator, and, at a later stage, the actors? We think it would be useful if professional change agents have knowledge of and insight into all the colors. This would assist them in knowing their limits and being conscious of where their incompetence starts. Such insight would offer them a possibility of adapting a strategy toward their own style. If this fails to produce a strong enough change strategy, then at least the orchestrator should learn to say "no, this is not something I can pull off" and then help the initiator to find a replacement that fits in better with the situational puzzle (see Figure 5.5). The colors might be of use in facilitating such conversations between the most important change agents at this point.

The (im)possibilities of combinations

In an earlier work (de Caluwé, 1997), we described blue-print, red-print, and green-print concepts as consecutive phases in a change process. We have not pursued this idea here. In painting, mixing many colors together produces a brown sludge. This is also true in change management, where it produces vague points of departure, conflicting styles, and so on. Nevertheless, it is still possible to think in terms of consecutive color phases, as long as the colors each have sufficient space and time to do their work. Typical consecutive phases in, for example, a large scale ambitious change processes would be as follows:

- ◆ *a yellow-print phase*, within which the most important actors and groups negotiate to determine the change goals and agree upon the approach to the change

♦ *a blue-print phase,* within which the business processes and organizational structures and systems are designed, with little participation of the employees

♦ *a red-print phase,* within which staff is allocated to the work processes, functions, and jobs and ample communication takes place to explain and motivate this effort to the employees

♦ *a green-print phase,* within which the organization learns to function according to what's intended with the help of learning and training programs. People start to bring the new structures and systems to life.

♦ *a white-print phase,* within which the change is incorporated and those involved give personal meaning to it. We have demonstrated the importance of this phase before through our research (de Caluwé, 1997).

It can be useful to think of the main phases in this way in some change processes. Other phase combinations are, however, also possible: Yellow is often followed by blue to help define efforts and projects. Blue sometimes also anticipates yellow: a hired gun (the expert report) is brought in to get the main players in line. Blue is often combined with red and green to firmly establish new strategies, structures, and systems in competencies or behavior. Red often supports blue as a "smoothing" agent. Green often supports blue and red, to improve along the way by learning. Red and green are often found on their own, while white is reasonably independent of the other colors and appears spontaneously as the result of increasing environmental unrest and/or complexity, or is (deliberately or accidentally) introduced by management.

Thinking in such phases also has disadvantages. If the phases are rushed, the whole process can lose much or all of its credibility. It might be possible to complete a blue restructuring within six months, but a green culture change demands uninterrupted long-term attention. Thinking in phases gives change in general a blue tinge, as though everything can and will follow according to plan. Using a white-print phase at the end of other color phases is really a contradiction in terms; self-steering tends to turn everything that has been so carefully built up on its head. Self-steering follows its own direction.

In some cases it is also possible to carefully combine colors at more or less the same time as long as a clear leading color remains. Within one basic strategy, green, for example, it is possible to carry out blue supporting interventions. It is, for example, worthwhile to use blue-print thinking in designing a simulation game as long as its implementation remains a deep shade of green. Or it might be useful to establish priorities for the game's goals with the help of yellow-print thinking with the most important players. Or use white-print thinking to set up a pilot study, when a lot of energy is already present: people volunteer and want to take it on as part of their own change programs.

5.3 Intervention Plan

The change strategy is fleshed out in the intervention plan, which can be defined as "an integral, consistent, feasible and relevant plan for interventions in an organization aimed at the actual implementation of the intended outcomes of a change." This phase has a different character than diagnosis and the search for a change strategy, where the emphasis was mostly on reflection; here the emphasis is directed more toward action. The size and scope of the plan can vary considerably; a plan for a meeting does not have to be worked out in as much detail as, say, a multi-year process. And the very nature of a white-print approach precludes the possibility of going into as much detail as might be possible with a blue-print approach.

In the previously quoted definition, we use the words *integral, consistent, feasible,* and *relevant.*

- ◆ Integral means that all steps and elements in the plan and the coherence among them have been considered beforehand.
- ◆ Consistent means that all the elements in the plan support the same system of clear outcomes (they are preferably based on the same color).
- ◆ Feasible means that they meet the pre-conditions of manageability and workability.
- ◆ Relevant means that the plan is seen to markedly contribute to the intended outcomes.

But how do you go about making such a plan? We believe that the following three activities are generally helpful: brainstorming, arranging, and detailing. We will look at these in some detail in the following sections.

5.3.1 Brainstorming

Using the intended outcomes and the chosen strategy as a starting point enables those involved to brainstorm about interventions and the partial outcomes or sub-goals that they can achieve. We purposely avoid using the word *results* in this context because of its quite definite character, which does not fit in with all the color prints.

The intended outcomes and the strategy often give an indication of who should be involved in these brainstorming sessions. In the yellow and blue approaches, the number will be limited to include the initiator, the orchestrator, and possibly a few sponsors. The white, green, and red approaches will usually involve a larger number of actors. This can help to generate more ideas and viewpoints, lower resistance, and help spread psychological ownership of the change process more widely.

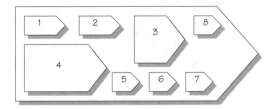

Figure 5.6 Intervention Plan With Eight Interventions

What must be discussed during these sessions? What kind of interventions should be thought up? In Chapter 4, where we dealt with the main elements of planned change, we argued that you can distinguish three elements in *change processes*, namely, the actors, the phases in the process, and the communication, and further, that these parts should be addressed before drawing up an intervention plan as well as become part of that same intervention plan.

Tichy (1983) even goes as far as thinking up different activities for each element. He has a political process plan to keep the actors "in line," a cultural process plan for communication and sense making, and a technical process plan for the more goal-oriented activities that can be easily subdivided. We find this division too artificial and rigid because when listing interventions, you soon discover that one and the same activity often has an effect on more than one dimension. For example, convening a group of directors to obtain their formal approval for something is a political as well as a communication process. And although quality circles can be regarded as a technical improvement process, they could just as easily be a learning process or even lend themselves to a political process if decentralized decision making becomes an issue.

Nevertheless, the division between actors, steps/phases, and communication is a useful tool to achieve a (heterogeneous) mix of interventions that will improve the feasibility of the whole change process. This is, after all, the whole point of making an intervention plan. Another aid to stimulating ideas is to list all the possible interventions. We examine this further in 5.4. At the end of the brainstorming process, the question is whether the sum of these interventions look like they have the required depth and scope to do the job. Also this is a time to chart remaining dilemmas. Which questions are still unanswered? Are there any conflcts that need to be resolved? What is out of the question or what is imperative?

5.3.2 Arranging

When the interventions have been listed, we have to find a place for them all. This requires three processes. First, dividing them into sub-processes aimed at specific intended outcomes. This gives an overview and helps keep track of interdependencies but, more important, makes it possible to give different people responsibility for specific sub-processes, a measure that allows for broadening the "psychological ownership" and spreads the risks. Of course, the need to coordinate increases accordingly, and thus it is searching for the best balance between overview and ownership, which is color dependent. The second process is concerned with phasing these sub-processes. In what order are these activities arranged? And, do they depend on one another? The third process is concerned with whether the "chemistry" between the interventions works well enough.

All this results in the outline of an intervention plan: an aggregate of parallel and consecutive interventions that form an integral (coherent), consistent (color matched), feasible (it can work), and relevant (contribute to the intended outcome) whole. The following is a visual representation of the result of such an arranging exercise.

In Figure 5.6, Intervention No. 8 follows No. 3, and No. 3 follows Nos. 2 and 1, while Nos. 1 and 2 are carried out at the same time as No. 4. The eight interventions have a common (intended) outcome, but each intervention has its own outcome as well. The eight interventions reinforce each other, and some build on the results of the ones before.

It is important to gain insight into the considerations that underlie such an arrangement. An example is the discussion about a change program in a school. Would we first train/retrain potential middle management, then restructure the school and then make them responsible for the results of new educational units, or would we approach it the other way around? Some saw first supplying training and then handing out responsibility as the way to go. How could we hold people responsible for results if they did not yet have the competencies to achieve them? Others thought that the motivation to learn would be best developed after people were made responsible for results, and not before. It is not yet apparent who is right even though both approaches have been used; but what makes the example relevant here is that phasing is not only a logistical activity but one that must be woven into the chosen change strategy. This illustrates the third part of the arranging process: checking if the "chemistry" works well enough. This question is especially relevant when the intervention plan contains different colors: either in different phases (as sketched in the example), or in different parts of the organization. As colors can even each other out, their seperation in time and space should be sufficient. Learning processes in a political environment, for instance, need safeguards like agreements on confidentiality.

5.3.3 Detailing

The intervention plan is not yet complete. When drawing up an intervention plan, in addition to the content—the interventions, the intended outcomes, the sequencing,

- The chief executive or head person manages the change effort
- The project manager is given the temporary assignment to coordinate the transition
- The formal organization manages the change effort in addition to supervising normal operations
- Representatives of the major constituencies involved in the change jointly manage the project
- Natural leaders, who have the confidence and trust of large numbers of affected employees are selected to manage the transition
- A cross section of people representing different organizational functions and levels manages the change
- A "kitchen" cabinet representing people whom the chief executive consults and confides in, manages the change.

Table 5.9 Examples of Role Divisions in Change Processes (Cummings & Worley, 1993)

and so on—attention must be given to a number of management aspects, such as the organization of the whole process, duration and timing, resources, milestones, and the exchange and provision of information. In a way, each of the main elements of planned change as covered in Chapter 4 can be used as a checklist when detailing the intervention plan.

Organization of actors

This concerns the division of roles: Who is responsible for what? Who will work together? Who will help? Who provides encouragement? Who makes the decisions? Who is within the system that undergoes change and who is not? Will the change cut through all hierarchial layers or not? How do we get the necessary disciplines on board? It is all about thinking through the social dimension of change. Cummings and Worley (1993) argue that the change agents should not necessarily be the same people as those who are responsible in the existing structure, because the management of change requires people with an adequate degree of influence and competence. They sketch a number of structures from which a choice can be made (Table 5.9).

Of course, the choice depends largely on the chosen strategy. In yellow-print situations the tendency is to shy away from an all too participative approach or to give large groups of employees a major role. This approach will lean more toward representation (apt political jargon). We would like to refer you to the remarks in Chapter 3

(Table 3.2) regarding how progress is being secured/anchored in different colored change processes.

Milestones

What outcomes can we expect along the way? And how can we mark them? For more than one reason, milestones are a good way of creating clarity. On the one hand, there is the importance of assessment and monitoring. Whether this is done through empirical measurements and reports to principals (blue) or done by and for the people concerned on the basis of perceptions (white, green), you want to somehow determine progress. But there is yet another reason: to celebrate successes or to reflect on disappointments. Rituals around milestones can breathe extra life into the change and can symbolize passage to the next phase.

Aspects of duration and timing

When determining the general time frame, including completion times and milestones, it is important to mark a clear starting point. How do we indicate that the change has begun?

Another activity is to look at critical paths: Which interventions depend on one another and how can transfers of responsibility or information best be assured? It is advisable to calculate in a sufficient amount of reserve time; change processes are to a large extent unpredictable. We would also recommend planning the initial activities in some detail. Perhaps it will be necessary to adjust the plan when the first interventions have been carried out. It would also be wise to build margins into deadlines as delays can easily occur.

Resources

This involves determining such necessary support, facilities, money and so on, including their deployment over time. Here, too, margins are vital to being able to build in a degree of flexibility beforehand. In any case, it is advisable to at least have an idea of how much "internal time" will have to be spent on the change. Very often out-of-pocket expenses, including hired hands, represent only a small fraction of the total cost of the change effort, whereas internal time spent takes up most ot the costs while often remaining less visible. Decision making based on this distorted picture is not advisable. In some cases, not only costs, but also such items as profits and returns can be mentioned.

And finally, the information aspect

This deals with the way in which information is produced, kept, and shared. Agreements on these points can improve efficiency (in blue processes, for example), but often more crucial is the sensitivity of information connected to personnel matters (red processes) or the strategic use of information in power approaches (yellow

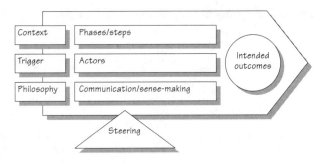

Figure 5.7 Elements of Every Intervention

processes). Anyone working in politics knows the value of information and the effect of leaking it to the appropriate people at an opportune moment.

Finally, a word of caution. The words and concept Intervention Plan could convey the false impression that change can be seen as the designing and implementation of a blueprint. We would like to remedy this impression. Intervention plans will often be adjusted along the way based on experiences of the change agents and results of the change process. We regard a change process as something that requires constant monitoring and adjustment. Nevertheless, drawing up a complete plan is an extremely useful exercise for the following reasons:

♦ It encourages reflection on the "leitmotiv" and the development of sufficient focus (the dominant color and the dominant themes)
♦ It encourages reflection on its integrality, consistency, feasibility, and relevance
♦ It encourages flexible and timely steering of the whole process (by means of built in reflection and adjustments)

5.4 Interventions

The intervention plan contains an arrangement of interventions, some of which run parallel, while others run in sequence. But what exactly is an intervention? We define an intervention as *one or a series of planned change activities intended to help an organization increase its effectiveness* (see also Cummings and Worley, 1993, and Chapter 7 in this book). We also go back to our method in Chapter 4 where we named six elements of change processes: outcomes, history, actors, phases, communication, and steering. These six elements are not only used to structure the entire change process, but also form the building blocks of *every intervention*. The following points must be determined for each intervention:

♦ History: What went before? What is the context and the trigger? Is the accompanying philosophy green or blue?

Policy	Organization	Personnel
Technical		
Goals and method 1 2 3 4 5	**Tasks and responsibilities** 1 2 3 4 5	**Expertise** 1 2 3 4 5
• Formulate concise goals • Draw up strategic plan • Make financial estimate • Set priorities • Focus on quality/quality standards • Keep memos brief • Involve groups in drafting reports • Determine budgets	• Adapt organizational structure • Define and actualize tasks and powers • Create clear feedback procedures between management and staff • Rethink work division in geographies and locations of work • Speed up computerization	• Maintain and improve level of expertise • Organize forward-looking training • Seperate HRM • Recognize internal expertise • Promote training in social skills • Recruit young people
Political		
Influential actors 1 2 3 4 5	**Decision-making** 1 2 3 4 5	**Autonomy** 1 2 3 4 5
• Increase contact with Board members • Promote understanding of existing policies throughout the organization • Build up and maintain a network of relationships	• Monitor social policy and participation process by the workers' council • Involve personnel more in the workers' council • Make use of informal influence • Pay more attention to bottom-up communication • Monitor that leaders are carrying out agreed-on policies • Mutual adjustment in groups and teams	• Set out a carreer path for every staff member • Allow sufficient room to maneuver • Upgrade status • Balance individual freedom and interdependency
Cultural		
Organizational climate 1 2 3 4 5	**Cooperation** 1 2 3 4 5	**Attitude** 1 2 3 4 5
• Build up the corporate image • Break down barriers • Promote acceptance of policies • Boost market appeal and presence • Improve work climate	• Encourage meeting protocol • Involve everyone in discussions • Strive for co-operation within and between departments • Prevent isolationism • Promote open leadership and horizontal co-operation • Mutual transfer of knowledge	• Stimulate creativity • Create conditions for flexibility • Develop a participative management style • Optimize commitment and consensus • Use incentives

(Camp, 1996)

Primary Organizational Level Affected			
	Individual	Group	Organization
Human Process			
• T-groups	X	X	
• Process consultation		X	
• Third-party intervention	X	X	
• Team building		X	
• Search conference			X
• Organization confrontation meeting		X	X
• Intergroup relations		X	X
• Normative approaches		X	X
Technostructural			
• Formal structures			X
• Differentiation and integration			X
• Parallel learning structures			X
• Cooperative union-management projects	X	X	X
• Quality circles	X	X	
• High-involvement plants	X	X	X
• Total quality management		X	X
• Work design	X	X	
Human resource			
• Goal Setting	X	X	
• Performance appraisal	X	X	
• Reward systems	X	X	X
• Career planning and development	X		
• Managing workforce diversity	X		
• Employee wellness	X		
Strategic			
• Integrated stategic management			X
• Open-systems planning		X	X
• Transorganizational development			X
• Culture change			X
• Strategic change			X
• Self-designing organizations		X	X

Types of interventions and Organizational Levels (Cummings & Worley, 1993)

Figure 5.8 Continued

Model Category	Possible strategies	Technologies
Input	• Change the environment • Anticipate environmental changes • Alter characteristics of input	• Interorganizational linkages • Condition building • Organizational set analysis • Open-systems planning
Transformation process mission and objectives	• Clarify • Change • Build ongoing mechanism for re-examining and changing	• Strategic planning • Goal confrontation meeting • Multilevel planning
Networks	• Technical change (work flow) • Social structure change • Examine emergent networks and change through new prescribed arrangements	• Contingency theories of organization design • Autonomous work groups • Job enrichment • Role analysis technique • Sociometric network analysis
Communication	• Change the flow • Change the content • Change the quality level of distinction	• Redesign communication networks • Data feedback
Control	• Establish collaboratively designed control system • Clarify standards and corrective action mechanisms	• Management by objectives system • Management information system
Problem-solving and decision-making	• Develop routine and nonroutine procedures • Alter decision-making structure levels, patterns of involvement	• Data feedback-survey feedback • Responsibility analysis
Reward system	• Deal with individual differences • Relate to organizational objectives	• Scanlon plan
Conflict management	• Alter sociotechnical arrangements • Develop intergroup mechanism for handling conflict • Develop interpersonal skills for handling conflict	• Integrating mechanisms • Organizational mirroring • Confrontation meeting • Role negotiation • Third party consultation
Individual style	• Alter selection and placement of individuals • Train individuals • Develop individuals for future	• Life planning-career development • Assessment center • Selection criteria (re-)design • Leadership training • Technical skills education • Sensitivity training • Coaching and counseling
Interpersonal	• Increased interaction and communication	• Sensitivity training • Team building
Group culture	• Change the norms and values about work (interactions)	• Process consultation

Examples of Change Strategies and Technologies (Sutherland, 1978)

Figure 5.8 Examples of Two-Dimensional Intervention Overviews

♦ Outcomes: What do we want to achieve with it?

♦ Phases: How will we organize it in steps and phases?

♦ Actors: Who will initiate, coordinate, steer, or undergo it?

♦ Communication: How and who will develop its meaning? How can we get people involved?

♦ Steering: How will we evaluate and monitor? How will we make (interim) adjustments?

The intervention elements are illustrated in Figure 5.7. The history (context, trigger, philosophy) is placed half inside and half outside the figure because a previous

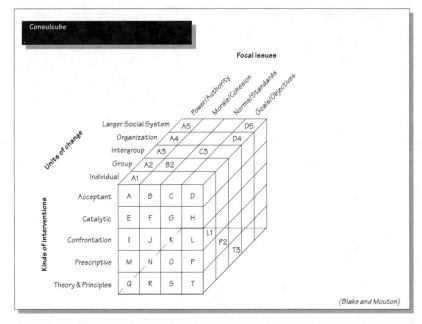

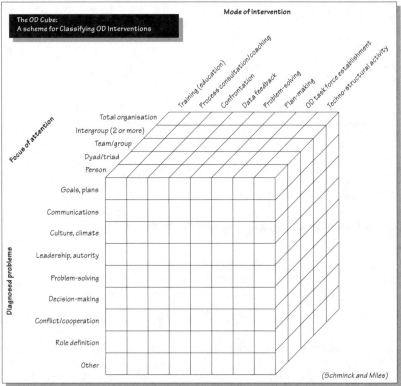

Figure 5.9 Two Intervention Overviews in the Form of Cubes

intervention can become the history of the one following it, just as incidents or external pressure can.

The intended outcome of any intervention can be characterized by one or more of the factors mentioned in Chapter 4: business processes, organization and management, interaction, or people. This is all part of the content of the change. The actors form the social dimension, the steps the structuring dimension, and communication the sense-making dimension (see Vinkenburg, 1995, and Table 4.2).

What kinds of interventions are there? Their nature and types appear to be endless. Fortunately there are a number of intervention overviews in circulation, just as every consultant has his own personal favorites tucked away on his own mental "hard drive." The added value of having an overview is that it simplifies the task of building up your own mix of interventions; after all, no one change agent is capable of knowing or mastering all of them.

It is sufficient, but at the same time it is also a professional duty for change agents to be at least familiar with of a wide range of interventions, that enable them to design the main features of an intervention plan. This is especially important for consulting agencies that offer a complete package of services. Overviews can help ensure that competencies within the firm are used to their best advantage for the benefit of the client. None of the published overviews is, of course, complete; what's more, their presentation varies, reflecting to a certain extent how the authors view change. We include five overviews here, each with a short explanation. Figure 5.8 gives three examples of two-dimensional overviews and Figure 5.9 shows two three-dimensional overviews.

In his all-purpose matrix, Camp (1996) offers approximately thirty possible solutions for problems in organizations. He arranges them in two dimensions:

◆ *Organization conditions*: policies, organization and personnel
◆ *Approach*: technical, political, and cultural

Cummings and Worley (1993) also use two dimensions, and they categorize approximately thirty interventions by

   ◆ *The organizational issues*: (1) human process issues, (2) techno-structural issues, (3) human resource issues, and (4) strategic issues. This dimension seems similar to Camp's "organization conditions," although Camp pays less attention to the last set of issues.
   ◆ *The organization level*: individual, group, organization

Sutherland (1978) arranges interventions ("change technologies") according to the strategy that fits certain organization components. He places these organization

	Level in the Organization	
Dominant Color	Individual	
Yellow	Personal commitment statement Outplacement Protégé constructions	
Blue	Management by objectives Hygienic working Working with a day planner	
Red	Career development Recruitment and selection Job enlargement/Job enrichment	
Green	Coaching Intensive clinic Feedback /Mirroring	
White	T-Group Personal growth Networking	

Table 5.10 Overview of a Sample of Colored Interventions for Each Level of an Organization

components in the left-hand column. These are very similar to what Cummings and Worley elaborate as "organizational issues." What Sutherland refers to in the middle column as strategies are the ideas behind the interventions (the intentions). In the last column he mentions some forty interventions ("technologies").

A number of authors go as far as to offer a model for arranging interventions with the help of three dimensions (see Figure 5.9). Blake and Mouton (1976) provide a "Consulcube" as an aid to consultants; it has the following dimensions:

♦ *Kinds of interventions*: This dimension concentrates on the role of the change agent, a dimension largely ignored in the overviews of both Camp and Cummings and Worley.

♦ *Focal issues*: This dimension concentrates on the type of problems. There is some similarity between this and Camp's "approaches." Blake and Mouton do justice to their own background by placing relatively little emphasis on technical aspects and concentrating more on cultural and political ones.

♦ *Units of change*: This dimension corresponds to Cummings and Worley's "organization level," although it is more detailed.

Group	Organization
Confrontation meetings Third-party strategy Top structuring	Improving quality of work life Forming strategic alliances Negotiations on labor conditions
Working in projects Archiving Decision making	Strategy analysis Business process redesign Auditing
Social activities Team roles Management by speech	Reward systems Managing mobility and diversity Triple ladder
Team building Gaming Intervision	Open systems planning Parallel learning structures Quality circles
Self-steering teams Open space meetings Making mental models explicit	Search conferences Rituals and mystique Deconstructing "sacred cows"

Schmuck and Miles (1971) designed a similar cube for organization developers, the so-called OD (Organization Development) cube. The dimensions they use are as follows:

♦ *Mode of intervention*: The kind of intervention, incorporating the role of the change agent

♦ *Diagnosed problems*: The content of the problem defined in such a way that it falls between Camp's two dimensions

♦ *Focus of attention*: The organization level as also defined by Cummings and Worley, although it is more detailed here

The first two two-dimensional overviews are manageable, offering nine and twelve different kinds of interventions, respectively. However, the three-dimensional cubes are very detailed. The Consulcube distinguishes 100 types of interventions and the OD cube distinguishes more than 350. The authors then, very wisely, leave readers to fill in concrete examples for these types. The cubes are best seen as providing "a way of looking at things," a perspective, not as actual methods for collecting and arranging interventions. We therefore choose to use a two dimensional overview of interventions.

Dominant Color	Examples of (Stereotypical) Statements
Yellow	You need each other The agenda has been predetermined with the parties involved Let us continue this discussion in a smaller group With those who have a mandate There will be a press release at 7 p.m.
Blue	You want to achieve a 12% cost reduction Within one year This can be achieved by taking the following steps That have proved their worth in practice With a monthly progress report sent to you An agreement is an agreement
Red	Our vision is to become No. 1 in the market And we will achieve this by investing in people And because we support each other We will pay out performance-related bonuses No one will loose out And these measures will be determined in consultation with the trade unions and after an internal survey
Green	I have asked you here today On the basis of your learning goals I would like you to read and analyze this case And to try out possible solutions in a clinic You gain in proportion to what you put in The idea is to experiment with new behavior You normally demonstrate this type of behavior And that has this effect on me You could also behave in this way or that

White	Leaders experience the organization as a twilight zone
	No matter what they have done they have failed, and fail
	    to get a grip on the situation
	While staff flaunt procedural rules
	And the market appears to develop more quickly than we are
	This creates a vicious circle and a feeling of impotence
	Dynamism does not flourish in conditions dominated by controls
	    and procedures
	There is a plethora of innovative ideas in the workplace
	Let people develop these no matter where they find sponsors
	    for them
	And allow them to exchange, test, and link their ideas
	And let the successful intrapreneurs act as coaches for others

Table 5.11 Statements as Small "Colored" Interventions

The Thought/Meaning Behind Each of the Statements
Emphasizing dependence between actors Restricting degrees of liberty Limiting the risk of loss of face Increasing room for negotiation Increasing time pressure
Stating and defining an unambiguous result Agreeing on project management aspects Making the process predictable Making use of existing knowledge and competencies Building in progress control procedures Not allowing the process to be dependent on changes in staff
Sketching a tempting prospect Making things attractive for people Stimulating vertical as well as horizontal exchange in relationships You scratch my back . . . Limiting uncertainty Building in a measure of care
Creating a group setting Basing the effort on existing learning issues Making use of practical problems Linking thinking and acting Emphasizing personal responsibility Creating security through rules and agreements Mirroring Using feedback rules Making somebody conscious of his incompetence
Placing a great deal of emphasis on observation, awareness Looking at the history of an organization Looking also at the interrelationships between diverse aspects In the light of the relationship of the organization with its environment To recognize (complex) patterns To give these patterns meaning Searching for where there is 'natural' will and power for change Breaking down barriers and obstacles Stimulating dialogues Creating new heroes

We prefer to use "color" as one of the dimensions for such an overview. Because we suggest change strategies to have one leading color, such arrangement of interventions, helps change agents find building blocks for an intervention plan. To a certain extent, the color gives clues in regard to the change agent's role and style, as well as clues in regard to the type of issues and problems that can be resolved. In this way our color classification corresponds to these kind of dimensions in the overviews of the above-mentioned authors. A red strategy, for example, can touch on HRM issues (Cummings & Worley), Reward systems (Sutherland) or Personnel aspects (Camp), while the change agent's role in the 'red' balancing act between organizational goals and employees' interests is often procedural, dealing with standards (Blake & Mouton) and standard training (Schmuck and Miles).

Color is the first dimension we use; the other is the level the intervention focuses on: individual, group, or whole organization. This distinction in levels is in line with Cummings and Worley and the designers of the two cubes. Each change agent can use the grid to arrange his own favorite interventions as well as the ones he leaves up to others. To illustrate the grid, we have entered three possible interventions into each cell in Table 5.10. The distinction between the cells is by no means watertight. As shown in Table 3.4, "knowledge management" or "mission formulation," for example, can have diverse meanings depending on the color print you have in mind. Because of this, an intervention like "strategy formulation" can be set up as a learning process within which views are exchanged and meanings sought (green); but it could equally well be set up as a highly analytical process based on research and benchmarks (blue). In spite of this, we feel that we can arrange interventions into the most "dominant" meaning usually attributed to them, partly determined by the "school" from which the intervention in question originates. The interventions mentioned in Table 5.10 are described in more detail in Chapter 7.

In conclusion: Interventions within interventions

Interventions can be conceived in all kinds of sizes, scopes, and depths. A three-year merger process can be regarded as one intervention, but so can one activity or even a single sentence. You might call this the "Mamouschka effect" (see 4.5), whereby interventions can be distinguished within interventions, and so on. You could say, "Within the framework of this intervention I will carry out this action," which is, in itself another intervention.

As an illustration, in Table 5.11 we list a number of change agent statements (micro-interventions) according to color. This level of interventions can be found mainly in the literature concerned with leadership, consulting skills, coaching, or conflict management.

5.5 The Case of "Organization X"

Situation (context and trigger)

We use this case to illustrate the phases in a change process. To put this into context, we first describe the general situation.

This case concerns a large insurance company that in comparison with its competitors has a problem with its cost ratios. There are also a number of threats: increasing domestic and foreign competition, increases in scale as a result of competitors merging, the professionalization of intermediaries (upon whom this organization relies heavily), the rise of direct writers, and unavoidable heavy investments in information technology. To make matters worse, the business is not sufficiently client oriented nor efficiently run.

The decision is made to undertake a drastic change operation. In the first phase, all the business processes are audited and redesigned. The organization structure is amended to reduce the number of management levels from six to three. Seventy of the 140 managers lose their positions as a result, and the organization will shed a total of 600 jobs (out of 2,800).

From the outset, the change process is split into three major phases. The first redesigning phase creates a so-called blueprint. This is followed by appointing staff to the new positions and the departure of superfluous personnel—the red print. In the third phase, an intensive introduction and training program is implemented to get the organization working according to plan—the green print.

The case starts when the blueprint and the redprint have been completed. We now have the task of designing the green print, and we begin with the important questions of the diagnostic phase.

Change idea

The change idea is the following:

There needs to be a paradigmatic shift from a predominantly hierarchical and bureaucratic organization into one that is flat, client oriented, and based on teamwork and output. This can be regarded as a strategic culture change (see Cummings and Worley, 1993).

New aspects for the organization include working in teams throughout the whole organization, close cooperation within the teams, and the introduction of team autonomy. Teams need to have cooperation skills, and their output will be judged using the so-called Balanced Business Score Card (see paragraph 6.3). Output-agreements will be made and monitored concerning the time allocated to processing a given volume of work, the maximum completion time, the maximum number of errors and complaints, and the number of commercial successes (hit ratio). Every team member shares the collective responsibility for this output. The team leader has no hierarchical power but must be regarded as a foreman who pitches in just like the rest. Management is expected to support team-oriented working by setting output goals with the team, by encouraging self-management by the team, and by stimulating cooperation. If we look at Figure 4.2, we can characterize the change idea of this third phase as follows: It is primarily concerned with characteristics of interaction. Working in self-steering teams assumes collective ambition (team goals), learning ability, openness, and respect. It requires people to be willing and to become able to cooperate and explore a more effective way to do business (in terms of improved hit ratios and quality).

Diagnosis

How do things stand at the beginning?

The aim is to change the organization's culture and to introduce a new organization paradigm. What, then, is the state of the present culture?

The following issues come to light during interviews:

"X is a prime example of an unbalanced, grossly overstaffed organization. It has a client-unfriendly, formal, and bureaucratic nature, which allows little room for personal initiatives or individual problem solving. "

"There is a job-for-life mentality and almost no willingness to change."

"Revitalization is essential, because some people won't get themselves into gear."

"No one knows how the teams will work, it's even unclear if people care for them at all. There is still a great deal of resistance against the new organization design. Lots will have to change before we can even begin to think about working in teams."

"The training sessions will be hairy and stormy events. This is a risky operation because now is the time to get things on the table and discuss everything. People will really have to speak their minds and say if they intend to cooperate at all. Some of the teams will end up in shambles and feelings could run high. The trainers will have to be therapists and specialists in group dynamics."

For the people in the workplace, the introduction and training program (the green-print phase) will be their first confrontation with the new way of organizing, with the demands put on them and with the competencies expected of them. Interventions need to be carried out that lead to the exchange of knowledge, the acceptance of new working methods, and that teach people how to function with them; or at least a good start should be made in this direction.

Most teams have only just been formed, and everyone still has to get to know one another and still has to develop some set of norms for their way of interacting.

The intended culture change is a huge undertaking. The intention is to influence every employee's way of working, working relationships, leadership style, behavior, and attitude. In view of the present situation, this process will take years. It is therefore important to get off to a good start, to carefully monitor what is happening, and to make provisions for follow-up possibilities that can be filled in at a later date—preferably team-specific possibilities—because teams will differ in what they learn and how they develop.

The change encompasses new complex concepts (teams, cooperation, leadership). It is especially important to be as clear and concrete as possible and to give these concepts substance.

If it is not introduced carefully, the change could easily create a negative attitude during the first round of training sessions. It seems especially important that expectations be managed by informing people, dealing with questions, and addressing resistance. People need to be given enough time to get used to the idea and test it. Trainings should certainly not be isolated events. Such trainings should be integrated into a much larger design of the change process. People need to become strongly motivated to take part in the whole process for it to work, and resistance should be carefully handled.

Other considerations are as follows:

The teams will differ widely in their stages of development and their competencies. Deep-lying unsolved problems may suddenly appear from nowhere, and the program must be able to deal with these and with diversity between teams.

In this (green) phase it is important that people learn, but how can you create a climate of learning in this organization's present culture? The approach can only be top-down given the circumstances, but learning requires motivation at the bottom. Will people want to learn and want to experiment?

There is a paradox. On the one hand, there is an extremely detailed blue print of both the work processes and the organization, while on the other hand, the teams are being given increased autonomy and authority and are being encouraged to manage themselves rather than being manageed. Can you realize empowerment in a top-down approach? Who are, or will be the carriers of the change and the change agents? External trainers might provide training, but how do you get all management to champion the change and stimulate its acceptance?

There must be regular checks to see to what extent the change has been accepted and is taking root. An overview of the change process is needed to assist in developing some kind of standards along the way that can be used as a benchmark when planning adjustments and subsequent interventions.

Improvement or renewal?

It is clear that the organization is involved in a major transformation, a fundamental renewal involving every single employee. As already mentioned, it concerns a strategic culture change, one that will try to influence the way of thinking and acting of every employee. Workers must learn to accept team autonomy, learn to work together as a team, and learn to be output-oriented. The new team leaders must learn their roles (steering without hierarchical authority), and managers must learn to work effectively with these teams. It will defenitely take two or three years to realize the change.

Resistance and energy

There is a great deal of resistance against the change on the part of the employees. This is partly generic, due to the existing bureaucratic culture where resistance to management's directives is the norm, also because there are so many of them. It is also because most workers neither know the details of the change nor comprehend why it is set up the way it is.

The teams are mostly new. The advantage of this is that groups can step out of possible dysfunctional existing group dynamics and start building up new working relationships. They can develop new ways of working from the start.

A number of people, including some managers, have had bad experiences with previous changes, including many changes being kicked off but later dying a slow and silent death. Would this happen again?

The need for change is well understood by most of management, but this is certainly not the case for people lower down the company ladder.

The change goals (change idea) are crystal clear and the management wants implementation throughout the whole organization (no exceptions). These are positive aspects.

The change agents' expertise and drive

Within management, and certainly at the top level, there is wide acceptance of the change goals. Desirabilty and necessity are clear, but many realize that they themselves are not sufficiently equipped to fulfill their role in both the change process and the new organization: a matter that must also be addressed. Managers and team leaders need to undergo some training and coaching to be able to act as change agents in the change process.

As external consultants, we knew what we were doing, but were less sure of what we were bringing about. It was somewhat of an adventure for us as well, one that was bound to teach us a lot.

Is it feasible?

In view of the above, we were inclined to answer this question positively. Also, there are clear indications what kind of change strategy might work. What requirements must this strategy meet? It needs to:

♦ give attention to processes of "bidding farewell to all that is familiar (but dysfunctional)"
♦ communicate the change idea widely and consistently throughout the organization
♦ create awareness at the initial phase of the change about new ways versus old ways of working before pushing for implementation.
♦ create momentum with a start up that is effective and has a real impact
♦ bring in powerful learning tools and introduce them carefully
♦ handle the "transfer of training" to the "real world" properly
♦ accompany the transfer from the old to the new situation with new rituals and symbols
♦ make the change as attractive as possible
♦ find ways to deal adequately with resistance
♦ develop the team leaders and managers first; they (especially) have a great deal to learn

Change strategy

The chosen change strategy needs to deal mainly with the knowledge and competencies of workers, the interaction between them and the way this is facilitated by the organization (see Change Idea, above). For this learning situations seem the best way to go, and thus the most appropriate basic color to employ would be green.

The change strategy has the following elements:

A. With regard to the content of the change:

♦ Work first on raising awareness and creating a feeling of "conscious incompetence"
♦ Use a tailor-made game/simulation as one of the learning tools to create microcosms of the desired change
♦ Have all of the employees take part

B. With regard to phases of the change process:

♦ It will commence a month or two after the personnel re-shuffle and the formation of teams and groups
♦ All the groups will be trained in a short period: within two or three months
♦ Prior to this, objectives and details of the trainings will be widely distributed though both personal communication and publications
♦ The training will start with the most senior staff members, then the next level, and so on; every level has a role to play introducing and assisting the change the next level down
♦ A psychological turning point will be created; a "rite of passage" from present to future

C. With regard to the actors:

♦ All the workers take part in their newly formed group
♦ Team leaders and managers will receive extra training to prepare them for their roles in the change process
♦ Managers are being committed by:
    ♦ first taking part in the training themselves
    ♦ then by personally introducing and winding up the training sessions of the teams that have started to report to them
    ♦ and finally by acting as co-trainers in several training sessions for teams

D. With regard to sense-making:

♦ A physical change of workplace is presented and used to encourage a new start
♦ One particular set of logos, symbols, and names is used to denote the change process as such, the game/simulations, the trainings, the teams, and so on
♦ An air of mystery is created by orchestrated secrecy. Participants say to curious colleagues "If you haven't taken part in the simulation yet, you can't really know what it is all about"

♦ A particular cognitive model on team work is created to supply new language and ideas. The model is set out in all kinds of materials
♦ "Heroes" and "anti-heroes" are publicly identified

E. With regard to the conditions:

♦ Every team has undergone intake interviews with the trainers in which possible resistance is addressed and their own learning needs and wishes are discussed
♦ Each team has a follow-up session three months after the training
♦ The process is regularly monitored by means of questionnaires, trainers' reports, and observations.

Intervention plan

The plan contains the following interventions:

♦ communication and information meetings with management
♦ communication through the staff magazine
♦ one-day meetings for groups of 100 workers to introduce the change, the change process, and the change agents (managers and consultants/trainers)
♦ training for management in team-effective leadership
♦ training of team leaders in order to motivate them to thoroughly prepare for the training of their own teams
♦ intakes with each team to make an inventory of learning wishes and to clarify the point of the training
♦ training the teams with the team leader in a game/simulation
♦ follow-up sessions three months after each training
♦ the distribution and discussion of the "critical success factors for teams"-model before and during training
♦ each group draws up a plan of action for itself to further implement the change
♦ all the participants fill in questionnaires during intake, training, and follow-up; this enables monitoring of the change
♦ each team has a checklist—in the form of the team diagnosis—which they themselves can use to discuss their performance and team functioning at their own convenience
♦ all the trainers meet regularly to exchange experiences and learn from one another.

Future interventions

After this intervention plan had been completed, we asked ourselves: How far did we get? What have all these initial interventions brought the organization? How should it be continued? Are the intended outcomes of the change still realistic?

This evaluation was made with the help of empirical data, including questionnaires and a variety of observations and impressions.

This leads to interventions designed and implemented after the initial intervention plan. They include:

A. Following up the follow-up

Teams that so wish are given extra training and coaching according to their needs. The rationale behind this is that the so-called consciously incompetent teams will by now recognize their own shortcomings and that training from now on can be tailored to meet their specific needs.

B. The team leaders' development process

Experience during the initial intervention plan made us aware that team leaders require additional training. Their job is not easy, and in view of the fact that a great deal is asked of their personal skills and attitude, we felt that extra, intensive training was necessary.

C. Intervision sessions

Intervision groups of managers and team leaders are formed to discuss their personal effectiveness in the new organization and to learn from each other.

D. Improving decision making between managers and team leaders

A manager and his team leaders practice ways of more effective decision making that will be less harmful to team development and collective team decisions.

E. Continued monitoring

The organization regularly sends out the previously mentioned questionnaires to enable further monitoring of the change process.

Note: A more extensive description of this case and an empirical study of the effects can be found in de Caluwé and Geurts (1999).

6: Examples of Diagnostic Models

In this chapter we take a closer look at the diagnosis. We focus on the change agent's "toolkit," with its diagnostic models and mind-sets. We limit ourselves to examples sufficiently different from each other so as to provide a wide spectrum of the types of models. Each change agent can add his favorite models to the list. In fact, we see steady accumulation of diagnostic tools by individual change agents as a valuable part of ongoing professionalization.

We classify the diagnostic models on two dimensions for the reasons given in section 5.1.2. The first dimension concerns the level: Does the model focus on the individual, the group, the entire organization, or its environment? The second dimension concerns the approach:

♦ Does the model focus on business aspects? This involves the characteristics and effects of (primary or secondary) business processes. The associated viewpoint stems from business science, business administration, business economics, and the like.

♦ Does the model focus on organizational aspects? We refer here to the characteristics and effects of the design and management of organizations. Most of these models are static: They describe what an organization looks like or should look like. This viewpoint stems from organizational science.

♦ Does the model focus on change aspects? This concerns the characteristics and effects of the underlying factors and forces driving those involved. On the one hand this refers to history playing out its role. It addresses life cycles, natural progressions, developmental issues, and so on. On the other hand, we refer to layers of reality of which those involved are not necessarily aware but that nevertheless guide their behavior and thus aid or frustrate change aspects such as group dynamics, power games, cultural trends, and mental models. Most of these models are dynamic. Their viewpoint stems from the social sciences: history, psychology, anthropology, semiotics, and the like.

	Business Aspects	
Individual	**6.1.** **Eisenhower Principle*** Curriculum vitae Timesheets	
Group	**6.2.** **Profitability formula for professional firms*** Fishbone diagram Task division scheme	
Organization	**6.3.** **Balanced scorecard*** Portfolio analysis Activity-based costing	
Environment	**6.4.** **Competitive structure*** Environment analysis Experience curves	

Table 6.1 Matrix With Diagnostic Models
*We describe these models in detail; we summarize the other two.

Table 6.1 outlines the twelve cells resulting from this classification.

The availability of diagnostic models for each cell varies. Business models focus strongly on the organization and environment levels, organizational models focus more on the group and organization levels, and change management models cover practically all levels. We describe the first-mentioned model for each cell in some detail; the other two models in a cell are only briefly outlined. Table 6.2 shows the framework we use to describe each model. Emphasis is placed on the content of the diagnosis: the scheme, the perspective, the model. We have excluded the diagnostic *process* from the descriptions (see instead 5.1.1). This is not because we do not find this important but because, in our opinion, the models can often be used in many different ways. For instance, a model designed by Porter (6.4) regarding the competitive structure of an industry *can* be used in an independent research approach by external experts who present the results of their long, well-considered quantitative analysis to a select group of managers. But we have used this model equally effectively in participative strategy development in which a group of about twenty people attempted to reach conclusions concerning the desired positioning of their organization. The emphasis in that case was on qualitative information, underlying mind-sets, and the creation of involvement, dialogue, and learning mind-set. This chapter does not go into the diagnostic process—the actions or the interventions—but is restricted entirely to the diagnostic *content*, the models and concepts.

Organization Aspects	Change Aspects
6.5. **Core qualities*** I/R professionals Competencies	6.9. **Biographical fit*** Power sources Levels of learning
6.6. **Team roles*** Team conditions for success Roles for staff units	6.10. **Optimal conflict level*** Learning curve Process/Result orientation
6.7. **Culture types*** Organizational configurations Organizational Iceberg	6.11. **The clock*** Passage of resistance Two forces for change
6.8. **Network organization*** Public/private cooperation Industrial ecology	6.12. **Field of influence*** Megatrends National cultures

Description of the format of the diagnostic model
1. Underlying notion Change agent's philosophy
2. Description Characteristics of the model and implications for action
3. Comments Applicability in terms of domains or phases of a change process
4. Approach Business aspects/organizational aspects/change aspects
5. Level Individual/group/organization/environment
Name and short characterization of two related diagnostic models (in terms of approach and level)
References for all three models

Table 6.2 Format for the Description of the Diagnostic Models

6.1 The Eisenhower Principle, Curriculum Vitae, Time Sheets

The Eisenhower Principle

1. Underlying Notion

People (individuals) easily allow themselves to be triggered by other people's expectations of them and to be swayed by the issues of the day. Parkinson's law applies here: "Work" tends to spread itself out over the maximum time available, or, in our opinion, even tends to exceed it. This is not only demotivating for the person in question but also is not in the best interest of the organization. This problem is aggravated as organizations become more professional or face a more dynamic environment; under such circumstances management has to rely increasingly on the self-steering abilities of its employees, including their personal time management. It can have serious repercussions on the organization's functioning if employees are unable to do this effectively. Various models are available to assist employees to manage their time. Business thinking does this by systematic analyzing and planning of activities. The assumption is that people will be able to have more control over how they spend their working hours if their activities are rationally characterized and structured.

2. Description

The Eisenhower principle maintains that activities should be characterized by both their urgency and their importance. It is emphasized that the nature of the two properties is entirely different. An urgent task requires immediate attention but need not necessarily be of great importance. Urgent tasks are often reactive in nature: they are imposed by the system (e.g., administrative obligations) or by bosses or clients ("look into this or that"; "this needs to be addressed"). Important tasks more often are of a (pro-)active nature and have a longer-term perspective. Some of these tasks stem from the individual's ambition, the vision he has about the work, his desire to exhibit a personal "style," and so on. Figure 6.1 gives clues as to how to prioritize one's activities based on one's assessment of their importance and urgency. The main aim of the exercise is to ensure that the most important rather than the most urgent activities survive. The following holds true for all urgent activities: if someone else can do it for you, that's fine. Important activities, in contrast, should receive the most attention and preferably from you personally. Things that are neither urgent nor important should be "forgotten."

3. Comments

This model can have relevance for all employees, regardless of their positions in an organization. The more somebody is expected to manage her own work and

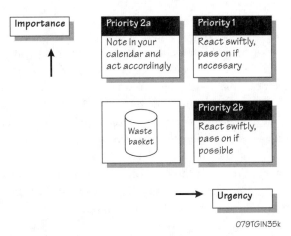

079TGIN35k

Figure 6.1 Prioritization Matrix

the more frequently she is confronted by new demands and expectations in her working environment (clients, colleagues, etc.), the more relevant the model is. This last aspect of "demands and expectations" makes such a model particularly relevant to managers and members of staff departments. This model is restricted by the fact that time management is not only a question of systematic planning but also depends on self-knowledge, clarity of one's goals and vision, and strength of character, as well as communication and social skills. If someone has prioritized his activities but nevertheless cannot say no, time management remains a problem. Does someone tend to jump in too quickly and take over other people's problems? Is he able to call others to account for their contributions?

4. Approach
The model focuses on business aspects. However, the discussion may sometimes widen to include the division of tasks/responsibilities (organizational aspects) or the psychological makeup of the person in question (change aspects).

5. Level
Individual. However, the model can also be used for groups or small organizations.

Related Diagnostic Model 1: Curriculum Vitae
The underlying notion of curriculum vitae is that individuals are able to steer their own "employability" by consciously reflecting on and investing in their own curriculum vitae. Career counseling uses the CV format, among other

things, as a tool. The CV's content: one's education (e.g., titles and courses), experience (e.g., expertise, roles, arenas), contacts (e.g., membership in committees, societies, boards), and achievements (e.g., assignments, publications) can all demonstrate and elucidate one's vision and talents. There is also the question of the CV's style: it can convey to a certain extent one's uniqueness, one's personality, and make one stand out from the rest. There are also limits to this model and a word of caution seems appropriate. Employability is sometimes used as an excuse to place the responsibility for employment entirely on the individual ("If things don't work out, it's your own fault") and deny the influence and responsibilities of organizations, governments, and similar others. People at the bottom of the social ladder sometimes face many hurdles that prevent them from finding work that suits them in this world of CV competitiveness.

Related Diagnostic Model 2: Time Sheets

In order to gain an insight into one's work patterns and the distribution of one's valuable time, it can be useful to record one's activities. The insight gained can assist as a reality check, in prioritizing activities, canceling unimportant tasks, and evaluating their costs and benefits. For instance, time sheets allow consultants to keep track of the number of direct (billable) hours they spend for clients versus the number of indirect hours they spend on the development of their organization or their profession. Based on this overview, the consultant can decide to limit the number of indirect hours spent on the organization or to delegate part of these activities to an assistant. This kind of diagnostic method can, of course, be applied to many sorts of work or activities.

References:

Blanken (1994)
Eisenhower (1990)
Groote, Hugenholtz-Sasse, and Slikker (1995)

6.2 Profit Formula for Professional Organizations, Fishbone Diagram, Task-Division Scheme

Profit Formula for Professional Organizations

1. Underlying Notion

Being able to steer the financial results of an organization depends heavily on having insight into the determining factors of the organization's performance and the extent to which they can be influenced by the organization itself. In other words: unraveling the operational processes, thus gaining solid financial indicators that are then monitored and used as a basis for operational management. It is exactly this type of unraveling that allows such management to do justice to the diversity of services that can be part of the organization's portfolio: one unit in the organization might be capable of achieving the same financial results as another, but each might have its own recipe for success that is suited to its type of clients and services. Different operational indicators and management are then required. Unraveling also allows for distinguishing between businesses that are so different that their operational management should have little in common. A good example is the much-needed distinction in operational management between such opposites as professional services and manufacturing industries.

2. Description

Maister argues that "profit per partner" should be viewed as the professional firm's equivalent of the manufacturing industry's "return on equity." The general idea is that it is the partners themselves that constitute the firm's equity investment: sometimes they are literally the providers of financial capital. In most cases they also represent the intangible equity: should they leave, the shareholders could consider the firm to be loosing its key assets. It is especially important to understand that profit per partner can be achieved in many different ways, all of which are legitimate. A partner can generate profit by providing a certain client base with standard services that realize a small profit margin. It can enable people to work many billable hours without undue stress because internal training and development demand little time and the methods and techniques are routine and clear-cut. Thus a good profit can be achieved, certainly if the tariffs are not too low. The labor cost can be kept down by deploying junior employees whenever possible, given the routine nature of the work. On the other hand, however, there can also be partners who have a "high-tech, high touch" approach with their clients. Here, more seniority is demanded: the leverage decreases and, possibly, the utilization (number of hours for client vs. hours on other matters like innovation, etc.) If the margins and the tariffs are high, the same profit per partner can be achieved. According to Maister, things start to go wrong when a firm no longer takes these differences into account and justice is not done to its variety in services *and* professionals. Worse still, to steer entirely on the basis of, for example, utilization and margin, no matter how good these may be, does not guarantee a satisfactory end result. Partners who are high achievers can seem to be doing badly and vice versa. The "profit formula" is a quick-and-dirty diagnostic tool to examine the "hygiene" and "health" of a business. Hygiene refers to short-term profitability—guarding against low utilization

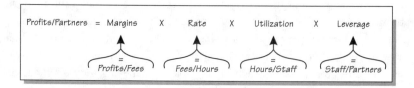

Figure 6.2 Maister's Formula for Professional Firms

(making sure everybody has billable work) and low margin (canceling projects that cause heavy losses and keeping the overhead down). Health refers to long-term profitability: striving for better leverage, higher rates, and professionally challenging projects. Unraveling one's performance, as done in this formula, provides clear indications of how to improve one's performance.

3. Comments
This specific formula can be applied only in professional service firms, provided each partner has sufficient steering possibilities. Its use is not limited in time, but its accuracy depends on the availability of internal systems that monitor the given indicators effectively.

4. Approach
Focuses on business aspects

5. Level
The formula is always applicable at the level of each individual partner's business. It remains useful when used on a higher scale (profit/unit instead of profit/partner) as long as on that level in the organization a comparable service is still provided to clients. The formula loses its value at the organizational level because at that point it lumps all services and all partners together.

Related Diagnostic Model 1: Fishbone Diagram
The fishbone diagram is an aid to mapping out the failure factors and risks in plans and processes. It can be used to facilitate and support group discussions on this subject. The principle originates from Ishikawa and is also set out by Hugenholtz-Sasse (1995). The key lies in identifying the main factors that have an influence on the outcome of a plan or process. One well-known shortlist of main factors is: people, machines, materials, and methods. Another, more based on human behavior, is: Are we required to do this, are we allowed to do this,

are we willing to do this, are we able to do this? These factors form the main fishbones. Next, all the aspects that can go wrong are identified for each of these main bones. For example, in "methods": the unreliability of registering time or the failings of a distribution net. The analysis will be a repetitive exercise in complex and risky plans and will preferably be carried out before a new step in the process is embarked upon. The analysis is usually broad and the details are only filled in gradually. For example, after using a fishbone diagram to inventory the risks, an analysis of the extent of the risk and the possible preventive and curative actions can be carried out.

Related Diagnostic Model 2: Task-Division Scheme

This is a simple aid for dividing tasks/responsibilities within the framework of a specific, collaborative effort. An inventory is made of all activities and the outcomes related to them. All activities are expressed by verbs, all outcomes by nouns. Next a list is made of all those contributing.

In the task-division scheme all this information is linked: each task is assigned, in terms of activity and outcome, to an individual, and only to an organization, department, group, or sector if the identity of the specific person has yet to be determined. The task may be content based and thus related to a phase in the change process or it may be managerial. The nature of the contribution must also be stated; for example "does," "is responsible for," "approves or decides," "initiates," "advises," "cooperates," "tests," "files," and so on.

References:

Maister (1993)

Groote, Hugenholtz-Sasse, and Slikker (1995)

6.3 Balanced Scorecard, Portfolio Analysis, Activity-Based Costing

Balanced Scorecard

1. Underlying Notion

Based on the assumption that many organizations pay a disproportionate amount of attention to financial management, it is necessary to determine other management factors that merit comparable attention. This can help close the gap between long- and short-term goals, because financial indicators can easily lead to short-term reflexes. This search for "balance" is the dominant feature of the balanced scorecard. The premise is that without such a balance there can be no healthy development and derailment becomes inevitable. What is more, it's felt that balance can be actively maintained and monitored in a top-down manner.

2. Description

In its original version the "balanced scorecard" consists of four perspectives:

◆ Financial: To succeed financially, how should we appear to our shareholders?
◆ Internal business process: To satisfy our shareholders and customers, in what business processes must we excel?
◆ Learning and growth: To achieve our vision, how will we sustain our ability to change and improve?
◆ Customer: To achieve our vision, how should we appear to our customers?

The scorecard is normally constructed on the basis of a vision or strategy. The perspectives are worked out in terms of objectives, measures, targets, and initiatives, preferably in combination with one another. To use the scorecard diagnostic model even if the organization does not already have one, the change agent needs to create a scorecard and work out the four perspectives himself. The diagnosis provides insights into such aspects as the balance among the four perspectives, the interdependencies among them, and the emphasis on thinking (objectives and measures) versus action (targets and initiatives).

3. Comments

In change processes where a balanced scorecard is constructed, it can be used as a diagnostic tool *later* in the process. But the scorecard can also be used in a less instrumental manner: for a quick qualitative bird's-eye view of the organization's performance at any given time. It is best used at higher levels in an organization, where all four perspectives fit both within one's domain of responsibility and (hopefully) one's general outlook.

4. Approach

Primarily focused on business aspects.

5. Level

Organization level

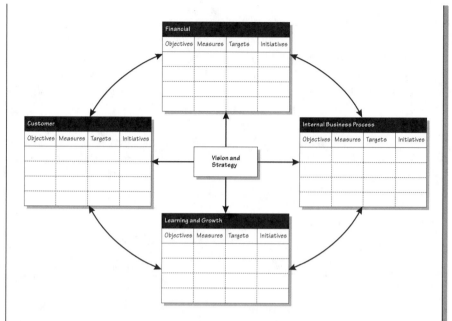

Figure 6.3 Balanced Scorecard

Related Diagnostic Model 1: Portfolio Analysis

The analysis assumes that four rules determine the cash flow of a product. First, it is assumed that high margins and high market shares go together (see also the "learning curve" diagnostic model in section 6.10). Subsequently, it is assumed that market growth demands investments to hold market share, while this lowers (short-term) profits. The same applies to procuring a larger share of that market. The final assumption is that no market can grow indefinitely; the payoff from growth must come when the growth slows, or it will not come at all. In any case, the pay off can no longer be reinvested in that product. On the basis of these rules, the Boston Consulting Group distinguishes four types of product/market combinations in terms of market growth and market share.

This characterization is especially helpful to organizations that have many product/market combinations (PMCs)—diversified organizations, for example—to help them assess how "healthy" their portfolio is (are all the PMCs at the end of their lifespan?), and to help them make decisions concerning investments and divestments. The four types of product/market combinations are

♦ "stars" with a high market share and high growth; although they demand investment, they can assure a future for the organization

+ "cash cows" with a high share of the market but no more growth to speak of;
  they demand little investment and provide the returns necessary for investment in stars and question marks
+ "dogs" with a low market share and little growth; they are evidence of
  having failed to create a leadership position in the growth phase; generally it
  is best to scrap these products and cut the losses
+ "question marks" with a low market share but a high growth; these are the
  product/market combinations that could become the "new stars"; they constitute the hope for the future but they demand high investment and not all
  will be successful

Related Diagnostic Model 2: Activity-Based Costing

The notion behind activity-based costing (ABC) is strikingly simple: Products
cause no costs, but the activities involved in producing them do. If you do not
know the details of the cost of the various activities involved, you will not be able
to calculate and thus predict what, for example, a threefold growth in production would do to the average cost of a single product. In the absence of activity-
based costing, it is often assumed that overheads, personnel costs, and so on, will
grow proportionally, something that is hardly ever the case. If the costs of activities are known, it is possible to determine accurately the fixed and variable costs
involved in creating any of the products. The variable costs can then tell you
what threefold production would do to the average cost of a single product. An
additional advantage is that ABC also allows more precise strategic planning.
For instance, information about the costs of operational processes is useful when
deciding on and planning investments that are the result of product and process
redesign. ABC fits in well with existing systems in the operational sphere (quality systems, logistic systems, etc.). Roughly speaking, the diagnosis consists of
four parts:

+ grouping similar activities in so-called activity centers
+ selecting "cost drivers" that indicate the relationship between the activities of
  an activity center and the creation of a product
+ differentiating costs into activity centers
+ differentiating the costs of the activity centers into the products on the basis
  of the cost drivers

References:
Kaplan and Norton (1996)
Henderson (1979)
Boons, Roberts, and Roozen (1991)

6.4 Competitive Structure, Environment Analysis, Experience Curves

Competitive Structure

1. Underlying Notion

The essence of strategy formulation is coping with competition. In other words, it is a power game with players that are in the same particular branch or sector of industry. This goes beyond competitors only and includes customers, suppliers, and others. To be able to maneuver successfully in this arena, an insight into the underlying power structure is deemed essential. The analysis is a rational exercise, and the knowledge gained provides the groundwork for a strategic agenda for action. The performance of an organization is considered the sum of the given competitive structure and the position the company chooses to defend itself against the collective forces or to influence them in its favor.

2. Description

Porter distinguishes five forces that together determine the attractiveness of a given sector of industry. The stronger these forces, the less attractive the industry is in terms of possible profits and growth. He argues that these forces determine what costs a company can charge to clients and suppliers and what costs simply have to be borne by the company. They also determine what investments are necessary for a company to ensure a good competitive position for itself. A company can go beyond coping with these forces and might take the offensive by altering the balance of power. For instance, it can lobby for legislation that creates entry barriers for others. Vertical integration or capital investments in large-scale facilities might also create such barriers. A company's strategy can thus change the structure of a branch: it is a question of anticipating changes in the competitive structure and foreseeing the impact of your interventions. The five forces as shown in Figure 6.4 are:

♦ Industry competitors: The determining factors in their mutual relationship are, among other things, industry growth, concentration and diversity of competitors, product differences, and the ratio between fixed and variable costs. Furthermore, intermittent overcapacity in the branch, brand identity, switching costs, and exit barriers also play a role.

♦ Buyers: The bargaining leverage of this group and the price sensitivity of the product are the determining factors here. This is influenced by, for example, buyer concentration versus firm concentration, buyer volume, buyer switching costs versus firm switching costs, the ability to backwardly integrate, the existence of substitute products, the extent to which the product differences affect the quality and costs of end products, and more.

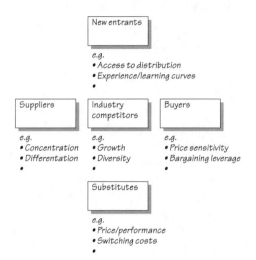

Figure 6.4 Porter's Five Forces

◆ Suppliers: Again, bargaining power is the determining factor. This is influenced by the number of possible suppliers and the impact of their inputs on cost or differentiation. Matters such as volume, presence of substitutes, switching costs, supplier concentration, and the possibility of forward integration play a role.

◆ Substitutes: Relative price and performance are the determining factors. How easy it is for customers to switch over? Might they be concerned about the parts that make up the end product ("Intel inside")? How actively are the substitute producers looking for new applications for their technology?

◆ New entrants: In contrast to substitutes, these are parties who want to deliver a comparable product. Of importance is how easy it is to gain entry: Is there an experience curve that hinders entry (see below in this section)? Is there a certain volume that must be produced in order to deliver comparable products in terms of quality and costs (economies of scale)? How big are the necessary investments? Are there any patents or government regulations that stand in the way? Will it be possible for new entrants to use existing distribution channels?

3. Comments

The model is rooted in a worldview based on struggle and of survival of the fittest. Possibly, this is most opportune in weakly regulated economies and less so in their opposites. In the original publication, Porter devotes little or no attention to underlying trends that help shape the competitive structure, like demographic trends or environmental crises (see later on in this chapter). Another important factor is the delineation of the battlefield: Who is considered to be part of the same industry? Can cars be replaced by bicycles or perhaps by working at home? Is a café a place to eat and drink something (with the snack-bar as part of the competitive structure) or a place for recreation (with the theater as substitute)? It thus would appear that the model often requires supplementary analyses and choices to ensure that the "rational analysis" paints a useful picture and doesn't leave out some very powerful forces. Nevertheless, the model is extremely versatile and can be applied to all kinds of industries and contexts. It is equally suitable for quantitative expert-approaches as for qualitative action-approaches.

4. Approach
Business aspects. Organizational aspects are addressed in only a limited way.

5. Level
Environment level, because it concerns the branch of industry or the sector as a whole.

Related Diagnostic Model 1: Environment Analysis
External analysis seeks out the trends in the environment that either provide opportunities or threaten the organization and that cannot easily be influenced by the organization itself. The assumption is that a company's enterprising strength is limited or facilitated by such developments, and that these developments are discernable. The ability to identify external developments depends partly on the magnitude of these developments, the powers of perception of the people in the organization, and the (expected) consequences of the change. Some authors use a checklist of factors as an aid in this analysis and a means of avoiding lacunas in it. Weggeman, Wijnen, and Kor (1992) describe the DESTEP acronym. These letters stand for

♦ Demographic (birth and death statistics; age distribution; emigration; immigration; composition of households; local/regional/national/international diversity)
♦ Ecological (environmental limits; natural phenomena; climate trends; availability of raw material, etc.)
♦ Social (outlooks on life; individualization; globalization; resistance movements; boycotts; education)
♦ Technological (new scientific developments; new combinations of materials; robotization; computerization; material extensification; R&D climate; patenting)

♦ Economic (competition; market developments; currency developments; inflation; macro-economic systems; trade restrictions; financing; [intellectual] property rights; market mechanisms)

♦ Political (legislation; enforcement; democratic/totalitarian systems; government stability; national cultures; intensification/extensification of government control)

Related Diagnostic Model 2: Experience Curves

A study carried out in the sixties showed that the production costs of services or products often decreased if a company produced more "units." This phenomenon was proved to apply to all branches of industry, from car manufacturers to insurance companies, from established products to recent innovations, and from high-tech to low-tech products or services. The decrease in costs is specific to each branch rather than to individual companies and can thus be easily mapped out by industry audits. The underlying dynamics can be explained by a number of factors. These are the efficiency of the employees (which increases with experience); increased specialization; improved working methods or the redesign or renewal of production processes; better use of production technology; the deployment, where possible, of cheaper labor; and the standardization of products. Knowledge of "experience curves" is of great importance. The curve can indicate entry barriers for new players: Their costs are higher, which will impede their marketing position. What is more, existing players can try to speed up their learning curves. For example, one can invest in the skills, cooperation, and innovative powers of employees. Or the scale of production can be increased: As more people are involved in production, the potential for mutual learning, specialization, and the cost-effectiveness of expensive technology increases.

References:
Porter (1979)
Weggeman, Wijnen, and Kor (1992)
Abell and Hammond (1979)

6.5 Core Qualities, I/R Professionals, Competencies

Core Qualities

1. Underlying Notion

People are not blank canvases. Each individual possesses deep-rooted characteristic traits that shape his or her personality. These traits are almost impossible to change, nor can they be easily cultivated. This implies that an individual's development depends strongly on his recognizing and applying his characteristic traits productively. In this way, personal development means that a person deepens her own personality instead of trying to become "someone else," a "new person." It also implies that attempting to deny or escape from these deeply rooted traits hinders further development.

2. Description

Ofman (1992) uses the term *core quality* for characteristics that are part of a person's nature and that express his individuality. The core quality is always available and is not acquired, but it is sometimes concealed. Each core quality involves certain dynamics: it determines what irritates you, where you become ineffective, what the challenge is in your development. These dynamics can be mapped out by means of a "core quadrant" (see Figure 6.5). This quadrant can be read as follows: Each core quality has its shadow. If the quality gets out of hand (too much of a good thing), it becomes a "pitfall." The opposite of this pitfall is the person's "challenge": a complementary quality. Potential conflicts with the environment can be expected when someone is "challenged" too much: his "allergy." At the same time, this allergy is the opposite of his core quality. The core quadrant that so evolves is an aid to increasing one's self-awareness. As an example, the core quality "clarity" and the other corresponding elements are mapped in Figure 6.5. Someone who understands that aloofness as a pitfall and groveling as an allergy are inextricably linked to his "clarity" is more able to accept these side effects. Such awareness softens the bad news of his pitfall and allergy, and thus his resistance to face them. At the same time, this awareness can serve to help someone steer his personal development and his relationships with others, whether in or outside of the work arena.

Combinations of the quadrants of one person with those of another is a useful aid in examining problems concerning cooperation. Imagine someone with the core quality "caring," who is allergic to "aloofness." When he meets the person whose core quadrant is like Figure 6.5, they are bound to get into trouble with one another, as "aloofness" is not only the pitfall of one of them, but is the other's allergy. If the interaction is examined with the aid of core quadrants, these problems can be alleviated considerably when both parties are able to recognize how they co-create the conflict as a result of their core quality's dysfunctional side effects. Furthermore, they can even become allies in their respective personal development: to fuel the desire to move beyond pitfall and allergy to their respective challenges, and to be each other's "early warning signs" for moves that do not work well.

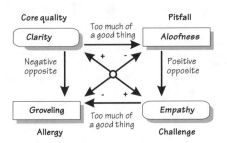

Figure 6.5 Ofman's Core Quadrant

3. Comments
The model can be used to discuss interactions in contexts where people find it useful and legitimate to discuss things on a personal level if doing so can make a difference. This can be a coaching relationship or a self-steering team, for example. Furthermore, the model can be used for self-diagnosis or as a tacit diagnosis by a change agent of certain people and their interactions. Generally speaking, the model can be applied for interactions only when a change process is already under way, because people have to get to know each other a little first. In more formal settings, the model is not applicable because people do not feel free or safe to reflect on personal interactions and dilemmas.

4. Approach
The model addresses organizational aspects. For example, it can be used to decide on team composition or to structure cooperation. It certainly also addresses change aspects because it focuses on the underlying forces that drive people or interactions.

5. Level
Individual, or at the cooperation level between two people. Applicability at group level is limited because the original meaning of the personality traits anchored in the individuals is lost. At the group level, core competencies, as was introduced by Hamel and Prahalad (1994), are a better and even somewhat related tool.

Related Diagnostic Model 1: I/R Professionals
Weggeman distinguishes between types of professionals. One such distinction is between the "Improvising" professional and the professional who relies on "Routine." The I-professional is someone who is continually producing new information based on his creativity and talent for improvising. She scores high

on flexibility, has one unique assignment after another, is driven by knowledge, and has learned how to learn (double-loop learning). Lawyers, journalists, artists, policy advisors, politicians, and detectives spring to mind. The R-professional is someone who, more or less routinely, is able to achieve a high level when applying a certain skill. He strives for perfection through mastering his chosen field: he has a long line of similar assignments. He is driven by experience and scores high on efficiency. He continually increases his knowledge of the same subject (single-loop learning). Here, glassblowers, surgeons, classical musicians, fighter-jet pilots, and sheep-shearers come to mind. The distinction between the two is important, because the most effective style of leadership for each group is different. With regard to the R-professional, managers are expected to act as trainers and coaches and, in these roles, they steer the output as well as the work process of the professional, with the focus on the tasks at hand. The boss of a group of I-professionals, in contrast, had better refrain from interfering with his staff's work process and direct his attention mainly to clearly specifying the required output and creating and facilitating a good work climate. It can be helpful to diagnose whether a professional behaves in the way that is fitting to her profession. Some I-professionals, especially after many years on the job, have been heard to say, "I've seen this all before" and then go about adapting the client's problem to their own repertoire of cherished recipes.

Related Diagnostic Model 2: Competencies

When diagnosing individuals, a model can be useful for mapping out their skills. There are many models available for this. One much-used one is a three-way division into kinds of knowledge, kinds of skills, and kinds of attitude. For professionals we use a checklist to which a number of elements specific to them—such as networking and self-steering—have been added. Such a checklist consists of five main categories:

- ♦ Professional knowledge and skill: specialism, degree of generalism, ability to create organizational synergy
- ♦ Interaction skills: dealing with clients, working in teams, communication skills, presentation skills, ability to deal with conflicts
- ♦ Organizational and environmental knowledge: internal networks, professional networks, knowledge of the organization, knowledge of the competitive structure and societal trends
- ♦ Self-steering: learning ability, self-awareness, empathy, flexibility, balance, drive, courage, creativity
- ♦ Specific management knowledge and skills: project management, leadership qualities, management of professionals, functional management aspects (e.g., Public Relations or Information Technology).

References:
Ofman (1992)
Hamel and Prahalad (1994)
Weggeman (1992)
Vermaak (1999)

6.6 Team Roles, Team Conditions for Success, Roles for Staff Units

Team Roles

1. Underlying Notion

All people have specific characteristics and competences that they bring to their work. A team role is the individual's contribution to the team's goal, given his qualities. Each role inherently possesses strengths and weaknesses. In order to have the necessary strengths available and the weaknesses compensated, a team needs a diversity of roles to be fulfilled. One searches for complementarity. No one person is able to take on all roles, as a role has to "fit" you. However, a person might be comfortable in more than just one role. The notion behind the model of team roles is not merely to describe them but also to "manage" them. To this end, by means of tests and discussions, the present team roles are mapped out and compared to an "optimal or workable composition." The idea is that on the basis of this twofold insight, the team can decide on an improved division of roles. This often includes "role sacrifices" (whereby team members take on roles they are not keen to fulfill but are capable of doing for the team's sake) and agreements on role development.

2. Description

Figure 6.6 illustrates eight roles that, according to Belbin (1981), often occur in teams and that complement each other nicely. For each role he describes typical behavior, telltale signs, traits, and so on. We briefly characterize the roles. The "coordinator" focuses on the team's goals and controls the procedures and roles. He is often the chairman and commands respect, is able to motivate, and has an eye for people's strengths and weaknesses. He does not need to make a contribution to the content or play a creative role. The "shaper" looks for patterns in the discussion, comes up with "game plans," and puts the team on the right track. He is enthusiastic and often convinced of his own abilities but can be impatient and intolerant of team members who are more reflective. The "plant" is an innovator who provides creative solutions and inspiration. She avoids well-trodden paths, she is an individualist, and, sometimes, she builds castles in the air. The "monitor" or "evaluator" is good at analyzing problems and evaluating (other people's) solutions. He is level-headed and cautious. He often is averse to emotion and can have a restraining influence on the team. The "company worker" transforms decisions into concrete solutions. She carries them out efficiently and systematically. She is a great believer in action and discipline; she cannot cope with vagueness and is not easily diverted from her course. The "resource investigator" searches for knowledge outside the team, he is good at networking with external relations, he has good social skills and lots of enthusiasm but is not always available for concrete (routine) tasks, especially when perseverance is required. The "team worker" monitors the team spirit, supports team members, and optimizes internal communication. She is sensitive and a good listener. She hates tough confrontations and often lacks decisiveness. The "completer" or "finisher" dots the i's and crosses the t's. He feels responsible for the final result and is conscientious and watchful. However, he can also harp on about things and rush people.

The whole idea is that each role has its added value and should be represented. This means that a team should be large enough to accommodate that. Some roles can be present in substantial numbers, like company workers and team workers. For other roles this would be dysfunctional: several coordinators and/or shapers on the same team would get in each other's way.

3. Comments

It is a good idea to discuss team roles when the team first comes together, because this can be instrumental in helping to organize the mutual cooperation. The model can also be of help in recruiting people and putting together a "balanced" team. The model can again be used as an evaluation tool after, say, six months or a year. Its limitation lies in the fact that social interactions are not all that "makeable": Not all roles can be developed just like that, and people are not always willing or able to make the necessary "role sacrifices." Any discussion of team roles also requires a degree of safety. For example, if team members have political agendas, discussion of team roles can be misused to manipulate the internal pecking order or to grab leadership. A further limitation concerns confusion about the term *team*. Every team is a group, but not every group is a team. A team typically consists of between five and fifteen people who share responsibility for an entire task. There needs to be interdependency among the activities of the team members. If this is not the case, each individual in the group can work individually and there is no necessity to fulfill the team roles.

the coordinator   the shaper   the plant

the evaluator   the company worker   the resource
                                                     investigator

the team player   the finisher

Figure 6.6 Belbin's Roles

4. Approach

Focuses on organizational aspects: How can teams be organized to ensure optimal performance? When people want to develop their ability for specific roles, the model can also support, for example, learning processes (change aspects).

5. Level

Suitable exclusively at group level

Related Diagnostic Model 1: Team Conditions for Success

The notion behind the concept of team conditions is that there might be universal characteristics for all teams, and that an overview of these conditions can be used as a tool to evaluate and improve a team's functioning. Vroemen (1995) uses a model with six conditions, each of which contributes to a specific desired team effect. These conditions are described below:

♦ Clear goals: These provide a challenge, thus giving the team direction and focus.
♦ Joint responsibility: This creates involvement and so contributes to team spirit.
♦ Open communication: This creates clarity. It helps teams to provide good dissemination of information to its members but also helps teams to handle conflicts.
♦ Mutual respect: This acknowledges and even creates diversity. It builds up the team members' confidence in one another and allows for differences within the team to be made productive.
♦ Adjusting flexibly: This creates development. The team is better able to tune to the environment and capitalize on this.
♦ Showing initiative: This creates action. The team discovers its creativity and energy. Daring is appreciated and stimulated.

Each factor helps to form an effective team, but the factors are also interdependent. They need and built on one another. For example, without open communication it is difficult to have respect for one another. And with little respect, open communication easily leads to quarrels. Ideally, the team conditions are improved concurrently.

Related Diagnostic Model 2: Roles for Staff Units

The underlying notion of Kloosterboer and Sterk's (1996) model is that staff departments are always faced with the dilemma of how much they should focus on "central" headquarters (HQ) versus "local" divisions. Centrality implies that the staff devotes their attention to the preparation, implementation, and monitoring of the central policies (thinking in terms of planning and control). "De-centrality" implies that staff concern themselves with consulting and implementing local policies (thinking in terms of autonomy and support). As the "third party" placed between central and de-central, a staff department is faced with a loyalty dilemma and, in the eyes of those involved, often chooses the wrong course. Central management often thinks that the staff takes itself too serious and pays too must attention to its own specialty or to all kinds of "local" units. As a result, central management is inclined to take the staff's advice with a grain of salt. Divisions often regard the staff as stooges of HQ, as armchair scholars who spy on them and impose all kinds of red-tape bureaucracy. This results in divisions keeping staff at arm's length, asking them to come in to do only chores that lighten the workload of one's division. In turn, the staff feel that they are underrated by (all) others, that neither HQ nor the divisions know enough about their specialty, and that this is the reason for all sorts of unnecessary mistakes. Kloosterboer and Sterk provide a model containing four staff roles based on the degree of focus on either HQ or local units. The model is suitable for analyzing the staff's current dominant roles, to assist the staff in choosing between the staff roles given certain situations and issues (contingency approach), and to decide on a dominant positioning. Each role has its (dis)advantages. The roles are

♦ Policymaker and controller: The focus is entirely on HQ. What is good about this role is its efficiency, its control, the possibility to organize synergy, and the clear backing from management. It is suitable in cases where, for example, statutory legislation or important concern-wide policies must be implemented, as room for negotiation is then intentionally absent. Staff has to be willing to put up with disadvantages like distrustful local divisions and an HQ that unloads tricky implementation chores onto them.

♦ Help desk/assistant: Here all tasks are focused on local units. A benefit of this role is contact with the shop floor and the ability to solve concrete problems. It is suitable when there is a local division management load that needs to be lightened or if implementation is not going as planned. Drawbacks of this role are that it can turn into fire fighting; great diversity in policies between divisions can arise, and staff can easily become over-worked.

♦ Expertise center/service unit: Here, the staff positions itself as an independent unit, providing service only when requested to do so. A benefit of this role is that a small, cohesive, and high-quality group can be established. It is suitable when there is not too much tension and difference of opinion between HQ and divisions (on the staff's subject matter), when both of them realize their shortcomings in that area and turn to the staff for help. In turn, the staff needs to accept that they may stand passively on the sidelines when HQ and divisions do not deem their involvement necessary. Also, there is a risk that HQ and divisions start looking externally for similar services or even decide to outsource them.

♦ Mediator/director: Here, staff takes the initiative and involves HQ and divisions on its own account to create new and better solutions. The staff claims a role in bringing the parties together and in orchestrating agreement and commitment. This is suitable when important decisions require active involvement of both parties and this involvement is not forthcoming. This is also the role with the highest risk. It requires great effort, and if things go wrong both "camps" will blame the staff. However, if the staff succeeds, they can become proper "heroes" and opinion leaders in the organization.

References:
Belbin (1981)
Vroemen (1995)
Kloosterboer and Sterk (1996)

6.7 Culture Types, Organizational Configurations, Organizational Iceberg

Culture Types

1. Underlying Notion

Organizational culture is sometimes defined as the actual behavior of the employees in an organization that arises from (a system of) implicit and explicit assumptions, values, and norms. In this sense, culture is regarded as something that can create strong cohesion and direction. In discussions, "organizational culture" is often misused as a container term that can mean just about everything as long as it is intangible. Nevertheless, the premise remains that various types of culture can be recognized and that these types can be influenced or even created. This is thought to be important for assessing and establishing the right "fit" between different but mutually dependant parts of an organization, between collaborating organizations (especially, when it comes to mergers), as well as between an organization and its environment. A view that is quite widely held is that mergers can fall through if the organizational cultures differ too much—"I don't know where you're from, but that's the way *we* do things around here." Internal tension, too, appears inevitable between, for example, an administrative department where emphasis is put on precision and proper procedures and the atmosphere is a bit bureaucratic, and a marketing department where creativity, action, and improvisation are the order of the day. A change agent who succeeds in analyzing and characterizing culture types can at least understand what causes tensions, throw the differences open to discussion, and maybe even make them productive.

2. Description

One of the best-known characterizations of organizational culture is that of Handy (1988). He distinguishes four contrasting types of culture, stating that in real organizational life these four types are less encountered than mixtures of these types. However, in most organizations one of the types still dominates the "culture-mix." Handy uses seven factors to typify each of the culture types. We give a brief summary here:

♦   Power cultures: Here, relationships between employees are determined by the strength of individuals' personalities and positions. The opinions of a small group of powerful people dominate when decisions have to be made in the organization: they are like the spider in the middle of the organizational web. As long as their assessment of the situation works, the organization can act decisively and react well to its environment. However, when this power center falls away or becomes dysfunctional, the organization is strongly affected. The organization cannot easily replace leadership. The larger an organization becomes, the more vulnerable this type of centralized culture makes it.

♦   Role cultures: The employees strive to achieve the greatest possible certainty and stability. Relationships are determined by rules, regulations, and rationality. Decisions are made by authorized people according to set procedures and roles. The behavior of the organization is predictable and clear. As long as its environment remains stable, an organization based on role culture will be effective. However, in a dynamic environment the organization would be slow to adapt. People would rather have the world adapt to them than the other way around.

♦   Task cultures: The behavior of the employees is determined by their task, and the required resources are marshaled to get work done effectively and efficiently. This takes precedence over hierarchy, decision-making procedures, organizational systems, and the like. Those directly involved base their decisions on what they deem necessary for getting the job done. People are flexible and result oriented. The organization can be likened to a net in which projects and tasks are a more important coordination mechanism than the formal structure. The drawback is that this pragmatic attitude sometimes takes too much precedence over professional quality or proper procedures.

♦   Person cultures: Here, the need of the individual for self-fulfillment is the central issue. Expertise is valued above all else. Decisions are made by consensus rather than by management. The quality of arguments matters, not the position of the people voicing them. Management is viewed with skepticism. In the most extreme form, relations are based on the sharing of (scarce) facilities such as offices, support staff, IT, and so on. The disadvantages of this culture are its susceptibility to ideological conflicts, its unpredictability, and the resulting risk of disintegration.

3. Comments

The importance of understanding and characterizing organizational culture is beyond dispute, and Handy's model has value. The limitations of the model lie in its generalized traits. The model is a good "quick scan" to help gain an

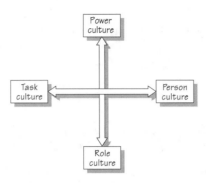

Figure 6.7 Four Culture Types

understanding of a specific culture, but no more than that. The next step might be to examine the stories, history, heroes, symbols, and rituals, among other things, to find the unique characteristics of the organization and discover which of these either promote the organization's goals or form a barrier to achieving them. Insights like this provide greater perspectives for appreciating and changing the culture, although the "makeability" of cultures remains limited. In our view, norms, values, and convictions can hardly be enforced by means of external pressure. Even limited change in this sphere demands great patience and skill from change agents.

4. Approach
Culture diagnosis is a process that helps to characterize an organization. However, the diagnostic model can also be regarded as addressing change aspects, for instance when it helps to assess frictions between different (sub)cultures or between the current culture and a desired culture.

5. Level
Organizations, or substantial parts of an organization

Related Diagnostic Model 1: Organizational Configurations
Mintzberg (1989) distinguishes seven now well-known, organizational configurations. His premise is that organizations are made up of six building blocks: the operational core where the primary process is carried out, the strategic apex that sets the direction, the line management that links the two and organizes the work on the basis of the goals. Next are the techno-structure that standardizes the work (like trainers, administrators, and planners) and the support staff that

provides services (like a mailroom and a cafeteria), and an ideology that infuses the whole thing with life and meaning. He goes on to say that each of the seven configurations consists of a coherent interplay of the six building blocks nicely suited to situational factors—such as the dynamics and the complexity of the environment, the age and size of the organization, and the technical system used to produce outputs. The seven configurations follow:

♦ The *simple structure* or *entrepreneurial organization*. For example a contractor, characterized by little specialization, limited educational training, action-focus, centralized management. The strategic apex makes all decisions; staff and line management are practically non-existent. The environment is easy to oversee but dynamic. The organization has the necessary flexibility, but has limited ability to distribute work internally. The organization is often quite young and relatively small.

♦ The *machine bureaucracy*, such as social services, characterized by high specialization and standardization of jobs, extensive planning and control, the functional arrangement of departments, and a focus on rationality. The techno-structure that standardizes the work is the dominant element. There is also a considerable support staff. The environment is predictable and stable. The organization is efficient but not always effective. It has often been in existence for some time and is reasonably large.

♦ The *professional bureaucracy*, such as a law firm, characterized by complex but also often routine work. There are many specializations but little formalized planning and control. The administrative systems help regulate interdependencies among the different disciplines. The operational core dominates, and power over many decisions, both strategic and operating, flow all the way down to them. There is a very small techno-structure but a lot of support staff. The professionals' training is highly important to standardizing and elevating skills, and the stability and the complexity of its environment allows and calls for this respectively. Ideological conflicts may occur in the organization.

♦ The *diversified form*, such as multinationals, which are characterized by a predominantly market-oriented structure, vertical decentralization into rather autonomous divisions, performance control on the basis of divisional results, and little interdependence among the divisions. Line management is the dominant building block. The divisions are often machine bureaucracies in themselves, but at the central level it looks different; for example, the techno-structure is smaller than the service staff. The environment is very diverse but stable. The organization is generally extremely large and often has a long history. There are sometimes identity problems.

♦ The *"ad-hocracy,"* or *innovative organization*, such as expeditions or film-making, characterized by many horizontal relationships, task-orientation, flexibility, and multidisciplinism. Work is often done by using the project approach; authority is often project related and changes over time. The "important experts" are the main building blocks in the organization. The staffs are small. The environment is complex and dynamic, and the organization is able to play with this successfully. The organization may be young, but this is not necessarily the case. The larger it is, the greater the possibility that continuity cannot be sufficiently guaranteed.

♦ The *missionary organization,* such as special-interest groups or farm co-ops, characterized by a powerful ideology that strongly overlaps personal goals. In theory there is a lot of freedom, as this overlap and the standardization of values form the dominant means of coordination. However, it is precisely the norms, values, and traditions (as part of the ideology) that limit this freedom as well. The work is not strictly divided, and there is little specialization or formality. Usually these organizations are not young for it takes time to institutionalize ideology. There is a danger of isolation or assimilation.

♦ The *political organization,* such as political parties, characterized by a lack of stability, many conflicts, ever-shifting internal coalitions, and diverse external coalitions. The determining building blocks change with the times. Power is the name of the game and it is played in the political arena. The organization can have a temporary nature because its instability makes it vulnerable.

Related Diagnostic Model 2: Organizational Iceberg

French and Bell (1984) assume that organizations are more defined, driven, and inhibited by aspects that lie hidden under the surface than by those that are visible to all. Many change processes fail to appreciate this. The authors state that as a result of not taking these "hidden aspects" into account, both the rates of success and the impacts of change processes drop severely. French and Bell's model is designed to at least analyze this "invisible world." They argue that interventions on the informal (or hidden) aspects should generally have first priority in any organizational development, as soon as the formal authorities have legitimized the change effort. Gradually, a more balanced approach to the two worlds can be approached until they come to balance each other. These two worlds are

♦ The (small) top of the iceberg: the formal and overt aspects. Here, it is a matter of goals, technology, structure, policies, procedures, products, and finances.

♦ The (large) base of the iceberg: the informal and covert aspects—beliefs, assumptions, perceptions, attitudes, and feelings that can all bear relationship to both the formal and the informal aspects of an organization. Furthermore, values, norms, and informal interaction also make up the base of the iceberg.

References:
Handy (1988)
Mintzberg (1989)
French and Bell (1984)

6.8 Network Organization, Public-Private Cooperation, Industrial Ecology

Network Organization

1. Underlying Notion

Primarily, the idea is that the age of organizational dinosaurs providing both top quality and top innovation in each and every part of their production chains seems to have passed as a result of the current climate of "hyper-competition," characterized by the terms "high tech, high touch, high speed, and high flex." The fashionable response of organizations is to focus on a number of core competencies and to outsource the rest. This response is still on the rise as the advent of quality management and information technology at suppliers and customers has made it easier to predict, monitor, and control their mutually dependent work processes. The underlying notion is that it is easier to improve the operational processes if the organization limits itself to doing what it is good at. The notion that innovation can be speeded up by combining the technology of various players also plays a role.

The result, then, is that the interdependence of the organizations involved is greatly increased and so is the need to enter into stable relations with a limited number of key suppliers, sometimes also co-producers and buyers. The next step is to organize this cooperation in "networks" in a suitable way.

2. Description

There are many ways in which cooperation within networks can be organized. The different forms can be more easily recognized and designed if there is a typology available. Also, strategic choices for certain forms would be facilitated if this typology elaborated on (contingent) advantages and drawbacks. Here, we give a brief description of the main forms in a free translation of Van Aken's (1997/1998) ideas.

   ♦   On one end of the spectrum is the *monolithic organization,* an organization where ownership, control, and identity are linked in one center. The advantages are obvious: few conflicts of interest, clear chain of command,

and obvious loyalty. The network character of and within such an organization is minimal.

♦   One step farther is the *network organization,* a single legal entity but with clearly distinguishable units that make use of all kinds of horizontal relationships and contracts in order to achieve their goals. At the top, the unity is intact, but this can be different on the work floor: The different units may develop their own subcultures, give priority to their own bottom lines, and exact a certain degree of autonomy. Stimulating the necessary synergy among units is one of the main challenges for the strategic apex.

♦   An *organizational network* is one in which different organizations work closely together as partners, often in several areas. This comes up for discussion only if there is a considerable overlap in the missions of the parties involved. Cooperation is intentionally designed, is often formalized, and is not a temporary affair. A "virtual organization" is a phenomenon that fits in this type: a cooperation in which clients do not or need not realize that they are dealing with more than one party. A good example is the franchise formula used by McDonald's or Benetton. Airbus is another example. There is no unity of ownership, but sometimes there can be a common identity—"We work at McDonald's." Unity of management is sometimes implemented to a certain degree, thanks to a rigorous division of strategic management and operational management. All issues are resolved at the top so that the people on the work floor can carry out their work as if they were working for one monolithic organization. Strategic flexibility provides a great advantage for this type of organization (partners can be added or removed), as well as extra possibilities for entrepreneurship, the accountability demanded of each other, and financial resilience (bankruptcy of one partner does not destroy the others). These advantages explain why franchising is sometimes preferred over merging. The drawback is that strategic planning and conflict resolution obviously require much attention.

♦   A looser collaboration can be found in the *organic network.* Here we again find various owners but now also find various identities. There is no center/apex that plans and controls, nor a selected few that work this out together. Instead, there is lots of nonhierarchical coordination. Participation in an organic network is easier than forming a network organization because units can enter into alliances without requiring the whole of the organization or the top to follow suit. The organic network allows for limited cooperation. This cooperation often happens spontaneously, and the extent to which the missions overlap may be limited. Cooperation is often temporary, linked to a project. What is more, it does not need to have an external focus: Cooperation might be restricted to joint research or to sharing a knowledge center. If need be, the cooperation can gradually be increased and include more units and more strategic choices. It then moves slowly in the direction of the "organizational network."

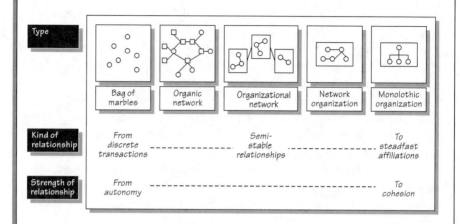

Figure 6.8 Spectrum of Network Formats

♦   At the other end of the spectrum we find the *bag of marbles:* separate organizations that merely carry out discrete transactions. This is no more than a question of buying and selling from each other in the "marketplace."

3. Comments
Because the model encompasses a wide spectrum of types of cooperation, it is widely applicable. Nevertheless, it is most relevant for organizations in a turbulent environment where participating in networks can enhance their ability to maneuver and make use of the dynamics of their environment. It is especially suited as a discussion model for the strategic top of the organizations involved.

4. Approach
Organizational aspects

5. Level
Level of the environment, assuming that the focus is not on internal networking within an organization

Related Diagnostic Model 1: Public-Private Cooperation (PPC)
Kouwenhoven (1991) defines PPC as an interaction between governments and corporations aimed at achieving synergy in the realization of convergent goals, exhibiting social as well as commercial characteristics, on the condition that the

parties involved retain their respective identities and responsibilities. PPC forms, then, a sort of compromise between mutual adjustment (the exchange of plans and taking each other's activities into account) and public-private partnerships (PPP): a structured cooperation based on common goals in an organization to be set up jointly.

PPC creates structured cooperation (like PPP), but each party maintains its own organization and identity (like mutual adjustment). There are many examples (infrastructural projects, health care, etc.) of all three forms. In PPC the parties search for complementarity in their goals, commit themselves in terms of efforts (not results), and create mixed working groups to sort everything out in more detail. Kouwenhoven provides a model that expresses a few of the principles that are necessary for the success of a PPC. These principles can be checked by the change agent. They include the following:

♦   Start conditions: First, there must be considerable interdependence and convergence of goals. Second, there must be a network in place and a broker available.
♦   Process conditions: There must be mutual respect as well as an agreed procedure for conflict resolution. There must be clarity regarding strategy, contribution, risks, returns, responsibilities, and authorities. These must all be laid down unequivocally. There must be an adequate project organization, business-like and client-oriented attitude and behavior, sufficient coordination, clear phasing, and adequate support and control. Finally, everything must be legal and above board, and the rights and interests of third parties must be protected.

Related Diagnostic Model 2: Industrial Ecology
The underlying notion is that organizations can learn from Mother Nature. There, one species' waste is another's food, and there is no question of squandering resources or causing pollution. On most industrial sites, however, factories stand next to one another that have no relation to one another: no interdependency and no added value. The diagnostic model concentrates on finding out whether or not there is another way, a diagnosis that is particularly important during the design and organization of new industrial sites because it is during these early stages that it is possible to direct efforts to ensure that various industries complement one another. The model often rattles the dominant mental models of those involved. People are used to chain management: cooperation with purchasers and suppliers. But industrial ecology goes way beyond that. A famous example is the Danish town of Kalundborg. Here, the power station supplies its residual heat to the pharmaceutical industry and to the

homes in the town. Its fly ash and gypsum are supplied to the cement and plasterboard factories on the site. In turn, the pharmaceutical industry supplies organic waste to the local farmers (as fertilizer) and its wastewater to the plaster-board factory. The oil refinery supplies the power station and the plasterboard factory with fly ash for fuel, plus cooling water to the plasterboard factory. Rich wastewater enables a fish farm to flourish.

The diagnosis concentrates on possible manufacturers, their production processes, possible alternative technologies and resulting in- and outputs. The diagnosis results in various possibilities for cooperation that challenge the tradi-tional images and limits of the industries involved, while visualizing a new, local, hybrid organization.

References:
Van Aken (1998)
Van Aken, Hop, and Post (1997)
Kouwenhoven (1991)
Frosch (1989)

6.9 Biographical Fit, Power Sources, Levels of Learning

Biographical Fit

1. Underlying Notion
Expectations about age-appropriate behavior are embedded throughout the fabric of adult life. A comparison is sometimes made with nature: We are expected to grow, to blossom, to bear fruit, and to die. Thinking in life phases in connection with the work arena can assist individuals to prepare for the future, to accept what they encounter (there's nothing wrong with me, it comes with the territory), and to take charge of their lives. It also can assist organizations in shaping their human resource policies, such as recruitment and training pro-grams. There are many models of life phases. Differences can be substantial between different cultures and eras, but are much less pronounced between recent Western models.

2. Description
Various authors, including Lievegoed and Erikson, recognize phases lasting from six to ten years. Roughly speaking, human physical vitality is at its peak

between twenty and forty. People in their twenties are trying to find a place and a profession for themselves. They are impatiently exploring new territories, battling their insecurities, experimenting when support is available, and gradually gaining acceptance and showing results. In their thirties they are ready to make choices on the basis of this exploration. Now, they want to take on greater responsibilities and are ambitious to build a life and a name for themselves: the right job, partner, house, and so on. They are great achievers at this time and have lots of stamina. Their productiveness and goal orientedness can sometimes lead them to become workaholics or to overvalue themselves at the expense of (their relations with) others. Physical vitality often starts to decline after this period. Many forty-year-olds have earned their way and earned respect. From being specialists they have often turned into generalists and they have developed their own styles. They can get away with functioning on automatic pilot, but that does not inspire them. They also get called on a lot by the organization, but this can feel like a burden. In terms of both energy and fulfillment, people ask themselves what the point is of continuing like this for years to come. It is a time for reevaluating one's priorities, of doing what is right instead of what works. For some, this turns into a mid-life crisis, where they try to stop the clock with love affairs, wild job changes, and the like. Some blame others for their predicament, while others achieve a stronger independent position. By the time people reach fifty, many feel it's time to take a step back. The drive to experiment, achieve, or lead lessens. Many realize it is nicely within their limits (physical and lifespan) to focus on inspiring others rather then leading them, to help others achieve success rather than claim it themselves. Those who resist this shift can become bossy and cynical toward their (younger) colleagues and thus isolate themselves. Their psychological fitness then decreases with their biological fitness. Those who make the shift can become important sources of empowerment in their fifties and can remain psychologically fit well into their seventies and eighties. In their sixties, they focus on matters that are (professionally and personally) closest to their hearts, often broadening their horizons out of interest. The archetype here is that of the wise old man. Naturally these are generalizations, and different people will encounter many different things in the same life phases or go through them at different speeds. Self-management remains key, rather then following any model, and the mastery a person has in this respect will show in areas other than just his work life.

3. Comments

The model is most suitable when the relationship between change agent and client allows for such personal observations and when the change agent has

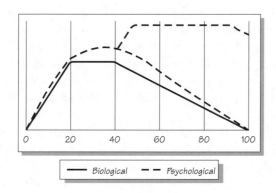

Figure 6.9 Biological and Psychological Age

considerable insight into his own personal development. The model is especially relevant when important career decisions are at stake, such as during a person's mid-life period. It can also assist personnel departments in shaping their HR policies. The models are somewhat deterministic and conservative in nature, which argues against using the models too mechanically.

4. Approach
Focusing on change aspects

5. Level
Individual

Related Diagnostic Model 1: Power Sources
Power can be defined as the degree to which someone is able to compel other people to do what she wants, or to avoid being compelled by others to do something she does not particularly want to do. In part, it is a question of perception. For example, if an employee thinks that his boss knows more about a given matter than he himself, the boss has "information power" over the employee, even if this knowledge is nonexistent or the boss makes no use of it. Insight into power is very important in yellow processes where coalitions have to be formed, or when change agents have to assess whether they have sufficient power to pull off an intervention successfully. Kor and Wijnen (2000) distinguish a number of sources of power or authority. Power can be based on

expertise, charisma, personality, or physical strengths (the archetype of power). It can also be based on the access one has to information via the networks one maintains. All of these sources of power are available regardless of one's hierarchical position. In effect, professionals often have more of this kind of "personal" power available than managers do. Managers, however, have power based on their formal position. This relates to other sources: the ability to impose sanctions or to reward. These can be expressed in terms of money but also in terms of equipment, parking places, promotions, travel, and the like. Another formal source of power is the ability to give direct assignments or orders. Power can also be derived from the connections one has or the people who (formally) support one.

Related Diagnostic Model 2: Levels of Learning

Bateson distinguishes six levels at which people can learn about themselves or can support other people learning about themselves. His argument is that it is important to distinguish between these levels because each level is presumed to have its own questions and, therefore, its own kind of answers. All levels are equally important, but not all at the same time. In self-reflection or coaching it is important to realize which level and which corresponding questions offer the best perspectives. Someone who is reevaluating his norms and values is not helped much by skills training or new cognitive models. Another important aspect of the difference in levels is that every person has a natural tendency to concentrate on a few levels only. A change of level is desired if someone is "stuck." The six levels and their corresponding questions are as follows:

- ♦ Spirituality/inspiration: What am I connected with? What am I part of?
- ♦ Identity/mission: Who am I? What am I here for?
- ♦ Conviction/value: What is important? What are my goals?
- ♦ Ability/direction: What am I able to do? What can I do?
- ♦ Behavior/action: What am I doing? How do I act?
- ♦ Environment/reaction: What makes me react? What triggers me?

References:

Lievegoed (1976)
Erikson (1982)
Vermaak (2000)
Kor and Wijnen (2000)
Bateson (1972)

6.10. Optimal Conflict Level, Learning Curve, Process/Result Orientation

Optimal Conflict Level

1. Underlying Notion

The term *conflict* has a negative connotation. Conflicts seem to be things we want to avoid. The idea here, however, is that without conflict or tension there can be no movement or progress. Creativity and innovation thrive on dualities, on clear juxtapositions of differences, like the tension between a need for internal stability and an urgency to respond to environmental changes. Or the tension between common sense and experimentation; or between action and reflection; or budgets and deadlines versus contemplation and discovery. These are examples of conflicts between values, qualities, and ideas, but the notion also includes conflicts between the people who represent these and the solutions they propose for dealing with such conflicts.

2. Description

Vandendriessche (1996) sketched a curve (Figure 6.10) that underscores how creativity is highest when there is an "optimal level of conflict." If there is no pressure or conflict at all, then people with opposing views must not have been debating their views. Especially in organizations of professionals, opposing views are always in abundance, for example, what constitutes good work or collegiality. Minds must not have met, or must have seen no reasons to meet. When such peace and quiet is the case, there is often stagnation and little willingness to change. In those cases, Vanderdriessche recommends putting on the pressure. One way to do this is by demanding higher performance, waking people up to the stagnant reality, and setting up confrontations between opposite sides. Yet if the pressure becomes too great and conflicts abound, the atmosphere may become overheated and thus thwart cooperation too. Too many conflicts can result in the parties' avoiding each other or not taking the time to discuss their different points of view. The conflict level can then be decreased by listening exercises, reconsidering goals, allowing for experiments, and accepting ambiguity. The model can be used as a diagnostic model: Just how prepared is this group to change, and how creative is it? The model also indicates which interventions are suitable.

3. Comments

The model appears to be suitable for groups where there is substantial task dependency, where people need each other to achieve their goals. It is especially

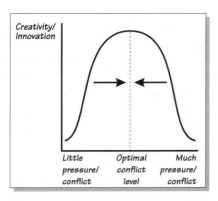

Figure 6.10 Optimal Conflict Level

relevant when organizations operate in dynamic environments, as this often requires innovation and the close cooperation of various disciplines. In static environments, the normative stance of this model probably has less to offer. One could make a convincing argument that routine jobs done by an individual bike technician could be carried out without needing an optimal level of conflict.

4. Approach
Change aspects: The model focuses on underlying forces that help or thwart change and are largely unconnected to either the character of the business processes involved or the way the organization is set up.

5. Level
Here, the model is applied to a group. It is unsuitable at the individual level because it involves interaction between people. The model can also be applied at the organization level, especially when the organization represents different types of subcultures and is not very large. It can then reveal useful information about the conflict level between departments or in the organization as a whole.

Related Diagnostic Model 1: Learning Curve
De Caluwé (1997) and others observe a curve that appears in many learning processes. The notion behind the curve is that the process of learning is often erroneously assumed to be linear: You learn something and gradually get better at it. This seems to be true at the start of the learning process, when stimuli are provided by external sources, as in a course. Participants follow instructions, first

successes are achieved, and from this they gain *extrinsic* motivation. The learning curve shows that this phase is followed by a relapse. Early successes are not followed by others, and participants begin to realize how difficult the new skill or idea actually is. They become conscious of their incompetence and ask themselves if it is really worth the effort. The relapse may not quite put them back where they started, but close to it. At this stage, there is a possible turning point during which time the learner reflects on her situation: "How important to me is this thing I'm learning? Am I convinced that I will eventually master it? Is it worth the effort?" This turning point is crucial: It is the possible transition from extrinsic to *intrinsic* motivation. A frequently occurring mistake in organizations is that managers try to avoid this dip in the learning curve by setting up "booster" sessions, refresher courses to jack up the motivation and the skills. Research shows that these interventions merely serve to postpone the turning point and, in this sense, are a waste of energy. If someone has passed the turning point and doesn't drop out, an upward trend in his learning commences. People internalize what they've learned, develop their own style, and integrate the new material into the skills and knowledge they already possess. The model is useful in helping to analyze the stage someone has reached on the learning curve, and it also helps to keep the expectations of those involved at a realistic level. "Dips" are an intrinsic part of learning. Failing to understand this leads to unnecessary disillusionment.

Related Diagnostic Model 2: Process/Result Orientation

The underlying notion here is that a group needs to focus not only on results but also on the way it reaches them: the process of cooperation and implementation. A unilateral focus undermines a group's ability to make change happen. The extent to which this applies provides us with four types of groups, each with recognizable characteristics. These characteristics facilitate the analysis, and the perspectives for action are obvious. The four types are:

♦ Success! The focus is on the process and on the result. There is euphoria within the group and among the superiors.

♦ Understanding! The focus is on the process. Understanding is limited to the members of the group; the superiors are not satisfied because they perceive little outcome or dynamics.

♦ Sigh—sigh! The focus is on results and hard work. Difficulties often arise between the members of the group and there can be long-lasting negative feelings. This is not always noticed by the superiors.

♦ Drama! Both the result and the process receive insufficient attention. There is dissatisfaction all around, both within the group and among the superiors. Serious interventions are unavoidable; often the process must be tackled first.

References:
Vandendriessche (1996)
Geschka (1978)
de Caluwé (1997)

6.11 The Clock, Passage of Resistance, Two Forces for Change

The Clock

1. Underlying Notion

An organization is not a static phenomenon. It develops over time as a result of its internal and external relationships. In this development various life stages can be distinguished, each with special characteristics and problems. It is helpful for change agents to recognize these phases, as interventions should preferably be appropriate to the organization's life stage. Some organizations should be helped to extend a particular life stage, others should be helped along to the next one, whereas still others should be "rejuvenated" so they regain their original health. The assumption is that failure to take history into account and to recognize these dynamics will result in poorly designed change processes. This is especially true when an organization's problems are not caused primarily by its present actions, but more by blind repetition of past success stories.

2. Description

H. Looten (see, in part, Alberdingk Thijm and Jansen, 1996) uses the image of a clock as a metaphor for an organization's development. The hands of the clock move between eleven and twelve o'clock. Eleven o'clock represents the start of (a part of) an organization: a fresh new venture with new staff, new products, and growing markets. It is a time of investment, of scoring successes. The atmosphere is hopeful and enthusiastic, and the organization grows. This growth leads in the second phase to a need for coordination. The organization is a bit too chaotic and improvisational. Order is introduced by delineating product-market combinations, creating departments, and, where possible, standardizing production processes. The organization is still healthy. At the end of this phase—11:30—this striving for order (structures and procedures) has overextended itself, resulting in a certain amount of rigidity. People are too slow to seize market opportunities and the market share decreases. The organization starts depending on its financial reserves, conflicts arise, and key figures, those who helped start the company, bid it farewell. Up until 11:30, when the problems first become noticeable, there are possibilities for revitalization: initiate new experiments, break through the existing structures, support entrepreneurial efforts. The clock is thus set back in the direction of the organization's pioneers, though not completely. However, once the clock has struck 11:30, this possibility is no longer viable. The financial situation precludes investments, and reorganization must be undertaken before anything else: cleaning up portfolios and lines of communication and dispensing with dysfunctional employees. The house must be put in order again. This intervention sets the clock back to the second phase, and revitalization may possibly follow. If, however, reorganization does not take place, the clock strikes 11:45 and the organization is in the fourth phase. The ever-increasing conflicts then become obvious to the world outside, and finances are in a poor state. Sometimes, as a desperate measure, a large project is embarked upon: a great leap forward. However, the necessary competencies and cooperation to make it a success are lacking. With swift action and drastic measures the clock can still be set back for parts—the healthiest ones—of the concern. This is accompanied by layoffs at the top, large cutbacks, and selling or closing down nonviable parts of the concern. By 11:55 it is all or nothing. If there are no drastic interventions, the organization perishes. Sometimes part of it will survive past twelve o'clock; a group of people or a division might rise up like a phoenix from the ashes of the organization and make a new start as pioneers in a the first phase in Looten's clock model. The model has characteristics similar to the models of Zuijderhoudt and Greiner (see section 2.3.2).

3. Comments

This model lends itself to "quick and dirty" diagnoses. It is not well suited to lengthy, expert assessments of an organization's development, but quite apt for boardroom settings when people discuss their organization's development. The model is especially suited for the beginning of any change process, for then it is especially relevant to know how much urgency the change effort has. For example, if you know there is an 11:55 situation, you would never suggest a lengthy participative approach to change, even though that might otherwise be very suitable to the organization in question.

It is, in other words, a good "quick scan."

4. Approach

It focuses on change aspects, although organizational aspects and business aspects can be used.

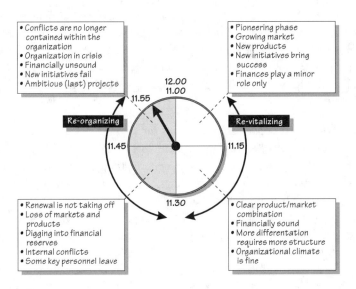

- Conflicts are no longer
  contained within the
  organization
- Organization in crisis
- Financially unsound
- New initiatives fail
- Ambitious (last) projects

- Pioneering phase
- Growing market
- New products
- New initiatives bring
  success
- Finances play a minor
  role only

12.00
11.00
11.55

Re-organizing

Re-vitalizing

11.45

11.15

11.30

- Renewal is not taking off
- Loss of markets and
  products
- Digging into financial
  reserves
- Internal conflicts
- Some key personnel leave

- Clear product/market
  combination
- Financially sound
- More differentation
  requires more structure
- Organizational climate
  is fine

Figure 6.11 Looten's Clock Model

5. Level

Organization level, or (e.g., in a diversified organization) for divisions in a company that have clear identities

Related Diagnostic Model 1: Passage of Resistance

The basic assumption of this model is that change automatically causes resistance: There is uncertainty and people lose control, maybe even their positions. Furthermore, change efforts often entail extra time and energy and interfere with existing plans and any promises that were made in the past. However, those involved do not put up equal resistance. The model differentiates between them: Every (major) change starts with one or a few people who wish to initiate the change. They, naturally, show no resistance. A number of people are open to their ideas and support them, the so-called early adapters, but they do not yet constitute a "critical mass." Then follows a crucial period. The change can be brought about only if and when a number of "conservatives" allow themselves to be convinced of the need for the change and join forces with those in favor. If not, the change effort is fruitless and should probably be aborted. The initiators feel that they are fighting for a lost cause. If, however, the change is accepted by most of the conservatives, then the majority of the organization, the late followers, will also slowly relinquish their opposition and follow suit. Often, a few conservatives remain opposed to the change: They may be the change agents of the future, but in many cases they are people with whom one will part ways. The importance of the model lies in recognizing to which group actors belong, where the change process is in terms of the passage of resistance, whether the change seems "politically" viable, and what next actions are called for.

Related Diagnostic Model 2: Two Forces for Change

Otto and de Leeuw (1994) distinguish two types of drivers for change: the will to change and the need to change. The underlying notion is that the presence or absence of both forces has far-reaching consequences for how to set up the change process. The model should be applied at the level of the "object" to be changed: this could be an organization, a group, or an individual. Otto distinguishes four combinations of the two change forces:

♦   There is a clear need to change but little willingness to do so. He characterizes this as "the alcoholic." Here, strong direction "from above" is required in order for the change to succeed. The organization is told by its superiors that it "must" change, and this is substantiated by the "facts" of its present situation (reality check). The resistance level is necessarily high and so is the chance of failure.

♦   There is a clear need to change and a strong will to do so. He characterizes this as "the rehabilitator." Here, environment factors as well as the organization itself contribute to the success of the change. The change can be self-propelling: The people involved can make it happen on the basis of a common vision of the future and on the basis of self-management. However, if the urgency is great as well, such as in an "11:55 situation" (see section 6.11), then the rate of change needs to be high, which often necessitates formal direction by superiors backed by facts and figures.

♦   There is no great need to change, but nevertheless a lot of will to do so. He characterizes this as the "health freak." Here, change is carried out by self-steering individuals or groups. Change is "freely permitted" by superiors and driven by people who are vision-driven. Sometimes the process is facilitated by the organization.

♦   There is little need to change and not much willingness to do so. Otto characterizes this as "a club with beauty marks only." Nobody cares enough about the minor improvements that might be attainable, so there will be no change.

References:

Alberdingk Thijm and Jansen (1996)
Wijnen, Weggeman, and Kor (1999)
Otto and de Leeuw (1994)

6.12 Field of Influence, Megatrends, National Cultures

Field of Influence

1. Underlying Notion

Change processes can be regarded as a political game, an arena where the influence the actors have on each other determines both the process *and* the outcome of the change. On the basis of this principle, it is important to map out the most important actors, their kinds of influence, the relationships they have to one another, and their agendas. On the basis of this information, a change agent can design a strategy to increase the chances that the planned change comes about as intended. This can include coalition building with relevant actors as well as circumventing other actors.

2. Description

A force-field analysis focuses on drawing up an inventory of networks and characterizing them. Whatever the change effort may be, there will always be groups of actors with interdependent relationships, which means that none of these actors is able to exert total influence on all the others. The limits of the analysis are set by one's ambition: maybe one is just looking to collect strategic information (an "early warning system"), maybe one wants to go beyond that and actively feed strategic information to the network, or one might even want to initiate or influence future developments. The greater the ambition, the broader and more in depth the inventory of the network must be. Other limits might be set by delineating the nature of the network: Is it a work-related network only, for example, a network connected to the implementation of a project? Or is it a market network (a power game with competitors) or a theme-related network, for example, concerning the organization of the Olympic games or debates on environmental issues? Each network has its own, relevant actors. Sometimes these three types of networks overlap one another, and then all three need to be included in the inventory:

♦   work-related: suppliers (knowledge, resources, etc.), clients (also users or "victims"), decision makers (sponsors, principals, supporters), champions, and implementers

♦   market-related: (potential) competitors, industry associations, normalization/certification institutes

♦   theme-related: national and local governments, interest groups, advisory bodies, media, academia, and research institutions

The next step is to evaluate the influence of these actors. Here, too, there are three categories:

♦ position of influence: degree and type of power (see also "power sources" in section 6.9) and credibility

♦ connections and relationships that provide additional influence: "who knows who" and what the nature and strength of these relationships are

♦ direction of the influence: attitude toward the intended change, specific interests, arguments and points of view

There are various ways to outline this in schematics. Figure 6.12 shows one of the possibilities, a "field of influence" or "network web." Sociograms can also help in charting relationships among the most relevant actors, and matrices can be used to "score" the influence that people have on one another. Theme-related networks are hardest to identify; they often have emerged rather recently and are related to "new" or recent issues. Furthermore, they are generally poorly institutionalized. They are also very dependent on individuals. It is not merely a matter of the "Friends of the Earth" or the local interest group being well known; what counts is also the notoriety, credibility, expertise, and the like, of its spokesperson in that region or on that issue. That's the person you will have to do business with. When formal procedures are absent or not dominant (as in these theme-related networks), positional power always takes second place to personal power (see section 6.9.). Who are you inclined to believe about the damage to the environment caused by PVC: the environmental group or the manufacturer?

Inventorying and evaluating the network can be done partly by a media search and partly by "snowballing" through the network. Media research can provide many names: authors of articles, letters, and books; authors mentioned in reference lists; persons mentioned in interviews, advertisements, newsletters, mailing lists, newsgroups, proceedings of seminars, minutes of important meetings, or government reports. The degree to which people are quoted, who their co-authors are, the functions and positions they occupy, the memberships they seem to have, the people they seem to represent, and so on, are instrumental in the evaluation. The snowball method is based on interviewing the "names" found and asking them who the opinion leaders or the key players are and why. Generally it takes no more than thirty interviews to provide both a good overview and a qualitative evaluation.

3. Comments
The force-field analysis is particularly relevant at the beginning of a change effort. It is precisely during this period, for instance, that the search is on for sponsors and supporters to anchor the process. In yellow-print processes this

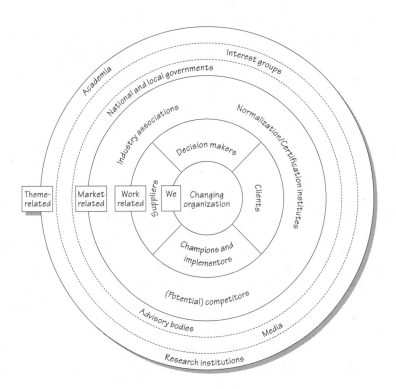

Figure 6.12 Field of Influence

analysis is absolutely vital. The playing field may change during the course of the process or need to be "worked on," which could mean that further analysis might also be useful in later phases of the change process.

4. Approach
It focuses on change aspects: the (power-)dynamics of the change at hand. The insights gained can have consequences for other aspects, such as the formal positioning and organization of a project.

5. Level
Environment. It is also possible to use the model to map out internal actors in large organizations, but it does not by definition limit itself to this. Any actor wielding considerable influence needs to be included in the analysis, which means that external actors will be included when relevant.

Related Diagnostic Model 1: Megatrends

The notion is that, apart from environment analysis related to competition (see also section 6.4), there are less tangible historical trends that exert influence on the organization, both from the outside in and from the inside out. An insight into these historical trends and their extrapolation into the future offers change agents the possibility of making sense out of developments they are confronted with. Mapping out megatrends is an exercise where one takes notice of patterns that emerge across various disciplines; over a longer period of time; and preferably across professions, societies, and national borders. Questioning and engaging the "profound thinkers" from various disciplines turns out to be more useful for this than quantitative investigations. Nothing can be proved, but hunches can be somewhat substantiated. Once spotted, the relevance of the megatrend then has to be assessed for the specific organization or change effort one is involved in. In the management literature, Naisbitt, Drucker, Popcorn, and Forrester are familiar names that have provided information on megatrends, the most famous example being Naisbitt's 1984 bestseller, containing ten megatrends:

- ♦ from industrial society to information society
- ♦ from forced technology to high-tech/high touch
- ♦ from national economy to world economy
- ♦ from short term to long term
- ♦ from centralization to decentralization
- ♦ from institutional help to self-help
- ♦ from representative democracy to participatory democracy
- ♦ from hierarchies to networking
- ♦ from north to south
- ♦ from either/or to multiple options

Related Diagnostic Model 2: National Cultures

Hofstede (1994) argues that every country invests considerable moral capital in its own mental software. This explains the widespread hesitation to throw cultural differences open to discussion. The causes of differences between nations, as well as between the ethnic, religious, or language groups within and across them, lie hidden in their histories and are based primarily on differences in values. Instead of decreasing, these differences appear to have increased in recent times. Hofstede shows how fundamental the influences of these cultural differences are on the functioning of both private and pubic organizations. Also, his work illustrates that the popular conception of organization culture (see section 6.7) is in comparison but a shallow phenomenon often restricting itself to symbols, heroes, and rituals dominant in organizational life.

Hofstede's view is that a person's ability for multicultural cooperation is first and foremost dependent on the person's insight into and acceptance of her own cultural background and associated values. Only then does she have a sense of certainty and identity that allows her to face and meet other cultures with an open mind. By so doing, insight into other cultures is gained and multicultural cooperation can become a distinct possibility. On the basis of a study carried out primarily among employees of the multinational IBM, Hofstede characterizes the cultures of many nations using five dimensions that provide strong indicators as to what is considered appropriate behavior within these cultures. In turn, each dimension also has consequences for the functioning of organizations. The validity of these indicators and his interpretations are likely to remain a matter of debate, but to give the reader a sense of Hofstede's characterizations we include here a very brief overview of the five dimensions and their effects on one aspect of companies: competitive ability. In change processes that face multicultural cooperation, it appears wise to take the dimensions and their effects into account.

◆   *Power distance* refers to the extent to which the less powerful members of institutions and organizations in a country expect and accept that power is distributed unequally. Within IBM it appeared that the Romance language countries (Spain, France, Latin America) and Asiatic and African countries were societies with large power distances. Small power distance societies are the United States, Canada, the United Kingdom, and the non-Romance-language countries of Europe. Small power distance can increase competitive capability because employees are inclined not to limit their responsibility to only their own task. Conversely, large power distance can contribute to competitive capability as a result of substantial discipline among employees.

◆   *Individualism versus collectivism* depends on the degree to which people are supposed to look after only themselves and their close family, or instead belong to in-groups or collectives that are supposed to look after them in exchange for loyalty. Within IBM, nearly all the rich countries scored high on individualism and nearly all the poor countries low. Individualism contributes to competitive capability, for example, by means of the mobility of staff; collectivism by means of loyalty to the employer.

◆   *Masculinity versus femininity* depends on the degree to which the roles of the sexes are either clearly separated or else overlap. Achievement and success are regarded as driving "male" roles, while quality of life and caring for others are regarded as driving "female" roles. The champions in terms of role separation are Japan, the central European countries (Austria, Italy, Switzerland, Germany), and the larger countries in Latin America (Mexico, Columbia, Ecuador, Venezuela). The United States and the United Kingdom follow suit.

Canada occupies the middle ground. Sweden, Norway, the Netherlands, Denmark, and Finland emerge as the most feminine countries: Here both sexes show overlapping roles. Masculinity contributes to competitive capability because of its drive for efficiency and mass production, while femininity achieves this by providing personal services and made-to-measure production.

♦   *Uncertainty avoidance* refers to the extent to which people feel threatened by ambiguous situations and create beliefs and institutions to avoid these. High scores are noted in Latin America, the Romance-language countries of Europe, the Mediterranean countries, Japan, and South Korea. Relatively low scores occur in the other Asian countries and the African, Anglo-Saxon, and Northern European countries. Strong uncertainty avoidance contributes to precision, and weak uncertainty avoidance stimulates innovations; both are important to competitive capability.

♦   *Short- versus long-term focus:* When short-term focus is high, a society often attaches great importance to social obligations and traditions. Hofstede sometimes uses the term *Confucian dynamism* in this respect. This correlates to people being quite normative, striving for stability, and expecting quick results. In contrast, long-term focus prevails when pragmatism rules and change is valued over stability and perseverance over short-term gains. Here traditions are of lesser importance and "many truths" seems to be the "new religion." The preeminently "long-term focused" countries are the Southeast Asian countries, but Brazil, India, and the Netherlands also have high scores. The real short-term countries are Pakistan, Nigeria, the Philippines, Canada, Zimbabwe, the United Kingdom, and the United States. Long-term thinking contributes most to competitive capability. This is because of its perseverance, the formation of stable relationships, and the availability of capital.

In general, Hofstede states that the countries that have the greatest problem with multicultural cooperation are those that register strong uncertainty avoidance: "If it's different, its dangerous," and/or register large power distances: "The whims of the mighty."

References:

Sas, Verberne, Postma, Vermaak, Mieras, and Taiti (1989)
Naisbitt (1984)
Popcorn (1991)
Hofstede (1994)

6.13 Concluding Remarks

In this chapter we have described thirty-six diagnostic models. Our intention was to demonstrate how insight can be gained at various levels of the organization and from different perspectives (business aspects, organizational aspects, and change aspects). Each of the models can provide the change agent with one more ways of defining the "reality of the organization." The theories outlined in Chapter 2 can also be used for diagnosis, which adds a further twelve views of reality. Forty-eight versions of reality is a modest number when compared to the enormous number of diagnostic models available. Currently, there is an effort under way to collect and characterize in more detail a much broader overview of diagnostic models.

The descriptions of the models are brief, particularly the descriptions of the "related models." We refer those of you who wish to make further use of the models to the literature cited in each section. Some of the descriptions explain how a model attempts to include more approaches and more levels. A balanced scorecard, for example, includes learning and growth as one of its four dimensions. This dimension resembles change aspects (as an approach), but its other dimensions have more in common with business aspects. As a result we feel the essence of this model is associated with business science.

The models are useful for gaining insight, and a few of them also suggest courses of action. For example, the models for "team roles" or "roles for staff units" were originally incorporated into theories that include strategies, steps, and tips to achieve improved functioning of teams and staff units, respectively. These courses of action are referred to only briefly here in order to separate the diagnostic aspect of this chapter from the intervention aspect in the next chapter. Nevertheless, these courses of action and their associated strategies and perspectives often imply the dominance of a certain color-print thinking. Many of the diagnostic models can therefore be regarded as connected to one of the five color paradigms of change. Take the force-field analysis, for example. In and of itself this analysis is a useful diagnostic exercise no matter what kind of change effort one embarks upon. The perspectives associated with it in the original literature, however, focus on ways to form coalitions and to reach consensus in the political arena: a yellow-print approach.

7 Examples of Interventions

In this chapter we go a step farther in detailing the change process. We concentrate on the interventions and modes of behavior used by change agents during the execution of an intervention plan. As discussed earlier, in section 5.4, we define an *intervention*

	Level in the Organization	
Dominant Color	*Individual*	
Yellow	**7.1 Personal commitment statement*** Outplacement Protégé-constructions	
Blue	**7.2 Management by objectives*** Hygienic working Working with a day planner	
Red	**7.3 Career development*** Recruitment and selection Job enlargement/Job enrichment	
Green	**7.4 Coaching*** Intensive clinic Feedback/Mirroring	
White	**7.5 T-Group*** Personal growth Networking	

*We describe these interventions in detail; we summarize the other two.

Table 7.1 Overview of Sample Interventions for Each Color and for Each Level in the Organization

as one or a series of planned (change) activities aimed at increasing or helping to increase the effectiveness of an organization.

This requires some explanation:

♦   An intervention can be *one* or a *series* of activities: For example, there is one training program for one group, or there are different training programs for various groups. Or the training program itself consists of an intake interview, the training itself, and a follow-up.

♦   *planned:* As is the case in the rest of the book, we are concerned here with planned change; the wish of the interventionist or change agent to influence in a certain direction.

♦   *effectiveness:* This refers to the intended outcome of the change. Perhaps some activities make a small contribution while others contribute more.

♦   *helping:* Because the intervention can be meant to directly influence or just indirectly support effectiveness, we use the word *or*.

In this chapter we describe a number of interventions as examples of what's available. We restrict ourselves both in the number and the depth of these descriptions

Group	Organization
7.6 Confrontation meetings* Third-party strategy Top structuring	**7.11 Improving quality of work life*** Forming strategic alliances Negotiations on labor conditions
7.7 Working in projects* Archiving Decision making	**7.12 Strategy analysis*** Business process redesign Auditing
7.8 Social activities* Team roles Management by speech	**7.13 Reward systems*** Managing mobility and diversity Triple ladder
7.9 Team building* Gaming Intervision	**7.14 Open systems planning*** Parallel learning structures Quality circles
7.10 Self-steering teams* Open-space meetings Making mental models explicit	**7.15 Search conferences*** Rituals and mystique Deconstructing "sacred cows"

1. *Underlying idea:*
   The central theme of the intervention, including the nature of the outcome and the main idea/purpose of the change agent

2. *Description:*
   Deals with activities that make up the intervention, describing the steps, the actors, and the communication that are part of a typical approach

3. *Comments:*
   Describes characteristics of the area of deployment and the intervention's suitability in certain situations or phases

4. *Role and contribution of the interventionist*

5. *Dominant color* (in terms of content and approach):

6. *Level* (individual/group/organizational):

Name and characterization of two related interventions
(in terms of color and level)

References (for all three interventions)

Table 7.2 Format for the Descriptions in Each Cell

in order to keep this chapter in proportion to the rest of this book, not to mention that it is not easy to strive for completeness, given the vast number of possible interventions.

We believe the examples we do present can give readers a feel for the spectrum of interventions available and insights into the differences among types of interventions. We hope that such insight will enable readers to place the interventions they encounter and/or prefer within this spectrum.

We selected the different types of interventions on the basis of two dimensions. The first dimension deals with whether the intervention is targeted mainly toward the individual, the group, or the organization, whereas the second dimension is concerned with the intervention's dominant color approach: yellow, blue, red, green, or white. These two dimensions create fifteen "cells" that are presented in Table 7.1. In each cell three sample interventions are mentioned. In each of the next sections we elaborate on the first intervention in a cell and give a summary of the remaining two interventions. The format in which they are presented in each next section is shown in Table 7.2.

7.1 Personal Commitment Statement, Outplacement, Protégé Constructions

Personal Commitment Statement

1. Underlying Idea

Employees have their own reasons and personal interests for doing a certain type of work, following a certain type of course program, or trying to work together with specific colleagues. Organizations, however, must guard their interests, too, and cannot give the employees carte blanche. The idea behind the personal commitment statement (PCS) is to create an effective negotiating climate that will do justice to the viewpoints and interests of both the organization and its employees. It is in both parties' interest to create a win-win situation.

2. Description

In some organizations, employees draw up a so-called PCS at the end of the year. In it they set out their ambitions and requests concerning work—focus of activities, type of training, product development, collaboration with others and so on—for the next twelve months. This (draft) document, often concise (1-2 pages only) and phrased in terms of outputs, is presented to the manager. In a subsequent discussion both parties attempt to negotiate a final version of the PCS, one that recognizes the wishes and demands of both the individual and the organization as far as possible. The PCS is a kind of social contract that forms the basis for coaching and performance appraisal during the coming year. The appraisal, for instance, is based on measuring actual performance and comparing it with the agreed-on targets in the PCS.

3. Comments

It does not take much time to design such a system, especially when compared with most other HRM systems like reward systems or competency management. Its introduction and application, however, are at least as difficult, partly because it does not follow the traditional task orientation of performance assessment and because it requires much of the skills and attitudes of the participants not to slide into formalistic discussions. Training or coaching is often necessary. The attitudes of the participants also determine how the PCS system functions in practice. If the manager feels that she can impose her will, the PCS starts to resemble Management by Objectives (7.2). If the worker feels that he should have the major say, the PCS can strengthen self-steering.

4. Role and Contribution of the Interventionist

We can think of a whole range of contributions, from designing the system to coaching individual managers in applying it. Another possible role is facilitating training or intervision (see 7.9) of a group of managers dealing with this subject.

5. Dominant Color

Because the process is concerned mainly with negotiation and achieving a win-win situation among individuals, the operational execution is yellow. The actual choice of introducing a PCS system is a red intervention, because the red approach attempts to improve the fit between the organization and the individual. The workers' activities agreed upon in the PCS can have different colors—a green learning process, for example. When the PCS is introduced with the intention of encouraging people to reflect on their own development and to include learning objectives in the contract, the PCS system supports a green change.

6. Level

Individual

Related Intervention 1: Outplacement

The idea behind out-placement is that when separation between an organization and an individual becomes desirable (e.g., resulting from conflict or underper-formance), a way is sought to make this separation as smooth as possible for both parties. Such "smoothness" is attainable when it serves the interests of both the individual (e.g., by limiting "loss of face") and the organization (e.g., by not upset-ting existing relationships more than necessary). Out-placement generally con-sists of allowing the person to stay employed by the organization, organizing lots of support—training, financial, and otherwise—in finding a new job elsewhere, and agreeing on a maximum term for leaving the company without lawsuits or other resistance. The actual "package" is the result of a negotiation process.

Related Intervention 2: Protégé Constructions

The idea behind this intervention is to deploy protégés in strategic positions to enable them to informally gain status and formally gain influence over others in the organization. People with power place protégés in certain positions where they can enjoy their patron's protection. They serve as examples of the ways a patron paves somebody's way based on the patron's agenda, and how a protégé can further his own interests by playing the role laid out for him.

References:
Vinke (1996)
Schoemaker (1994)
Maister (1991)

7.2 Management by Objectives, Hygienic Working, Working With a Day Planner

Management by Objectives (MBO)

1. Underlying Idea

Workers' behavior and work performance must be consciously managed. Workers also need to be well prepared, instructed, motivated, and supported in times of change. This can be greatly facilitated by setting clear goals for the employees and making them fully aware of what is expected of them. These goals are based on each worker's expected performance and the desired results of his group over a certain period, say, one year. The goals steer the worker's behavior in a certain direction, and they mobilize his efforts and activities toward achieving the performance expected of him. The concrete nature of the goals makes it possible to successfully monitor and control performance. MBO was once based on McGregor's (1960) "theory X," which states that people are inherently lazy, want the greatest return for the least effort, and are driven mainly by fear or greed. This view has mellowed somewhat over the years ("theory Y"), but the fact remains that MBO steers by determining and demanding performance from the top down.

2. Description

Organizations often employ a system where the goals are first set at the organizational level and then translated to departmental levels and so on until they can be translated to the individual level. The system of setting objectives is accompanied by a system of periodic monitoring of results on all of the appropriate levels of the organization. Comparing like with like (both internally and externally) and with previous periods or years is a favorite way of establishing benchmarks. Designing a total system like this takes months, and setting goals at all levels takes just as long again. The system can then run with periodic (e.g., yearly) updates in both content and procedures.

3. Comments

The intervention's strong point is the transparent relationship between expectations and performance at every level of the organization. At the individual level, MBO gives workers something to hold on to; their accountability and task are clear. The system is more difficult to manage when there is a degree of task interdependence between workers or when there are factors outside their control that influence the results. This is especially the case when their own managers, who also assess them, are responsible for some of these factors. MBO is best applied at the group level when task interdependency is present between workers.

There is a great deal to be said for making the process of goal setting bilateral and thus avoiding MBO's top-down character and even to include discussions on interfering factors. But this requires more skills and trust on both sides. If this does not seem feasible and the top-down approach stays, there is a risk of too much emphasis being placed on performance measurement and assessment with other aspects—learning, collegiality, and innovation, for example—being more or less forgotten. Workers' assessments and reviews can then degenerate into demotivating, one-way communication that can, in turn, eventually lead to pocket vetoes (see 2.2.3.) and a negative spiral.

4. Role and Contribution of the Interventionist
She can contribute to the design and operation of the system by introducing a series of rational empirical methods (benchmarking, research, data collection).

5. Dominant Color
Blue, because of its results-driven nature and its method of monitoring and assessing, as well as the strongly rational view of the process. Elements of other colors can also creep in; for example, making the system bilateral turns the process more yellow and the system more red.

6. Level
Directed toward the individual

Related Intervention 1: Hygienic Working
The idea behind this is that you can work effectively and efficiently if you work in an orderly fashion: Do one thing at a time, keep everything in its place, and know where to find things. A more in-depth version of this occurs when people's behavior and interactions in the workplace are restricted to work-related matters: private problems, emotional dilemmas, and so on, are kept out of the workplace unless they serve a clear function.

Related Intervention 2: Working With a Day Planner
Good planning, booking, and appointment making to structure work most efficiently can be one effect of using a day planner. Another is to create order and overview even though the work itself might be dynamic and complex. In recent years management has introduced electronic day planners in organizations to increase efficiency, for example by allowing for widespread access to each other's calendars in planning meetings, by including individual databases (e.g., for

addresses, phone numbers, etc.) and synchronizing these with the company's, by saving notes "on the road" or in meetings, archiving crucial files, and the like.

References:
Drucker (1964)
Lap (1992)
Schlenger and Roesch (1991)
Humble (1971)

7.3 Career Development, Recruitment and Selection, Job Enlargement/Job Enrichment

Career Development

1. Underlying Idea

Career development helps individuals reach their career goals. It is concerned with searching for, finding, and determining individual goals. In that sense it is highly personal and individual. In general, it concentrates on looking back at a person's career history, gauging his interests, determining his competencies, examining alternative career prospects, making decisions to (re)vitalize his career, and planning the progress of a chosen path. This process encourages people to opt for a certain profession, job, or organization of their own choosing and can take place within one organization or across a number of them. Organizations invest in this approach because it helps people continue to develop and to stay motivated. It also stimulates the in-house and external mobility of workers when people's careers can systematically be matched to the organization's career possibilities.

2. Description

In small organizations, good conversations between manager and employee on the latter's talent, the possibilities in the organization, and material and immaterial support to explore both can be very effective in developing a person's career. In larger organizations, HR systems often come into play. In these systems there is a wide array of tools to stimulate career development and planning, such as periodic career talks, assessment centers, coaching and mentoring, creating new challenges, course programs, sabbaticals, job rotation, and internships. The extent to which such systems are present reflects the ambitions and value that an organization places on the development of its staff. There is also often a strong link between the presence of these systems and the ambitions of the organization. Designing and implementing such systems takes at least a year. It is one thing to put these systems into place, but using them adequately and credibly is quite another. The role management plays in this is vital and generally requires some management training; the more active their coaching role, the more intense the managers' training must be.

3. Comments

The credible use of these career-planning systems requires a delicate touch. Individuals must not feel that they are being manipulated in a way beneficial to the organization or feel that they are being placed on a sidetrack and not being given a chance to develop themselves. Fastidious implementation is the watchword, and hidden agendas and unfair treatment must be avoided for the systems to work. The systems work best when individuals have a high degree of self-awareness and know what they want or do not want. When managers are able to respond to workers' interests and ambitions, this has a positive effect for the organization. However, if there is too big a gap between what the individual wants and what the organization can offer, or if managers are disinclined to pick up on what workers are saying, the systems can have detrimental effects on the organization as a result of frustrating expectations.

4. Role and Contribution of the Interventionist

Interventionists can help with the design and implementation. Together with management and the Human Resources department, they can determine the system's goals, scope, procedures, and roles. They can also give training in the skills needed to use the system and can even take on the role of individual (external) coach or mentor.

5. Dominant Color

Red, because of its strong orientation toward the fit between organization and individual, and toward the well-being, development, and growth of both. The systems can be designed using a blue approach, starting with a definition of results and a program of requirements. The training sessions are green in character: they are learning situations.

If career guidance is completely focused on the individual and includes attention for the individual's life outside the office, the process becomes green or even white. In this case, the personal growth of the individual and not the optimal fit of individual and organization becomes the main priority.

6. Level

Individual, as a starting point. When focusing on the systems aspect of career development, it fits the level of the organization as a whole.

Related Interventions 1: Recruitment and Selection

Modern selection procedures place a great deal of emphasis on the individual looking for career fulfillment or an environment where his ambitions can be realized, and on the organization searching for individuals who will help realize the organization's ambitions. In this view, individuals seek to fulfill their ambitions and use organizations as temporary and sometimes even parallel platforms that assist them in doing so, while organizations do the same thing the other way around (employees as "human" resources). There is almost no better illustration of the creation of a red "optimal fit" between the two.

Related Intervention 2: Job Enlargement/Job Enrichment

The notion behind this intervention is that people generally do not like doing monotonous work. Increasing variety in work by expanding a job's duties is the essence of job enlargement. Job rotation also accomplishes this, but spread over a period of time. A more fundamental approach is followed in job enrichment: specialized tasks are put back together so that one person is responsible for a whole product or an entire service. The notion behind this is that it is satisfying to "see the results of your own labors." It also allows for more knowledge of the results of one's activities (feedback) and thus allows for more autonomy and even improvisation. Taking into account these particular kinds of effects on employees when designing a job turns such design from a blue endeavor into a red one.

References:

Schoemaker (1994)
Thierry, Koopman, and Van der Flier (1992)
Van der Heijden (1999)

7.4 Coaching, Intensive Clinic, Feedback/Mirroring

Coaching

1. Underlying Idea

Giving specific one-to-one attention to individual learning goals can greatly increase the insights and the competencies of the person being coached. Such goals can vary greatly from wanting to solve recurring problems at work, to having support in tough times, to exploring one's potential pro-actively. Ideally, the person being coached should be in charge of both his learning goals and selecting his coach. The selected coach should then guide his client in finding his own solutions and possibilities.

2. Description

Coaching comes in many shapes and sizes, but it usually has the following steps in common:

♦ selecting a coach by looking for a good personal match as well as a familiarity with the kinds of topics to be dealt with and agreeing on the coaching process (length, roles, etc.)
♦ gaining insight into the (problematical) situation, into the client's own behavior, and your part in the (problem) situation
♦ developing new insights, skills, and so on, that lead to a different view, approach, or behavior that deals more effectively with the situation the client is faced with
♦ support in putting learning into practice or in helping to remove any other obstacles

Coaching takes place in a number of sessions, varying from a brief process of between three to six sessions, to ongoing coaching lasting one or two years. Generally the periods between the coaching sessions vary from one to several weeks. A session will last from one to two hours and is very intensive for both participants.

3. Comments

It is important that the coach and the client have a good relationship based on mutual trust. The client must have at least some insight into his own learning needs or incompetence, be motivated to learn by the chosen method of coaching and the selected coach, and take responsibility for his own learning process. Certain rules are necessary to create the right conditions, like agreeing on confidentiality. At the start of the process a coach must be selected based on the degree to which his competencies and personality are in harmony with the client's and the client's learning needs. Some coaches focus on a client's behavior and help modify it, for example by offering clear steps or hints; others deal more with (dysfunctional) convictions, help the client work though emotions, analyze inner conflicts, or explore "spirituality in the workplace."

4. Role and Contribution of the Interventionist

The coach listens actively and uses questions, feedback, visualizations, new perspectives, exercises, and so on, in an attempt to clarify the (problem) situation and to help search for an alternative, more satisfying approach. His role can be directive to a greater or lesser extent, and his "toolkit" varies depending on his background and the client's goal.

5. Dominant Color

Green, because it is concerned with learning. It can be red if the coaching is not really confidential or given by an "outsider," but is part of a manager's style of leadership. In this case, the coaching is not targeted only to the needs of the individual, but more toward finding a better fit between the individual and the organization. For example, if someone's behavior is so outrageous that it affects others, the manager will try to find a solution with the help of the individual concerned. For clarity's sake, however, we would like to distinguish coaching as a professional intervention from coaching as a leadership style: "the manager as coach."

6. Level

Individual. Coaching can also be given within a group, with each person receiving guidance in turn. When the facilitator does most of the coaching, it resembles a training format and also allows people to learn from each other's problems. When the facilitator leaves much of the interaction to the participants, this form is more like intervision, which has the added value of participants also learning how to coach others. In these training and intervision settings, collective learning takes place.

Related Intervention 1: Intensive Clinic

People are capable of formulating their own learning goals and taking responsibility for part of their own learning process. This concept is applied in intensive clinics where participants describe exactly which competencies they lack or feel they do not sufficiently possess. These competencies are then practiced in a kind of role play with actors and a facilitator. The facilitator coaches, interrupts, and builds in moments of reflection. Sometimes there are a number of consecutive exercise situations ("'stations'"). If participants who have a common learning goal replace the actors and each in turn takes part in the role-play, this can be regarded as a group-oriented form of learning.

Related Intervention 2: Feedback/Mirroring

Feedback sessions can be organized after one or more real or practice situations. The idea behind this is to look back on how someone has functioned or acted in a certain situation and what concrete effect his behavior has had on it. Specific feedback rules are applied to ensure a nonthreatening environment. The purpose is to hold up "a mirror" without judging the person, wanting to change the person, or apportioning blame. The idea is that the person involved becomes conscious of the effects of his own behavior (both positive and negative) where he might not have been to the same degree before. The insights gained allow him to cope better with similar situations in the future and thus increase his personal effectiveness. As a by-product, feedback/mirroring also can help improve relationships among those involved and, when done systematically within a group, help further a learning environment in that group.

References:
Moursund (1985)
Kor, Wijnen, and Weggeman (1997)
Evered and Evered (1989)
Sadler and Miller (1993)
Krijger (1994)

7.5 T-Group, Personal Growth, Networking

T-Group

1. Underlying Idea
To offer people insight into group dynamics and their individual effectiveness within group settings, there is no substitute for personal experience. Thus a setting for experiential learning is created. In these settings participants learn how their behavior influences others and how others' behavior influences them. They experiment with different behavior in groups and see what dilemmas, roles, and processes are likely to occur in groups.

2. Description
This intervention usually involves between ten and fifteen people who do not know one another. After setting some basic rules (like logistics, attendance, etc.) and explaining the goal of the T-group and his own role as a resource person, the facilitator sits back and lets the group take center stage. Under the watchful

eye of a facilitator they experiment with group processes, leadership, and interpersonal relationships. What goes on in the group becomes the "here and now" data for reflection and feedback. The facilitator refrains from giving directions or judgments even when pressed to do so but does feed back his observations of group dynamics. As a result, the participants are better able to understand themselves, their development, their competencies, and their incompetencies. This is also known as an encounter group or personal growth group. The depth of this intervention can vary; it may encompass the person as a whole or concentrate on a specific aspect like leadership style. It takes place in a series of sessions, each lasting a number of days, over a longer period.

3. Comments

T-groups need to be run completely from beginning to end to minimize risks of "unfinished business" in a group. Because of the confrontational nature of such groups, the participants also need to be highly motivated. The fully unstructured variant of this intervention, with no agenda and where the trainers only observe and interpret the group process, seems to be somewhat outdated. The fact that individuals take part without their colleagues and outside their workplace creates a "transfer of training" problem, whereby the effects T-Group interventions have on the organization are not always clear. Thus variations have emerged that use existing work groups ("team building"), are more task-oriented (using for example games/simulations), or are theme oriented (e.g., focusing on leadership styles). Examples of these more structured forms are dealt with in section 7.9. Especially popular are interventions that deal with role behavior and communication. These interventions are not suitable for organizations with dominant political processes (too unsafe) or where there is significant time pressure.

4. Role and Contribution of the Interventionist

T-groups require extremely experienced trainers who are skilled in understanding and intervening in group dynamics. Experience in therapeutic techniques is recommended.

5. Dominant Color

White, if the setting is unstructured. What takes place and emerges "here and now" within the group is the basic learning material. If the setting is more task or theme oriented, it is green because of its focus on preset learning goals and the stronger influence of the facilitator. Both colors make use of similar methods and skills such as observation, feedback, setting learning conditions, and so on.

6. Level

Mainly individual: participants in this group for their own sake. In a more structured (green) form, the group level becomes most important.

Related Intervention 1: Personal Growth

This way of thinking argues that a person's effectiveness depends on how well she knows and "manages" herself. This includes matters such as her recognizing and understanding her personal motivations, finding peace within and with herself, her ability to transform dysfunctional views, and her ability to deal with her emotions. The idea is that someone who embraces her own character is sufficiently self-aware, strong, and motivated to guide her life in the direction of her choosing and is consequently able to build meaningful relationships with others and meet the challenges in her working life.

Related Intervention 2: Networking

The idea behind networking is that people try to meet and seek out others to satisfy their needs, fulfill their goals, and find new meanings and perspectives. The objective can vary from learning and cooperation to sponsoring and new leads. Networking can create subcultures around, for example, a number of ideas, goals, lifestyles, or people, and produce a semistable informal group of individuals who, often without the knowledge of the outside world, maintain their own similar perspectives and norms on a number of common issues. Through networking, individuals can often pursue and reach their own goals more easily than would have been possible within their own part of the organization or social circle. After a time, if a network relationship fails to contribute anything, it will perish more or less automatically.

Note: Sometimes networking is interpreted as lobbying or forming coalitions; in that case, it is of course yellow.

References:

Schein and Bennis (1965)
Maslow (1976)
Camp and Erens (1994)

7.6 Confrontation Meetings, Third-Party Strategy, Top Structuring

Confrontation Meetings

1. Underlying Idea

These meetings are meant to mobilize both the thinking power and support of a group or (the key players of) an entire organization in order to identify problems, establish priorities, determine actions, and start to work on them. Various points of view are brought together with the aim of finding solutions through discussion, negotiation, and give and take. This type of meeting is very similar to MOS-style conferences where the emphasis is also on generating a consistent and widely supported set of statements of Mission, Objectives, and Strategy (MOS).

2. Description

The following steps may be used:

Step 1: Designing and preparing the confrontation meeting. Design would involve clarity on desired outcome of the conference, urgency, group dynamics, selection of participants, and so on. Preparation would include gathering of necessary data in advance, communicating expectations and homework, arranging logistics.

Step 2: Gathering together a large group of people who, after introductions, are broken up in interdepartmental groups of between five and fifteen members. Management forms its own group so as to allow for more open communication in the other groups. These groups start making an inventory of issues in the workplace. The scope depends on the design of the conference and might also include environmental analysis, determination of core competences, and so on.

Step 3: The groups list their findings—say on problems in the workplace or about the effectiveness of the organization—and report these back to one another in a plenum. The list of problems is broken down into categories that best allow (existing) groups to work on them.

Step 4: At this stage, problem-solving groups are formed to solve particular categories of problems—the marketing department tackles marketing problems, for example. The groups have different compositions than in Step 2. Each group devises a plan of action and a timetable.

Step 5: There are regular progress reports to top management, the team leader, or the whole group, after which the group reconvenes to fine-tune their plans. Sometimes this involves stepping back from the level of problems and actions and (in other small groups) looking at the emerging larger picture in terms of underlying patterns and overarching missions and objectives. In turn, such missions and objectives can be used as input to fine tune action plans.

Step 6: The meeting is rounded out by putting the plans together (at least visually) and agreeing to put them into practice. Follow-up is agreed upon and periodic follow-up meetings are often planned.

These conferences are often given in sizable plenary meetings with discussion in subgroups. The careful preparation and design that they require generally takes at least a month, and the conference itself can last for a number of days. The follow-up will take at least three to six months.

3. Comments
Cases have been documented where this intervention generated a significant amount of thinking power, acceptance, and energy. Because it creates a sense of unity and people negotiate with one another, the method clearly has a positive (mass psychological) effect. But there are also cases where the conferences end with ambitious statements and plans that little is heard of again. During these meetings, when too much emphasis is placed on achieving concrete outputs rather than on thorough analysis and negotiation, participants may be inclined to write down things mechanically, making many quick-and-dirty compromises. As a result, such plans of action are often replaced later by ones that have been drawn up by the powers that be. This intervention is a useful safety valve when there is a great deal of tension in an organization or when there is a (perceived) substantial gap between the top and the work floor.

4. Role and Contribution of the Interventionist
He can (help to) design and facilitate the meeting and carry out preliminary work like research and data collection.

5. Dominant Color
Yellow, because agreement must be found through negotiations across disciplines and hierarchies. It has much in common with the conclave method, where a group must reach agreement within a certain time. When emphasis is put on wide participation and dialogues, rather than on key players and concrete outcomes, substantial learning can take place in these conferences (green).

6. Level
Group. This can be a very large group and can even involve (almost) the entire organization.

Related Intervention 1: Third-Party Strategy
Bringing in an independent third party can be an effective tool to help resolve disagreements or conflicts. The idea behind this is that the discomfort of the conflict and the ineffectiveness of solving it lead the parties involved to more readily accept a third party who, by maintaining his independence, will be able to offer possible solutions that the parties could not otherwise have generated together. The solutions vary depending on the substance of the conflict (e.g., they can be based on interest, viewpoints, allergies, etc.) and on the context (e.g., urgency). Sometimes the solution lies in changing the organizational setup (decreasing dependency), sometimes procedures or a "final" verdict by the third party. Mediation, arbitration, and process consultation all have slightly different approaches, but the underlying idea of impartiality in conflict resolution is the same.

Related Intervention 2: Top Structuring
Top structuring is often riddled with questions about power distribution, interdependencies, coalitions, and likes and dislikes. As a result, designing and staffing a (new) top structure is a tough issue for the apex of an organization. Third parties are often brought in to assist in compiling a top structure, while paying close attention to such issues. Not heeding these issues is likely to render the resulting top structure unworkable. Because it is so much more than a matter of only proper (blue) design, top structuring can best be regarded as a negotiation game.

References:
Cummings and Worley (1993)
Koning (1987)
Gerrichhauzen, Kampermann, and Kluytmans (1994)

7.7 Working in Projects, Archiving, Decision Making

Working in Projects

1. Underlying Idea
The underlying notion is that people appreciate clarity. You therefore need to invest energy in defining beforehand exactly what the result of an activity or project should be, and what requirements it should meet in the end. This

clarity with regard to outcomes gives all those involved something to hold on to and to aim for. It aligns their mind-sets, as it were. Still more clarity should be provided by defining a plan to reach the desired outcomes. It is also needed to clarify the roles involved—the principal, the project leader, and the members of the project team—and to define the rules of the game in regard to their individual tasks and responsibilities. The plan supplies norms for the project, and frequent monitoring ensures that work can be adjusted along the way to reach the agreed-upon result.

2. Description

Many organizations structure their work in projects and use project teams to carry it out. This is a powerful method for unique assignments. If an organization has many such assignments, its whole organization can be geared toward this, and temporary project structures can be seen to overlay and overshadow the regular organizational structure. Conversely, this will not be the case in organizations that carry out mainly routine or improvised work.

In the project approach, the first order of business is to draw up a project brief. Work can begin when the principal has approved this. A project leader is found to direct the work and a project team to carry it out. The work in projects is done in a clear sequence of steps. A decision document is drawn up between each of the steps, to be discussed with the principal. Time, money, information, quality, and organization of the project are deliberately included in these documents and managed during each step. Projects vary in size, length, prestige, and the like. Multiproject management is advisable in organizations carrying out a large number of projects. This enables them to retain an overview of all the projects, manage capacities and budgets, and so on.

Introducing project management in an organization as its dominant way of working can take years. It requires training, coaching, intervision, model projects, and so on. More important, when most work needs to be done in teams, it requires considerable adjustment of the organization to deal with competing leadership (project management vs. line management), to allow for substantial autonomy, to further cooperation in teams, and the like.

3. Comments

The main advantages are the clear structuring, the unequivocal rules of the game, and the clear direction toward the result. There can be disadvantages: not paying enough attention to people (stressing the content and results of projects over the interaction process of the team), difficulty in adjusting the result along the way (once it has been defined you are "stuck" with it), and neglecting to take power plays or resistance into account.

4. Role and Contribution of the Interventionist

These can be manifold. As project leaders, they can champion ("difficult") projects, thus demonstrating the approach. They can support the team in the methodology by, for example, helping them to draw up a start-up document or by assisting in drawing up an interim project evaluation. They can also play a role in introducing the project-based working method to the whole organization. They can develop and give training programs and coach project leaders or help adjust the organization to support wide use of this approach.

5. Dominant Color

The approach is as blue as can be. The introduction often requires green processes (training, coaching, intervision).

6. Level

Group level for single projects. If the method is introduced throughout the organization because of a constant large number of projects, the organization level obviously also comes into the picture.

Related Intervention 1: Archiving

New thinking on the office of the future does not provide workers with their own work space, but divides the office into areas for carrying out various functional activities. Workers choose the office areas appropriate to the activities they have to carry out at various times during the day. This demands watertight agreement in the group on a number of issues, including archiving documents and protocols. Even personal archives are no longer managed at the individual level; they are often managed collectively and increasingly in a digital format. If such a system is to work, it must be unambiguous, consistent, and used across the board.

Related Intervention 2: Decision Making

Clear rules on how decisions should be made, how people are and are not supposed to contribute to a decision, who makes the final decisions, how information is distributed, and how implementation of the decision is sanctioned are all issues that keep blue-print thinkers occupied. After all, group processes are difficult enough to come to grips with, and the least they can do is get the rules straight for all those involved.

References:
Kluytmans (1994)
Wijnen, Renes, and Storm (1990)
Kor and Wijnen (2000)
Russo and Schoemaker (1989)

7.8 Social Activities, Team Roles, Management by Speech

Social Activities

1. Underlying Idea

There appears to be a strong correlation between a person's well-being and his productivity/performance. The human relations school teaches us that people require and thrive on attention and that colleagues sometimes want to meet each other outside the confines of a purely professional environment. Giving attention to the atmosphere, collective happenings, and informal activities in the department or in the team in which someone works improves relationships. Because cooperation is a function of such things as trust, loyalty, understanding, willingness to agree and disagree, and so on, improved relationships indirectly improve the work itself. Many organizations therefore have (small) budgets or facilities for departments or teams for this purpose.

2. Description

This can include a whole range of activities. Groups or departments organizing social activities (a day out, an evening get-together, or meeting for drinks), celebrating each other's birthdays, or decorating their own or common work stations using anything from a goldfish in a bowl to an expensive piece of art. The organization can organize open-house days, Christmas parties for workers' families, outward-bound expeditions, or company outings. All of these can be organized at either group or company level. The intensity and frequency can vary, as can roles: Was it management's idea and did the company organize it? Or is management just supporting and stimulating these kinds of initiatives from the shop floor? Support can consist of budgets, personnel, external resources, and so on. Social activities can take place during working hours or be kept separate.

3. Comments

The organization can do little more than instigate, stimulate, and facilitate social activities. Obligations to take part are generally counterproductive. The workforce itself must be sufficiently enthusiastic or it will come to nothing.

Quite often there are widely divergent needs/wishes with regard to social activities, with some desiring "friendships" in the workplace and wanting to expand social activities, while others wish to keep their private and business lives separate.

4. Role and Contribution of the Interventionist
Minimal. Can contribute ideas, facilitate the discussion on this subject, or contribute to the activity itself

5. Dominant Color
Red, because it covers the area of individual well-being within the organization

6. Level
Group, but there are often links with the whole organization

Related Intervention 1: Team Roles
Team members can contribute differently to the tasks of the team as a whole. The contribution that they make or the roles that they play can either complement others' or have the opposite effect. The idea behind Belbin's theory (see 6.6) is that deploying a certain set of complementary roles in a team ensures a good fit among the individual contributions, thus supporting the quality of the team's performance. Members have their own individual preferences or dispositions for these roles. The interventionist takes the individual's preference and possibilities as well as the team's interests into consideration when assembling a team (a red approach). He can also stimulate discussion on team roles, role conflicts, and the complementarity of roles once a team is already fixed. The intervention then takes on a greener shade (see also the next section on team building).

Related Intervention 2: Management by Speech
The thinking behind this intervention is that managers need to be visible on the "shop floor." Managers are encouraged to explain things to their staff, to be interested in their staff, and to coach their staff as well. Interaction is the watchword, and motivation and adding meaning are key objectives. The credibility of managers doing this lies in the degree to which they take staff's concerns seriously and how genuine and reliable their care really is. The belief is that people will give more to the organization if they believe they are valued and cared for by that organization, represented, as it were, by management.

References:
Belbin (1981)
Cummings and Worley (1993)
Kor, Wijnen, and Weggeman (1997)

7.9 Team Building, Gaming, Intervision

Team Building

1. Underlying Idea

Team building tries to help a group find ways of improving the manner in which they carry out their work, improving interpersonal skills, and improving the skills needed to solve problems collectively.

The idea is to make maximum use of the team's resources, including the level of motivation and the qualities and contributions of its individual members. Basically, team building helps teams to discover and address the things that are limiting them, which range from a lack of motivation to carry out joint tasks or a lack of competencies, to ineffective meeting procedures or group members failing to follow up on agreements.

2. Description

Team building is aimed at functional teams, a group of people who are charged with carrying out a specific task and who are depending on each other to get the task done. The team generally includes a team leader, who sometimes has to reconcile his or her team role with that of being manager (in a hierarchical sense) of the team members as well.

Team building can be targeted on

♦ activities aimed at better performance or the contribution of one or more individuals, including the manager or the team leader
♦ activities aimed at the work and behavior of the whole group
♦ activities aimed at the relationship of the group to the rest of the organization

The activities can be mainly diagnostic (What exactly is going on?), problem solving (How can we do this better in the future?), or both. To underscore the importance of team efforts, the process of team building itself should be a team effort as well, instead of something thought up on their behalf. In that sense, the role of the team leader is crucial. Does he take part in the session or is he absent? What is the role of the facilitator in the group? Is this facilitator an outsider or does the team leader take on this role? Preferably, these decisions as well as the objectives of the exercise are determined by the group in preparing for the actual team building. The team-building sessions are often quite intensive, away from the workplace, and last a number of days. Once again, many of the processes during these days are shaped more by team members—their qualities and their agendas—than by the facilitator. The meeting usually culminates in the drawing up of a broadly supported action plan that demonstrates how the team can reach results collectively. Sometimes there is a follow-up meeting.

3. Comments

Team building can be confrontational. Some teams like to invest time and energy in such exercises to support their individual development. For others, it has to be worth the effort in terms of effectively improving the functioning of the team to a level needed for the team's job. This is the case the more the following are true:

- ◆ task interdependency is substantial, given the complexity of the team's task
- ◆ the team members are willing to act as an integrated group, and the team leader behaves as part of the team
- ◆ there are clear problems that need fixing, especially regarding interactions within the team
- ◆ the team members are willing to learn and assist each other's learning

The remark about learning also implies that team building is extremely difficult to apply in cases where there is talk of an underlying conflict, of one or two team members dominating the team, of hidden agendas, or of members airing the team's dirty linen in public. Another unfavorable factor is a team leader who performs poorly or is not accepted by the team members. Issues like these dampen members' willingness to participate in a learning exercise and must be addressed before a climate of sufficient safety and openness can develop, which in itself is necessary for learning to take place and team building to become successful. It is often important for the facilitator to have a good eye for the stage of the team's development in order to better understand the team's dilemmas, needs, and possible resistance (see also section 5.2.1).

4. Role and Contribution of the Interventionist

She is firmly focused on the team's process. She creates a secure environment and space for the group to (learn to) solve their own problems. She also generally introduces and facilitates a procedure or a number of problem-solving steps to facilitate this learning and problem solving. The interventionist also monitors these procedures during team building, thus allowing the team to focus on the issues at hand. These procedures can assist in, for example, identifying problems, defining roles, setting priorities, describing interaction patterns, brainstorming for solutions, and so on. In order to help the group progress, the interventionist must sometimes use or introduce feedback and mirroring to raise awareness of certain patterns of behavior in the team.

5. Dominant Color
Green, because it concerns learning activities in general and collective learning in particular. People learn from and with each other. Groups often learn not only how to tackle acute problems, but also how to tackle new ones in the future; they are learning to learn.

6. Level
Group. This intervention often has only an indirect effect on the organization as a whole; for example, if many groups attend such sessions.

Related Intervention 1: Gaming
Gaming is a learning method in which people interact in a structured activity or simulation. The learning goals are previously determined and are by design incorporated into the game activities. The idea behind games is that people learn by doing and that reality can be represented in a simulation. This allows people to learn the same lessons in a simulation that they would in real life. In other words, they have to complete the learning cycle in a game: experiencing, reflecting, concept building, planning, and putting plans into action (see also 8.4). Every part of the cycle is extensively practiced during the game, and the entire cycle is repeated several times. This is a way to accelerate (collective) learning, because the same cycle often takes a much longer period to go through (given the nature of certain assignments) in the workplace than is the case in these simulations.

Related Intervention 2: Intervision
Intervision is often used to help professional workers think through issues they are faced with in the workplace. The thinking behind intervision is that quick suggestions, tips, or hints rarely help people with persistent issues. In these cases, it is more effective to look at other aspects of the problem, discern underlying patterns, come up with new perspectives, and become aware of personal

attachments to ideas and behavior that keep the problem in place. For this, coaching (see section 7.4.) is very suitable, but a group format in which people take turns being coached by all the rest works also: intervision. This group format produces as positive side effects people learning from each other's problems and also learning to coach. Intervision is normally carried out in small groups of four to six people. To avoid the discussion reflex and unasked-for advice, the participants usually opt for a clear procedure for discussing the cases, which creates space for joint exploration and learning. Especially when people are unfamiliar with intervision, the method must be carefully introduced and the first meetings must be facilitated to learn how the process works. Groups generally meet every couple of weeks over a period of four to ten months and then they cease to exist in an effort to prevent them dying a slow death. New intervision groups can be started in different compositions, as diversity within a group generally enhances learning.

References:
Caluwé, L. de, et al. (1996)
Vroemen (1995)
Steyaert (1994)

7.10 Self-Steering Teams, Open-Space Meetings, Making Mental Models Explicit

Self-Steering Teams

1. Underlying Idea
Teams that are made responsible for drawing up their own goals, determining their own working methods, and managing their own interactions and further development, can accomplish things other teams cannot. Self-steering allows them to oversee and coordinate more complex tasks and react more adequately to changes (e.g., shifting demands due to client wishes or the illness of a team member). Such teams also experience increased satisfaction from their work because they are able to see the results of their own efforts, the tasks are more varied, they are free to carry out the work as they see fit, and they are in charge of their own further development. The team members can make optimal use of each other's qualities and can interact independently with both internal and external clients and suppliers. They take full advantage of the opportunities their environment has to offer.

2. Description

The process of developing self-steering teams is difficult to describe in steps because of its iterative and dynamic nature, but it generally includes the following:

♦ *Laying the foundation.* First, knowledge is gained about how the organization works and whether or not self-steering teams would work in this surrounding. This inquiry can be done in a participative fashion by also supplying those involved with insight into the concept of self-steering teams and the process of creating them. Whether there is a fit is partly connected with the complexity of tasks, but also connected with the views and values about work itself: Are increased responsibility, empowerment, professionalization, and teamwork valued? And is this still the case when self-steering includes more interdependence, more confrontation, and possibly conflicts and costly failures along the way? If so, one needs to determine what has to change in the organization and, more important, in the competencies of the team itself to make it all work.

♦ *Design of the organization.* The goals and the composition of the team are determined. Goals are often determined in terms of outputs that are based on the delivery of whole products or services. Tasks are transferred to the team to ensure the team can take full responsibility for the delivery: for example, 80% of the actual tasks involved should be done by team members. The team's relationships and transactions with its environment are (re)defined, such as IT and administrative services and the like. As a rule, this always implies considerable adaptation of the support systems. The team's composition is based on complementary specializations needed to get the job done.

♦ *Start-up of the team.* The team moves into its own work space and starts discussing and designing its internal functioning. Questions include, but are not limited to, "How will we deal with the issue of leadership? How do we assign tasks internally? Do we replace each other? What kind of meetings do we need? How do we communicate with one another? Are there contact persons for the outside world? How will we learn from each other?"

♦ *Start-up and continuous improvement of teamwork.* The team becomes accountable for its work and it learns by doing. It does both collectively. The essence of self-steering now comes to the fore through constant reassessment of goals and effects, joint organization and cooperation, and the quality of learning.

Working in self-steering teams can yield extremely effective results. The introduction of self-steering requires a great deal of training, supervision, and trial and error as well as time and patience. This is preferably an action-learning process.

3. Comments

It is easier to introduce this concept into new organizations or into organizations about to undergo a transformation process. Self-steering disrupts an existing organization, and the results are by no means immediate. Failure factors include not allowing the team a sufficient degree of autonomy, goals being overly ambitious, the team being an isolated experiment within an old-fashioned organization, the boss not trusting the team enough to learn by trial and error, and the organization claiming to follow the trend of self-steering while in fact paying only lip-service to it. In addition, self-steering demands a great deal from the team members themselves; they must have the necessary knowledge and skills to be able to design and basically manage a "small organization" all by themselves. Being able to do all this jointly as a team and handle internal conflicts along the way are also requirements.

4. Role and Contribution of the Interventionist

During the introduction, the interventionist can be involved in training and explaining the concept of self-steering. She can help design the organization to allow for such teams. She can also play the role of action-learning consultant and develop and support the process of implementation. Already functioning teams can ask for help when and where they need it. This can vary considerably.

5. Dominant Color

The idea behind self-steering fits with white thinking. Learning situations will be employed during the introduction, which will gradually change from green to white. It is sometimes necessary to briefly remove obstacles for self-steering, such as changing the organization's structure or the power balance dramatically. These elements may look blue or yellow initially, but are born out of white considerations. When such changes take considerable time and stay yellow or blue, the top-down approach conflicts with the whole concept of self-steering.

6. Level

Group, unless it is a guiding principle for the whole organization, in which case it is organizational level

Related Intervention 1: Open-Space Meetings

The idea behind open space meetings is that energy and movement are encouraged by allowing people to create their own agendas and run their own meetings regarding the issues about which they have a genuine passion and for which they are willing to take some personal responsibility. During an open-space meeting, the differences between leaders and participants, between experts and laypeople, disappear. The interventionist only sets the stage (organizing the date, venue, and inviting participants), briefly introduces the concept, and "holds the space." The participants take the initiative to start discussions and form groups during the meeting. Relevant themes introduced by the participants are discussed in groups whose composition regularly changes. People are allowed to leave groups when they feel they are no longer learning or contributing. The meeting can last from one to three days. The longer the meeting runs, the more results are recorded and communicated across groups in some way.

Related Intervention 2: Making Mental Models Explicit

Mental models or mental frameworks are the often subconscious individual and subjective impressions that an individual has of reality. They are constructed and checked against what an individual perceives as being the reality of his daily existence. Being in the individual's mind, they are often implicit and are not (immediately) transferable or open to analysis or discussion with others. Making mental models explicit is usually a group activity aimed at raising people's awareness of their own and others' mental models. This process can use a number of techniques, including the Socratic method, questioning, observation, and reflection. The added value of this exercise lies in understanding "where someone is coming from," thus enabling better communication; in transforming your own mental models; or in jointly creating new ones that offer greater perspective (see also section 8.4.2).

References:
Eijbergen (1999)
Stoker (1999)
Van Amelsfoort and Scholtes (1994)
Geurts and Vennix (1989)
Bunker and Alban (2000)

7.11 Improving Quality of Work Life, Forming Strategic Alliances, Negotiations on Labor Conditions

Improving Quality of Work Life

1. Underlying Idea
This is one of the classic interventions from the 1950s. It was first defined in terms of the personal consequences of work on employees in terms of job

satisfaction and occupational health. The idea is that improving quality of work life (QWL) is worthwhile both as an end in itself and as a way of increasing employee contribution to an organization while lowering resistance to change. Many QWL processes involve representation of workers, be it through unions or workers' councils. The idea here is that a balance of power between management and workers helps by serving the interests of both parties, which in the end is beneficial to working relationships.

QWL tries to promote employee involvement in four ways. First, employees are given more say over their work. Their involvement in decision making is increased. Second, they receive adequate and relevant information on which to base these decisions and be socially integrated in their working environment. Third, they are given more possibilities to acquire the skills and knowledge necessary for their job, helpful for understanding the business they are part of, and beneficial for their career and growth. Finally, they are given recognition and fair rewards, both material and nonmaterial, to underscore the value of their contributions. Part of this is also making sure the working environment is safe and healthy and worker's rights are protected.

2. Description

Many processes of employee participation and employee consultation have characteristics in common with this approach. The change effort focuses on balancing the interests of the organization, represented by top management, and the interests of employees, represented by informal cross sections, workers' councils, or labor unions. Often a committee is made up of representatives of management and labor who draw up overall change objectives in which increasing employee involvement generally takes prominence because such involvement can serve both groups' interests. Often a number of subcommittees are formed to allow representatives from the various layers in the organization to deal with certain subissues, or temporary work task forces are formed to tackle certain projects. The outcomes of lower-level groups are generally joint activities based on higher-level agreements or joint proposals to be discussed and resolved at higher levels.

This approach demands that a great deal of time be devoted to meetings and is difficult to plan in advance. It often takes months to draw up clear goals, let alone begin to implement them.

3. Comments

The effects of this approach are mixed. We do know of cases where greater involvement and employee participation has led to the increased productivity and well-being of the work force, but there have also been cases where differences of opinion and distrust have increased, inevitably leading to opposite effects. The focus on interests of both parties in itself leads to antagonism if not resolved in a timely fashion through the defining of overarching interests. Decisive factors seem to be whether or not people are willing and able to reach agreements, and whether they have the necessary negotiating skills to do so. Deadlines, press conferences, an (implicit) threat of sanctions, or a threat against survival can help the process along. In many mergers or major restructurings such conditions are used as pressure in negotiation processes to encourage timely results, especially where such mergers or restructurings are likely to fail without the support of workers' representations.

4. Role and Contribution of the Interventionist
The role can differ, but it generally has to do with leading and facilitating the negotiations. This can be in the role of an independent chairman or in a supporting role (carrying out research, data collection). He can also be a mediator carrying out a kind of shuttle diplomacy, or he might use conflict resolution techniques.

5. Dominant Color
Yellow. The process is concerned with conflicts of interest, searching for the dominant coalition, and using negotiation to reach agreement. Carrying out supportive research can be seen as a blue activity. Many of the outcomes, in terms of increasing job satisfaction, can be regarded as red.

6. Level
Organization

Related Intervention 1: Forming Strategic Alliances
Organizations form alliances or merge to achieve a better market position allowing them to out maneuver remaining competitors better or even create a monopoly (this is against the rules, but yellow-print thinkers think rules were made to be broken). Common interests bring them together and they pool their resources and influence, which they then direct toward strategic aspects of their businesses, which might range from product development and knowledge management to marketing and distribution channels. The idea behind this is, "If you can't beat them, join them" (see also sections 6.8 and 6.4.).

Related Intervention 2: Negotiations on Labor Conditions

The so-called Polder model, a reference to the successful mix of policies underpinning the Dutch economy in the nineties such as wage moderation and labor market deregulation, is perhaps one of the best examples of the yellow approach. This model suggests that employers and employees in the Netherlands were able to successfully appease or bring together their specific interests, which resulted in the setting of collective goals and bringing about win-win situations. This was achieved through an elaborate system of semi-permanent platforms and even joint organizations where both parties met and hammered out agreements. These mechanisms still exist, and you can find a similar underlying philosophy at lower levels, like collective labor negotiations at the branch level, or periodic meetings of employers with a workers' council within individual companies.

References:

Cummings and Worley (1993)

Thierry, Koopman, and van de Flier (1992)

Sitter (1989)

7.12 Strategy Analysis, Business Process Redesign (BPR), Auditing

Strategy Analysis

1. Underlying Idea

To most people, strategy corresponds to some kind of plan, a consciously intended course of action predating implementation, with the latter consisting of changes in the organization as well as in the business processes. In this sense, "structure follows strategy" instead of the other way around. The construction of a strategy is based on structured and formal analysis. The analysis supplies the desired direction and design of the organization to bring it into line with both external and internal developments. The optimal future situation that would result is laid out, and the difference between present and future situations is determined. The subsequent action plan is aimed at gradually decreasing this difference.

The idea is that people can most skillfully accomplish this kind of analysis with a helicopter view of the situation (top management) and by specialized consultants who bring expert knowledge or methods to bear. These processes are expected to be entirely rational and free from irrational influences.

2. Description

Strategy analysis is carried out systematically. A frequently used framework is the SWOT analysis (Strengths, Weaknesses, Opportunities, Threats). Its steps are often elaborated on as illustrated below:

♦ Analyzing the strengths and weaknesses of the present organization, often with a focus on its strategy, structure, and business processes only. Some analytical models are used, such as a capability scan or BCG's portfolio analysis (see section 6.3)
♦ Charting opportunities and threats in the environment. Here again, multiple rational models are used, such as an environmental analysis or Porter's competitive structure (see section 6.4)
♦ Choosing the desired strategy and organization structure. Here scenarios are sometimes created and evaluated on the basis of a few key indicators.
♦ Designing a strategic change plan
♦ Implementing the change plan

People typically start with the mission, then the objectives, and finally the strategy (the so-called MOS approach; see Weggeman, 1996). It can easily take a year to draw up the full plan, given the number of tasks (like data collection, research, benchmarking, and competitive analysis), the limited number of people executing these tasks, and the decision-making processes of top management. Subsequent implementation often takes at least a year.

3. Comments

The problems that accompany this approach are well known: lack of understanding and resistance to the implementation among employees, based on the "not-invented-here" syndrome; the strategy not being up to date given the duration of a well-executed analysis; and the resulting strategy being too rigid and fixed for organizations with dynamic environments. As a result, people have come up with other strategy approaches while sometimes using similar diagnostic tools. Some have argued that "strategy follows structure" or that strategy comes about incrementally. Others have opted for more employee participation in strategy formation, arguing that you learn more from writing a statement of strategy than from reading one. These approaches, of course, also create their own problems. Participative approaches require much time and attention to facilitate discussions, to communicate outcomes, and to prevent the development of strong differences of opinion or a lack of consensus. They also lack the clarity and depth of an expert analysis. And if time is at a premium and the organization is under threat of survival, there is no real alternative to a quick-and-dirty version of the top-down analytical approach for coming up with a game plan.

4. Role and Contribution of the Interventionist

This can be a supporting role, including such tasks as market research, benchmarking, and data collection to provide those involved with empirical data to help them make rational decisions. The interventionist can also facilitate top management meetings or, in the capacity of a boardroom consultant, give her expert advice. She can draw up or assist in the drawing up of the implementation plan and help to implement it.

5. Dominant Color

Blue. This is a strongly rational process with a well-defined result and activities. Thinking clearly predates action, like it should in a proper blue approach. Other colors can play a supporting role during the implementation—red for job allocation, for example, or green in the training of new skills.

6. Level

Entire organization

Related Intervention 1: Business Process Redesign (BPR)

BPR is a set of methods designed to chart work processes, to analyze them (by putting them into a logical order, measuring duration, analyzing frequent errors or bottlenecks, etc.), and to redesign them using a number of logical, rational rules. This often involves using IT capabilities, for example, to take over routine transactions or supply knowledge systems. This redesigning is carried out primarily to speed up work processes, improve their quality, and make them cheaper. Redesigning usually results in a large number of detailed blueprints. This method is suitable for bringing antiquated work processes into the twenty-first century. Resistance to this approach on the part of employees can be vehement for the same reasons that are mentioned with regard to strategy analysis. Resistance can sometimes be tempered, because IT capabilities can also allow for an improvement of quality of work life (see also section 7.11).

Related Intervention 2: Auditing

This method uses a structured framework (e.g., a model or a fixed set of questions or issues) to carry out a systematic study (through interviews, study of documents, questionnaires, etc.) of an existing situation. Quite often audits tend to focus more on tangible aspects of organizations (business processes, structures, strategies, systems) than intangible aspects (styles, norms, interactions, quality, power distribution, etc.). Structuring the data in a chosen framework creates a picture of the organization or part of the organization being studied. Often these frameworks are normative and imply specific improvements based on the picture that emerges. In that sense the results of the audit often include evaluations and recommendations (see also the discussion on diagnosis in 5.1).

References:
Weggeman (1995)
Ansoff (1987)
Hammer and Champy (1993)

7.13 Reward Systems, Managing Mobility and Diversity, Triple Ladder

Reward Systems

1. Underlying Idea

The idea is that rewards in organizations are a powerful tool for increasing the performance of individuals and groups. On the one hand, they improve extrinsic motivation: the satisfaction of a good base salary, lots of fringe benefits, good facilities, and the like. On the other hand, a good reward system can also prevent intrinsic motivation (satisfaction derived from the work itself, the interaction with clients and colleagues, etc.) from becoming frustrated by, for example, linking pay to performance instead of to age or "number of years with the company," or by having flexible conditions of employment. Preferably, reward systems are congruent with other organizational systems and practices, such as the organization structure, HRM philosophy, and working relationships. These systems and their effects together create something stronger than their individual parts: they send a clearer message to the staff. For example, valuing self-steering and cooperation in a reward system would go hand in hand with flat organizational structures, a lack of bureaucracy, and a coaching (rather than a directive) management style. Such congruence can contribute to both the organization's and the individual's effectiveness.

2. Description

The influence of rewards on this effectiveness depends on a number of factors:

♦ that it is given in a timely fashion and explicitly related to achievements, so that it can be experienced as feedback for them
♦ that it is proportionate to a person's achievements and fair, in terms of similar performances receiving similar rewards both over time and in comparisons between colleagues

- that it is predictable and consistent in terms of expectations being managed in advance so people know what is being rewarded and what is not
- that the rewards are available, especially in a form that matters most to the persons involved. Increasing somebody's salary often does not offer the biggest incentive. There are many alternatives in terms of pay (like bonuses, shares, profit-sharing), flexibility (extra vacation time, a leave of absence, child care, variable working hours, working from home), extra opportunities for development (promotion prospects, sabbaticals, traineeships, study, special projects), or extra perks (computer, car, mobile phone).

Designing, implementing, and monitoring a meticulous, unambiguous system is the best way to facilitate these factors. Such a plan can take months to design and is usually drawn up by experts, occasionally with participation of (representatives) of employees. The actual implementation can take well over a year. This period includes the provision of extensive information about both the new reward system and the training of management to help them use the system properly and similarly.

3. Comments

We can make a distinction here between the design, the implementation, and the deployment of such systems. The design of the reward system must reflect the needs of the organization and the motivation of the workers. In organizations of professionals, for example, such things as possibilities for development, facilities, and flexibility are often deemed more important than pay in itself. Rewards based on seniority and age are regarded as being unfair. In other types of organizations the situation can be completely different. Communication of the rationale and procedures of reward systems is vital during implementation but also (each year again) when pay raises take place; everyone needs to understand the reward system. Even if the system is a good one, a lack of clarity about the system or secrecy about pay distribution can lead to substantial misperceptions that cloud the relationship between the reward given and the intended feedback. We have seen how this can breed mistrust and fuel grudges. Reward systems are even more powerful in demotivating people than the other way around when they are misunderstood by those concerned.

4. Role and Contribution of the Interventionist

As an expert, he can help design or evaluate a reward system. He can also train management in its use.

5. Dominant Color

Red, because it is concerned with the fit between the individual and the organization and with encouraging desired behavior and sanctioning the opposite. The design itself can be a blue process except when employees participate significantly in the design. A green process can be used for the provision of the necessary training.

6. Level

Organization

Related Intervention 1: Managing Mobility and Diversity

The demographic composition of many companies has changed dramatically over the past few decades. There are now more women, ethnic minorities, and disabled people in the workplace. Age has become less deterministic regarding the position somebody has in an organization, and performance has become more so. Generally, this is regarded as being fairer. All these differences can be regarded as an organization's strength, introducing a great diversity of talents, outlooks, and ambitions. Whether or not these strengths are tapped depends on whether the organization can deal with the tension that may arise as a result of this diversity. This aspect is increasingly important because of the growing mobility of the workforce, with an individual's time spent within any one organization decreasing. This mobility is partly in the interests of the organization, as it provides a source of new "blood" and new talents, but increasing mobility also makes greater demands on an organization, forcing it not only to deal with diversity constructively but to do so more quickly and effectively as well. After all, time is at a premium. This demands HRM systems that attempt to monitor and optimize diversity and mobility. They must also be able to cope with a variety of needs, expectations, and lifestyles by offering different reward systems, child care, different physical workspaces, different dress codes, and so on. Diversity also has implications for how work is carried out and how people cooperate with one another.

Related Intervention 2: Triple Ladder

The theory behind the triple ladder is that individuals can grow in a whole range of competencies. Every company has a number of different competencies critical to its success and survival—for example, research competencies, commercial competencies, and management competencies are essential for an R&D company. We can use the analogy of a ladder with each of its rungs representing a stage of competency development. Those standing at the top of the ladder can act as mentors or coaches to those lower down and can take on the most complicated tasks themselves. Those at the bottom of the ladder are expected to learn and start by carrying out simple tasks. If we are talking about three different types of competencies, the concept is known as a triple ladder. Not everyone has to climb every ladder; there are a variety of career possibilities depending on which ladder or ladders the individual chooses to climb (based on his talents and ambitions). Having only one ladder implies that management competences are valued above all else; this is generally not a healthy situation for any company. The introduction of a triple ladder system enables an organization to name the most important competencies and their levels, determine which workers are suited to which ladders, and to set out career lines. This helps prevent the development of an organization that looks for clones instead of valuing diversity.

References:
Maister (1993)
Vinke (1996)
Cummings and Worley (1993)

7.14 Open Systems Planning, Parallel Learning Structures, Quality Circles

Open Systems Planning

1. Underlying Idea

The autonomy of organizations is regarded as a myth, and consequently it is considered dysfunctional to look predominantly *within* an organization to figure out improvements. This is especially the case in dynamic environments and complex organizations. Instead, organizations are regarded as "open systems" and planning is based on the following assumptions:

♦ that the (selective) perceptions of the members of the organization play an important role in comprehending and acting in the organization's environment and that these often reinforce themselves

♦ that the members of the organization need to develop a common view of their environment and their own role therein in order not to contradict each other subconsciously or consciously and come into conflict with one another

♦ that this common view of members of the organization needs to be effective in responding to the environment or—better still—be able to influence their environment and cocreate it. This implies that the separation of organizational and external domains is thin: people need to be in touch with reality and in interaction with outsiders

♦   that all this can only happen through learning processes

2. Description

Open systems planning generally takes place over a period of months with a cross section of the organization, and includes several day sessions. During these days the environment is first mapped out. People distinguish different parts of the environment, try to walk in an outsider's shoes, and identify what these groups might need and expect from the organization. This exercise helps reduce biases in terms of the selection of external actors and in terms of the understanding of their perspectives. The sum of all these expectations reveals the implicit mission of the organization, which may be in contrast with what the mission statement says. Next, scenarios are created, varying from how things develop if everything stays the same, what happens if the environment changes predictably and the organization stagnates, to scenarios describing organizational responses to more surprising but still possible environmental changes. One of these scenarios then becomes the basis for action planning.

Walking in another's shoes, looking at a broader range of actors, sharing expectations, and exploring consequences are all ways to shake up existing views, create learning, and craft a common vision. Such a process requires a high level of involvement from a diverse group of people. Interaction and communication are facilitated in order to enable dialogue to take place. When differences in perceptions are persistent, data gathering or interviewing external parties helps in between sessions. Lots of information is gathered during these meetings, which is often documented. People often need to be reminded of the purpose of the intervention, which is as much in the learning process itself as in the resulting outcome: the outcome makes full sense only to those whose perceptions have been challenged in the process. They will have developed a more apt view of how the organization presently functions within its environment and what this should ideally be.

3. Comments

The interventions are unsuitable in situations where there are major power differences or strong political processes, because such factors do not go together well with open dialogues. An important precondition is that people are willing to learn from each other and about both the organization and themselves. To avoid falling back into old habits, the participants are expected to engage fully and creatively in the different steps while reflecting on their own thinking.

Substantial resources are involved, and the outcome is not predictable. Do we have the time and money to see this through? Is there sufficient diversity and enough to learn to justify it?

4. Role and Contribution of the Interventionist
She can contribute to the design of the process and check for the necessary conditions. After all, that is the job of a didactician, someone who knows how learning works and how to create settings for learning. She can also take on the role of facilitator or be the one who monitors the process and documents all the learning results.

5. Dominant Color
Green, because it concerns a learning process and a collective setting

6. Level
Organization

Related Intervention 1: Parallel Learning Structures
These structures help organizations solve poorly defined complex problems, offer a means of helping bureaucratic organizations to adapt, and suggest subtle ways to transform their formal structures. A parallel structure is set up alongside that of the existing organization. This additional structure works in a completely different and more informal way that develops from a conscious choice. The same people that are part of the formal structure usually also take part in the parallel one, but the norms and procedures are completely different. There is some kind of steering committee that is responsible for guiding the process, ensuring sufficient support by top management, and dealing with frictions with the existing structure. There is often talk of dynamic networking with changing but continuous participation. This intervention differs from work groups or task forces in that they are temporary and have a specific task, while parallel structures are permanent (although they may develop autonomously). This intervention is very common in major international production companies like the automotive industry and electronic goods manufacturers.

Related Intervention 2: Quality Circles
This originally Japanese idea came to the West in the 1960s. It proposes that workers are closely involved in solving their own problems and in improving production processes. Small groups of workers trained to use problem-solving techniques come together on a voluntary basis to solve problems. In this

intervention, quality management is not regarded as a control issue. Learning to solve your own problems is the main principle here, not only because it helps ensure quality, but also because it helps enhance flexibility, expand employees' capacities, and support group autonomy, all of which in turn often increase employee satisfaction. The management philosophy behind this demands that power, knowledge, and information are properly delegated.

References:
Argyris (1996)
Argyris and Schön (1978)
Schonberger (1982)

7.15 Search Conferences, Rituals and Mystique, Deconstructing "Sacred Cows"

Search Conferences

1. Underlying Idea

This is a relatively new method that aims to get an entire organization on the move. As many people as possible from across the whole organization are brought together to reflect on the past, evaluate the present position, and search for creative ways to shape their future. This method is also known as "futuring" or "visioning." The idea is that focusing on problems often creates even more problems. It bogs people down. Central to search conferences is the belief that for a leap forward to become possible, you must undertake the conference as a community rather than as top management, and that the energy to take the leap resides within the community itself.

2. Description

Search conferences need a clear reason to be held, something that gets people's interest. It might be a joint venture, going international, or a shift in technology. Such a starting point will make it easier for those involved to think big and be concrete. The conference is held over a couple of days, and participants are selected on the basis of their energy and willingness to contribute and be creative. Based on the idea that organizations are open systems, it is not just a large cross section of the organization that is involved (including the powerful players), but also important outsiders like major partners, clients, suppliers, and so on. The participants are assumed to have everything necessary to make the conference a success: no additional homework, experts, or research is needed.

During the conference small groups are formed that try to make sense of what's going on in the organization. During one round, people reflect on its history, recalling and discerning important events, turning points, and patterns. In another round, people look at what is happening in the organization's environment, and in a third round people examine what factors in the current running of the organization drive or frustrate its development. The rounds help gather a lot of information that is recorded and then exchanged. Next, people start visioning, using creative tools such as metaphors, painting, storytelling, and the like. Then the group gradually starts focusing on what the best bets are. At the end, people reflect on what they have learned and translate this in their own departments into plans for their collective and own work. These plans are exchanged and followed up on.

3. Comments

A successful conference usually results in increased energy for change and increased solidarity as a result of the frank exchange of views, of people thinking beyond their own frame of reference, and of building improved relationships within and beyond the organization. Especially when substantial changes are sought, top management tends to isolate itself. Here, many people are involved instead.

However, a search conference may easily backfire and end up in bedlam. Because of its creative nature and because it builds on people's energy, people can take it in any direction they see fit. Conflicts can emerge and grudges brought to the table. Crucial relationships with outside parties might be put under stress. For search conferences to work, participants must be geared toward being creative and constructive, while also showing the ability to reflect and the willingness to take on leadership roles and take risks. If this is not likely, or expectations cannot be managed well enough, this intervention is not suitable. It is not advisable in organizations with unresolved issues and power games.

4. Role and Contribution of the Interventionist

The interventionist can help check whether the conditions are right and can help prepare for the search conference. He can facilitate, but not manage the conference. His way of communicating, his degree of openness, and the amount of risk he is prepared to take can be an example to others, and he can also encourage the participants to explore new ways of thinking.

5. Dominant Color

White; this is primarily a process of searching for personal motivation, understanding underlying patterns, and searching for new perspectives

6. Level
Organization

Related Intervention 1: Rituals and Mystique
Rituals are collective activities that can be regarded as technically superfluous but socially essential. They point to and call up common values and norms regarded as essential by those involved; these could include solidarity, fellowship, and team building. Rituals can also contain an air of mystique. Their importance is difficult to rationalize, but lies in injecting meaning into established processes, reaffirming deals and values in the organization, or emphasizing the necessity of certain changes. New rituals can be created, though not always consciously or easily. Their existence, in any case, cannot be avoided. Rituals are a good means of marking milestones or transitions like celebrating rebirth after a major change process, making a new start, putting your house in order, putting the past behind you. They are also a way of collectively wishing someone well at the start of a new venture.

Related Intervention 2: Deconstructing "Sacred Cows"
When many people are disoriented and the situation is confused, it can be important to get "everything out in the open," to ask the questions that people really want to ask but for one reason or another are afraid to ask. Such disorientation can come about as a result of having gone through tough times or strong shifts of circumstances or environment, during which important issues have not been addressed adequately. The specific issues, the sacred cows, and the fact that they are not addressed often touch on cultural characteristics that perhaps once served a purpose in the organization but are now responsible for frustrating its renewal. Change agents can ask these questions, but preferably they stimulate and create a setting where people come up with these questions themselves. This can lead to interesting surprises, and sometimes one sacred cow can lead to another. Often there are one or two issues that turn out to be most important. They often come up last, and are usually posed by those most daring and produce sighs of relief and much attention from most others. Getting these sacred cows out in the open allows them to be discussed and brings them back into proportion: their sacredness is deconstructed. This can be extremely valuable, as it enables people to get questions off their chests that might otherwise preoccupy them. It further allows them to say goodbye to the past and realize they were not the only ones longing for renewal. As a result, the time may now be right for wiping the slate clean and making a new start.

References:
Weisbord (1992)
Cornelis (1995)
Knibbe (1996)

7.16 Concluding Remarks

In this chapter we have used a standardized framework to describe forty-five sample interventions. Our intention is to demonstrate what interventions are possible within the different colors and at different levels. Of course, there are many more interventions than are described here, and we hope one day to publish a more complete overview. A number of our favorite books have attempted to do this, and though none of them is complete, you will find many more interventions in works by Cummings and Worley (1993), Gerrichhauzen, Kampermann, and Kluytmans (1994), Camp (1996), French and Bell (1999) and Tichy (1983).

In some instances, the interventions in this chapter are written in an exaggerated and deterministic style. We have done this deliberately to emphasize the essence of their colors. It is clear, however, even in these descriptions, that interventionists sometimes modify interventions somewhat by adding a touch of a different color to accommodate more people and to take off "the sharp edges" in the hope of combating or removing perceived inherent disadvantages. In most instances, however, one color usually remains dominant.

What also becomes clear in the descriptions of the interventions is that words or labels can either disguise the underlying color and concept or leave it completely open. We gave a number of examples of ambiguous labels in Table 3.4—for example, knowledge management. In this chapter, again, in discussing the colors of interventions, we have shown how interventions can take on different colors. Also some subjects, like strategy formation, have been touched upon by many interventions: as "blue" strategy analysis, as "green" open systems planning, and as "white" search conferences. All this once again emphasizes the importance of the careful use of words and labels because of the different meanings that can be attributed to them.

We have used existing labels as much as possible and have not distinguished between labels that refer to an outcome of a change process (rewards, outplacement, self-steering teams) and the process leading to it (team building, confrontation meetings). This can be a useful division, however, because the outcome can be related to a different color than the process that leads to it. On the other hand, thinking in terms of outcome and process and the differences between them is typical for (light) blue thinkers. Such a distinction makes little sense to white-print thinkers; for them the purpose resides in the process and the process constitutes the outcome.

8 The Change Agent

From Expertise to Authenticity

The change agent is possibly one of the most important factors in effecting change: his quality of presence and his competence probably make as great a difference (if not more) as any intervention plan. But what exactly is a change agent? What sorts of shapes and sizes do they come in? And what makes someone topnotch? In this chapter we address these questions.

Change agents receive special attention in the professional literature. Even at the beginning of the planned change tradition, it was recognized that these agents could come from both within and outside of an organization. Recently Van der Zee (1995), Kor (1993) and Gerrichhauzen (1994), among others, underscore that the change agent can be an internal manager or member of staff, or an external consultant. Zaltman and Duncan (1977) go so far as to say that, ideally, a team consists of people from both sides. Boonstra (1992) agrees with this statement. We doubt if it is necessary that both internal staff and external consultants should always be involved simultaneously in a change process, but we are in full agreement with the conclusions of Van der Zee and Kor that, in principle, the change agent can come from anywhere. This is also the reason why we deliberately did not include the term *change agent* when we distinguished a set of actors in the change processes in section 4.4, because each of the actors involved can assume that position. It is nobody's prerogative in particular.

8.1 Roles and Styles

The behavior that a change agent exhibits or should exhibit poses an interesting question. Various authors present generalized do's and don'ts for change agents, but it is more widely accepted that what constitutes effective behavior depends on the situation at hand. Lippit, Watson, and Westley (1958) and many others emphasize that a change agent should adopt a suitable "helping role." On the basis of this contingency idea, various roles can be envisaged. The terms *role* and *style* are often used interchangeably in the literature.

Let us first take a look at a few simple models with which some authors classify the different roles of change agents (Table 8.1). Each model incorporates an expert/teacher role whereby the change agent provides the necessary knowledge and solutions. Each model also includes a facilitating role aimed at improving communication between people and enhancing trust and safety. Zwart as well as Drukker and Verhaaren present another role that is more aimed at assisting personal growth. The remaining roles that are distinguished are the catalytic agent and the programmatic role.

Westra and Van de Vliert (1989) interviewed some fifty consultants on the values they associate with the "ideal" consulting style and the degree to which the importance of those values is in line with their own most usual style. Their findings suggest that there are at least four clearly distinctive ways change agents act. Moreover, individual change agents appear to adhere to the specific style(s) that match their dominant values. Style is thus not just a contingent choice, but a statement of values as well (see Figure 8.1):

♦   Values like independence and courage show a positive correlation with interventions that are aimed at personal or behavioral development. Westra and Van de Vliert conclude that process interventions like these apparently demand a lot of guts from the consultant.
♦   Values like control and consistency correlate positively with a consultant who suggests concrete (and often technical) solutions. The role of expert seems to fit consultants with a cautious character.
♦   Values such as competence and ambition show a positive correlation with consultants' structuring of the problem-solving process. This structuring is based on the consultants' own visions of the problems at hand. It is also embedded in their systematic characters.
♦   Values like love and forgiveness correlate positively with an altruistic approach. Consultants concentrate on furthering their clients' achievement and not on demonstrating their own competences: They appear to have unselfish natures.

Finally, we refer to Quinn's (1988) model, which postulates as many as eight roles and eight styles. All these roles and styles are distinguished from one another by the degree of control/flexibility on one hand and by the degree of internal/external or long-/short-term focus on the other hand. This model is reproduced in Figure 8.2.

The last two models above introduce a special element into the discussion regarding possible roles and styles of change agents. Westra and Van de Vliert relate the change

Author	Roles	Description
Zaltman and Duncan, (1977)	Expert	Whereby direct solutions are provided to the client system
	Catalytic agent	Whereby the change is outlined and stimulated
	Process consultant	Whereby the communication between those involved is facilitated
Zwart (1993)	Teacher	Based on an expertise model of change. The change agent establishes his authority by means of his (technical) vision and the knowledge that he transfers to those involved.
	Discussion partner	Based on an acceptance model of change. The change agent seeks to build up a relationship based on trust so that problems can be discussed openly. She looks for solutions and method for which there is sufficient (shop floor) support
	Therapist	Based on an action model of change. The change agent has the "courage" and the capability to create movement, break though stalemates and address any powerlessness of those involved
Drukker and Verhaaren, (1980)	Expert role	The consultant solves the problem. Those involved play a passive role; the relationship is technical; the focus is on the content of the change
	Programmatic role	The consultant structures the problem-solving process. The client is taught a "better" plan of approach; the relationship is that of teacher and pupil; the focus is on the problem solving approach
	Behavioral development role	The consultant focuses on the organization's culture. He inquires into behavioral patterns and brings these up for discussion. He also assists the development of social skills. The relationship is supportive and time-consuming
	Personal development role	The consultant does not meddle with topical problems, but concentrates on the values and norms of those involved. She focuses on introspection, self-acceptance and new perspectives. The relationship is personal

Table 8.1 Change Agent's Roles

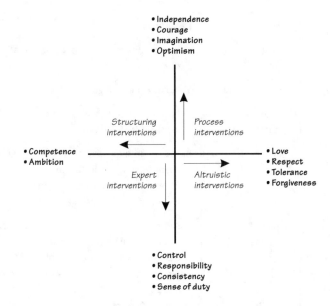

Figure 8.1 Styles and Values According to Westra and van de Vliert

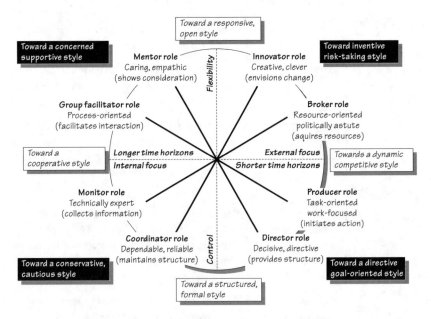

Figure 8.2 Competing Values Framework of Leadership Roles

agent's role to what she believes is "good" (her values). Quinn relates change agents' roles to the normative model they have their mind. Quinn places someone who favors the open systems model (see also section 7.14) in the "innovator" or "broker" role. In both cases, it is all about the change agent's implicit or explicit belief system: what she trusts to be "good" values and "good" strategies and, based on that, "good" roles for herself.

We firmly believe in such interconnectedness. In our own way we put forward a similar model, but based on color-print thinking. We suggest that there are close connections between a change agent's intention (often related to her values), her "color" strategy, and her role. We attempt to demonstrate this in Table 8.2 with a model consisting of five possible change agent roles. The aspects on which change agents tend to focus are also shown.

8.2 Competencies

What makes somebody a good change agent? What competencies should the change agent possess? Cummings and Worley list eighty-four competencies based on their review of the literature and studies in the world of organization development (OD) practitioners (Table 8.3). Quite an extensive list! They put the size of the list into perspective by saying that only about fifty of the competencies are regarded as being absolutely necessary for every "OD practitioner." The other thirty-five are just to give the experienced professionals that little bit extra. Another point they make that helps put things into perspective is that they consider that part-time change agents (employees or managers who do it "on the side") can take things a little more easily. Doppler and Lauterburg (1996) also come up with an impressive list: thirty-three competencies (Table 8.3). They, too, put things into perspective: Not everyone will (be able to) master everything perfectly, but if there are too many gaps somebody is bound to run into problems. They also share their belief that not all thirty-three competencies can be easily acquired. For example, personal characteristics (Part A) seem to them difficult to learn and the "special" skills (Part B) can be learned to only a certain degree. Not a reassuring message.

We agree with these authors that change agents need a lot of competencies if they are to be able to implement the full spectrum of (color) strategies. We do not deem this task impossible by definition, but it is certainly a tall order. When we consider ourselves, our colleagues, and our clients, we observe strong preferences and affinities in each of us for one or two of the color prints. On the one hand, this denotes what you believe in, what you like doing, and what you dare to do. On the other hand, it denotes what you are good at. We think that an important principle can be discerned behind this. It seems to us that it is a good idea for all professional change agents to be aware of the existence of the spectrum of (color) strategies available and the corresponding intentions, styles, interventions (and so on) of the change agent that would bring these to life. The main thought behind this is that they will then be more inclined and better able to recognize the limits of their own professional capabilities; to know when

	Yellow Print	*Blue Print*
Intention	I want to change the opinions and policies of actors/organizations. I help the most important players reach consensus.	I want to change one of the hard aspects of the organization (buildings, production lines, information systems)
Role/style	A facilitator who strives for feasible solutions, who guards his own power base and makes use of it when necessary (e.g., in mediation, arbitration)	An expert who strives for the best solution; who takes full responsibility for the implementation and monitoring progress (assuming he has been mandated to do so)
Focus	Focus on positions and context	Focus on expertise and results

Table 8.2 Intention, Role, and Focus of the Change Agent

it is necessary to refer elsewhere or to call in the help of others, and not try to maintain a pretense of perfection. It takes courage, of course, to admit to not knowing all the answers. On the bright side: It's only human. And in many cases, you serve as a good role model in change processes, in particular in green and white processes. It provides space for other people's imperfections and it often enhances trust and establishes rapport. Who would you rather see, someone straight from the classroom who knows all the answers or an older professional who has at least as many questions as answers? Aren't quick answers often a response to a need to reduce the uncertainty of both change agent and client? At the end of a roundtable discussion celebrating fifty years of consulting in the Netherlands, the Dutch "grand old men" of consultancy, Otto, Rubinstein, Ganzevoort, and Van Londen, came to the conclusion that "they were still confused but on a higher level" (de Caluwé and Vermaak, 1997). Obviously, this is not an obstacle to success.

Red Print	Green Print	White Print
I want to change a soft aspect of the organization (personnel composition, management style, HRM systems)	I want to change the people. I help people develop themselves, give each other feedback, and share lessons learned	I create space for change, I appeal to people's self-confidence and inner direction, and I "practice what I preach"
A procedure expert who strives for solutions that enjoy (shop floor) support, that elicit involvement, and that encourage motivation. If so requested, she can advocate particular solutions too	A facilitator who strives to help people solve their problems (together). He is an expert only as far as the communication and interaction between people is concerned. With regard to content he is, at most, a coach	A personality that strives for spontaneous evolution by catalyzing forces that create solutions and thwarting forces that block them. To this end she looks "under the surface" and uses any expertise or power she has
Focus on procedures and atmosphere	Focus on setting and communication	Focus on patterns and persons

One way of gaining awareness of the kind of change agent one is (or is able to be) is to compare the color prints with one's own vision on change (Chapter 3). Another way is to determine which of the interventions described in Chapter 7 are most familiar to you. A third way is to discern which style(s) in Table 8.2 would normally be your style of choice. A color test for change agents, based on such queries, is included in Appendix 2 to help you assess both your thoughts and your actions as a change agent. A fourth way is to consider which competencies you possess, because the sum of your vision, your interventions, and your style implies certain change agent competencies.

Any shortcomings you might have based on the lists in Table 8.3 need not be a problem. On the contrary, it can be quite a relief to meet change agents who acknowledge their shortcomings, who specialize in certain types of change processes and admit to being one sided in that sense. It is certainly no problem to make a good living if you restrict yourself to using only the one or two color prints you are good at. In Table 8.4 we attempt to outline specific competencies for each color print. The table is not

Core and Advanced Skills for the Future OD Practitioner (Cummings & Worley, 1993)	
General Consultation Skills ♦ Organizational diagnosis ♦ Designing and executing an intervention ♦ Process consultation ♦ Entry and contracting ♦ Interviewing ♦ Designing and managing large change processes – Management development – Assessment of individual competence **Intrapersonal Skills** ♦ Conceptual and analytical ability ♦ Integrity (educated moral judgment) ♦ Personal centering (staying in touch with one's own purpose and values) ♦ Active learning skills ♦ Rational-emotive balance ♦ Personal stress management skills (maintaining one's own health and security) – Entrepreneurial skills **Organization Behavior/Organization Development Knowledge and Intervention Skills** ♦ Group dynamics (team building) ♦ Organization development theory ♦ Organization design ♦ Communication ♦ Intergroup dynamics ♦ Open systems ♦ Reward systems ♦ Conflict ♦ Large system change theory ♦ Leadership ♦ Power ♦ Motivation ♦ Theories of learning ♦ Sociotechnical analysis ♦ Job design – Adult development/career and stress management – Personality theory (individual differences) – Trans-organization theory – Cross cultural theory **Interpersonal Skills** ♦ Listening ♦ Establishing trust and rapport ♦ Giving and receiving feedback ♦ Attitude in speaking the client's language ♦ Ability to model credible behaviors ♦ Counseling and coaching ♦ Negotiation skills – Language and nonverbal cross-cultural skills – Telephone intervention skills	– Communication theory-based skill, such as T.A., neurolinguistic programming, etc. – Suggestion skills (metaphors and hypnosis) **Research and Evaluation Knowledge and Skills/Research Design** ♦ Action research ♦ Diagnostic research ♦ Evaluation research – Theory building research – Case method research and writing methods **Data Collection** ♦ Research interviewing ♦ Participant-observation methods (from anthropology) ♦ Questionnaire design and use – Unobtrusive measures – Job measurement **Data Analysis** ♦ Elementary statistics – Computer skills – Advanced statistics **Presentation Skills** ♦ Training skills ♦ Public speaking and lecturing ♦ Political speaking and selling skills ♦ Writing proposal and reports ♦ Graphic and audio-visual skills **Experience as a Line Manager/Major Management Knowledge Areas** ♦ Human resources management ♦ Management policy and strategy – Information systems – Legal and social environment – Quantitative methods – Production (operations management) – Finance – Operation research – Economics – Marketing – International Business – Accounting **Collateral Knowledge Areas** ♦ Social psychology – Industrial psychology – Cultural anthropology – Policy analyses – Psychopathology and therapy – Systems engineering and analysis – Manufacturing research and development

NOTE: ♦ = needed skills; – = desired skills

Table 8.3 Competencies for the Change Agent

Competencies for Change Agents (Doppler & Lautenburg, 1996)

A. Personal Characteristics
1. Good physical condition (self-confidence, stability, stress resistant)
2. Positive demeanor (optimistic, constructive attitude)
3. Openness and honesty (direct, spontaneous, authentic)
4. Willingness to accept responsibility (personal engagement)
5. Focus on cooperation (as opposed to elite, hierarchic, authoritarian)
6. Courage to "take a stand" and make independent decisions
7. Fulfillment of responsibilities (agreements)
8. Intuition (access to emotions)
9. Sense of reality (feeling what is feasible)
10. Sense of humor (creating moments of relaxation)

B. Special Skills
1. Ability to create a climate of openness and trust
2. Good listener ("active listening")
3. Ability to convince and enthuse people (creating motivation and ownership)
4. Ability to integrate (putting teams together and having these teams pull together)
5. Handling conflicts (daring to take a stand and not avoid confrontation)
6. Process competency (ability to understand and steer developments)
7. Chaos competency (ability to function in complex situations)
8. Strategic competency (ability to discern complex patterns and decide on appropriate measures)
9. Intercultural competency (ability to work in diverse social structures)
10. Clear self-expression (clarity of thought, to the point, simple and lucid argumentations)

C. Specific Experiences
1. Self-awareness, self-reflection (consistent and intensive self-enquiry of personality, motives, and social behavior)
2. Individual consultancy (rendering expertise, support, and coaching)
3. Team work and team development (leading and developing small groups)
4. Communication facilitation for large groups (organizing and leading work conferences)
5. Project management (organizing and leading change projects)

D. Specific Knowledge
1. Basic psychology
2. Basic business economics
3. System theory/chaos theory
4. Group dynamics
5. Organization theory
6. Organization psychology
7. Organization development design (concepts/strategies)
8. Organization development interventions (tools/methods/processes)

	Yellow Print	Blue Print
Knowledge	− Strategy and policy theories − (Top) structuring − External trends and networks	− Expertise in regard to the content of the change − Project management
Skills	− Network identification − Feeling for power structures and balance − Conflict mediation and influencing tactics − Strategic interventions	− Planning and control − Analytical thinking/ research methods − Verbal and written presentation
Attitude	− Independence − Stability − Self-control − Self-confidence − Perseverance − Flexibility − Diplomacy	− Result oriented − Decisiveness − Independence − Intelligence − Accuracy − Dedication

Table 8.4 Competencies of the Change Agent by Color

exhaustive but is meant to provide an image of what matters most for each color and how different that can be.

8.3 Professional Career

The "grand old men" of consulting whom we mentioned earlier emphasize the fact that change agents should have an affinity with both the "soft" sciences and the "hard" sciences. They should understand a little about people, about interaction, about cultures, about social trends, and about themselves (the arts), but also be somewhat versed in analytical thinking, financial management, research methods, planning methods, and so on (the sciences). Few people are well versed in both fronts right from the start. Unfortunately, it is rare for people to move from the soft to the hard sciences in contrast to the other way around, according to the grand old men. Van Londen told how his firm used to be concentrated on the "hard" aspects of the profession and attempted to compensate for this by bringing social and behavioral scientists into the firm. Few of these psychologists and sociologists went down well with the clients, in particular in boardrooms. The main reason was that their knowledge of business and management processes was too limited. As very few of them felt like learning about these

Red Print	Green Print	White Print
– Management science, specifically HRM-methods – Motivation theories	– Learning theories/didactic theories – Organization-development thinking	– Chaos theory/systems theory – Psychology
– (HRM) systems design – Communication planning – Working in teams – Facilitating discussions/interview skills – Convincing, motivating	– Designing and facilitating learning situations – Creating a safe and open environment – Coaching/listening/giving feedback – Acting as a role model	– Pattern recognition and creation of (new) meaning – Challenging the status quo – Dealing with conflicts and creating dialogue – Dealing with insecurity/uncertainty
– Carefulness – Flexibility – Trustworthiness – Decisiveness – Loyal – Steadfast	– Empathy – Trustworthiness – Creativity – Openness – Flexibility – Self confidence – Inspirational	– Independence – Authenticity – Self-assured – Honesty – Flexibility – Self-confidence – Spiritual

matters—"Bookkeeping is a dirty word"—this problem turned out to be persistent. The other way around had more success. Van Londen and Otto shared that this also corresponds with their personal career paths; Ganzevoort and Rubinstein affirm:

> Beginning consultants with a background in the hard sciences gain a certain security from the orderly certainty of a Cartesian view of the world, where everything can be expressed in numbers and symbols. As the years pass, they often develop an interest in their own emotions and in the soft sciences. (de Caluwé and Vermaak, 1997)

The development from hard to soft sciences coincides naturally, as it were, with the stages many people go through in their life history.

Wolfe (1980) outlines five learning phases in the development of what he calls the "creative change agent":

♦ Conceptual grounding. In this phase, change agents familiarize themselves with basic models and theories. By doing so, they attempt to gain insights into concrete situations and also into themselves.

◆   Learning the craft. In this phase, change agents master a number of basic skills. Theory is no longer enough. Skills are acquired: for example, diagnostic, research, and intervention skills.

◆   Practice in the field. Change agents learn by "doing." They get their feet wet and gain experience. Thus an important step is taken toward building up an individual professional identity.

◆   Consolidating and integrating competencies. Now, change agents step back to reflect on their own experiences. What have they achieved so far? What are their weak points? Feedback from others is essential here.

◆   Creativity. Here, change agents develop their own concepts about change and their own methods. These help to make their professional identity explicit and to develop it further.

Lynn (1986) distinguishes four stages in the development of organization developers/ consultants:

◆   The beginner. At this stage, the change agent struggles with self-acceptance and credibility. He undergoes stress caused by the doubt he feels about his personal suitability for the work. The question, "Am I good enough?" lurks behind every interaction. Initial success and support from friends leads new practitioners to the conclusion that they are up to the job. Self-imposed perfectionist expectations fade away and a sense of confidence emerges.

◆   The technologist. At this stage, the change agent struggles with issues of influence and power with clients and other professionals. She seeks opportunities to make her "mark" in the profession. She is interested in learning specific techniques that give her greater control over the outcomes of the change. Through trial and error, she learns how to avoid rescuing clients and how to avoid taking over the client's job. At the end of this stage, she feels more grounded in her authority and power and, just as important, she has mastered a whole range of methods and techniques.

◆   The professional. At this stage, the change agent struggles with the dimension of independence versus entrapment. He relies increasingly on his creativity and intuition in helping clients craft change strategies. He is able to communicate openly and directly about his ideas and feelings. He is highly skilled in the negotiation of contracts where responsibility for the outcome is shared equally with the clients. He has worked through difficult personal and professional experiences, and has worked through dependent or counterdependent ways of relating to clients. He has greater mastery over interpersonal relationships by having learned not to be dominated by these relationships but to retain his independence and freedom of expression. He achieves increasing personal success.

◆   The master practitioner. At this stage, the change agent has the feeling that her autonomy and success do not give her sufficient satisfaction. She explores the possibility of interconnectedness with others as something that might outweigh pure personal freedom. She finds that being the "impartial observer" no longer works for her. This is a period of personal and spiritual development in which she searches for processes with which she can serve others. She comes up less with standard recipes for change and is much less after personal success. She prefers to listen to clients from a place of full acceptance and to understand their dilemma as completely as possible, upon which she naturally moves with the client to the next step in the consultation. She addresses the heart of the matter. In a way her presence is her main intervention.

These stages of development can be regarded as related to specific styles and strategies, as is expressed in color print thinking. There appears to be a "natural" sequence in colors. At the start of their careers, a blue-print approach will prove to be a useful starting experience for many change agents. A red-print approach can also be a good start. Green-print and yellow-print approaches demand more of the interpersonal skills of professionals. They must be able to build up good interpersonal relationships, win confidence, dare to express themselves freely, and intervene in tricky situations. A white-print approach seems to be something for experienced change agents who have had sufficient time for their personal development to enable them to accept themselves fully. Out of genuine caring they might put themselves wholly in the service of the client. Authenticity is the key word here.

8.4 Reflective Practitioner

How do change agents develop along the path from beginner to master practitioner? How do they learn? We see learning as a wondrous process that more often than not eludes our control. It is a process full of surprises and riddled with ups and downs as we, as many others, have experienced and are still experiencing firsthand. We could in no way have predicted or planned our professional development, neither the lessons learned nor the way in which they were handed to us. Much has been written about learning processes, and we are able to devote only limited attention to it here. We use Kolb's (1991) well-known learning cycle as a stepping-stone for exploring the art of professionalization, as we regard it as a good tool for the reflective practitioner.

Kolb introduced a theory about learning that puts great emphasis on learning by experience. He states that four phases must be experienced consecutively for learning to take place (Figure 8.3). The learning cycle begins with active experimentation based on the understanding a person has of his relationship with his environment. In this stage, the individual experiences problems or successes. He notices that some of his actions work and some don't. The next phase lets him reflect on these experiences. He attempts to understand his observations. His understanding crystallizes into concepts, ways of making sense of his observations. On this basis, new choices and decisions are made about how to proceed, and the cycle repeats itself. By continually repeating the cycle, worn-out behavior can be reevaluated and reformulated. Behavioral changes become possible and can lead to increased effectiveness of the person involved. According to Kolb, learning is an infinite and continually repeating process. It never stops. The learning cycle might apply to everyone, but each person still has her own

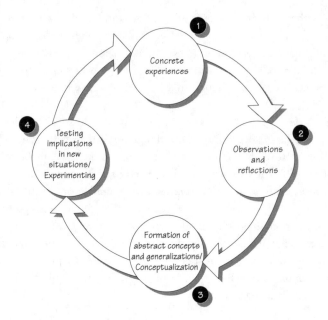

Figure 8.3 Kolb's Learning Cycle

particular style of learning. Kolb calls a person who is drawn to experiencing and reflecting a "dreamer"; if too much emphasis is placed on this at the expense of the other learning phases, you have someone who wallows in her feelings. When the accent is on reflecting and conceptualizing, the "thinker" comes into being. Too much emphasis on these aspects and we have someone in "an ivory tower." Placing the emphasis on conceptualization and experimentation produces the "decision maker"; the "reflex manager" is the result of too much emphasis here. Finally, we have the "action hero" or the "hands-on person," the result of much experimentation and experiencing. This can turn into a hit-and-run approach, an approach that can have a person making the same mistakes over and over again. Each learning style is legitimate and remains functional, but too much emphasis on any one phase breaks the learning cycle and so slows down learning.

With a certain amount of poetic license, other theories about learning and growing can be linked to this simple learning cycle. For each of the aspects of the learning cycle we have selected one theory that can possibly inspire change agents to intensify their learning. According to Shepard (1989), excellence in every phase of the learning cycle not only results in increased learning but also enriches one's life: alertness of all senses and organs, the discovery and creation of meaningful perspectives, autonomy to create a world worth living in, and lastly the establishment of expansive relationships. We examine this tempting perspective in the next four sections.

8.4.1 From Observing to Sensing

An important insight about "observing and reflecting" is that change agents can perceive their environment and themselves at multiple levels. Observing often implicitly refers to two of the senses in particular: what we see and what we hear. We might hear somebody say that the organization's culture is dysfunctional, but his body language can imply that he is neither very upset about this nor overly eager to initiate change. This we can see. You might notice from the corner of your eye that the parking lot of your client's firm is full or empty. This again we can see. However, other senses might also play a role. You might feel that you, for unknown reasons at that point, have a hard time trusting someone. You might be pleasantly surprised by sensing a good atmosphere in the office. Is there a feeling of insecurity in the air or do people get along well? The idea behind all this is that the alertness of our senses and organs allows us to collect many pieces of a jigsaw puzzle, each containing complementary information. Palmer (1990) emphasizes that if our senses are poorly developed, chances are the "message" that we are meant to receive will be brought to our attention ever more forcefully until we take notice. Put simply, a latent feeling of dissatisfaction can develop into an ulcer. Consequently, the challenge for the change agent is to hone her senses, to put up all her sensing antennas. The good news, according to Shepard (1989), is that this is, in itself, an extremely satisfying exercise: body and soul are alert. He calls the result the "tone" of the whole organism, thus broadening the meaning attached to "muscle tone."

There are many ways to distinguish the various levels of perception—our senses. Both modern psychology and mystical traditions furnish various maps that distinguish and explain the different levels; studies by Piaget, Werner, Loevinger, Arieti, Maslow, and Jacobson come to mind. Wilber (1980) bundles these findings in a division that recognizes three main levels. He uses these levels to describe the course of life of the human race and of individuals, from the cradle to the grave, as it were. He also explains that the levels do not exclude one another. In fact, each progressive level not only transcends the previous level, but includes it as well. In other words, with increasing consciousness, each person's sensory alertness expands (and vice versa):

♦   The first level is the level of the *subconscious*: the perceptions of the body, the senses, emotions, and sexuality. He states that these are the perceptions that most animals have in common with us and that are, in a sense, "pre-personal." This is also the level at which people will not be aware of problems or conflicts even though they might be faced with them because there is no sense of time, there is only the immediate experience of the here and now. This is the area of impulses and desires. In change processes your senses on this level can, for example, make you aware that people around you are tense, that people are pleased with how meetings go, that there is vitality in the organization, or that you are impatient and driven.

♦   The second level is the level of *self-consciousness:* the perception of the will, the logical mind, the ego, the creative spirit. Wilber indicates that it is here that personality plays a major role. A tangible difference between "me" and the rest of the world arises. Here, duality emerges clearly. This is the level at which people observe social interaction, where language is analyzed, where people have intentions, and where these intentions are gauged. What would your senses show on this level? For example, in change processes people can be seen to miss each other's point, flawed arguments can be spotted, fantastic ideas noticed, ambitions charted.

♦   The third level is the level of *super-consciousness*: intuition, sudden transparency or clairvoyance, the experience of interconnectedness and spirituality. Wilbur states that this level should be regarded as being "transpersonal": duality makes room for experiencing unity and cohesion. This is the level at which people can experience timelessness and altruism. Your senses on this level might tell you in change processes that even though you hear what people are saying, somehow a piece of the puzzle is missing: "It just doesn't add up." You might sense that the chemistry between certain people is not right, or that you meet someone whom you know right away to be of the same mind. Or you might be surprised by finding out you knew ahead of time what was going to take place.

8.4.2 From Conceptualization to Sense-Making

The second aspect of Kolb's learning cycle is conceptualization. Kolb's cycle is often considered useful when routine problems must be solved in a familiar environment. In such cases people attempt to improve their way of handling the situation within a well-known framework. In the professional literature the term *first-order learning* has been coined for this: learning by doing. Characteristic of first-order learning is that the underlying insights (theories, assumptions, reasoning) come up for discussion only rarely or not at all. The behavioral changes are all about doing the same thing better (not doing something altogether different!). Here, the question "how" is important; "why" questions are hardly touched upon. In *second-order learning*, "why" questions are dealt with in particular. The term *second-order learning* was introduced by Argyris and Schön (1978) and it means: examining the way in which one learns, questioning the methods one uses to solve problems, deliberately crafting one's own learning processes and thus also daring to recognize one's own capacities and incapacities. It will be obvious that both first- and second-order learning have their merits, but not equally for all cases. As one defines problems differently, the effects are different as well. Feltmann's (1984) three-dimensional intervention model provides us with a practical way of distinguishing among three ways of making sense of our perceptions and experiences:

♦   *Monoparadigmatic.* Here, change agents organize their own observations within the framework the client has. If no such framework is discernable, they use the one to which they themselves are most accustomed. Their focus is that of a "first-order" approach: finding a solution to a problem without questioning whether the problem stated is the *real* problem. "How" is the primary question that is raised. This approach is suitable for uncomplicated or relatively unimportant problems or for problems for which the solutions have been tried and tested.

♦   *Multiparadigmatic*. Here, change agents seek other, new frameworks to help them organize their observations. Usually, the help of another person is helpful in accomplishing this. It can be classified as a simple form of "second-order" learning: The change agent looks for new ways of examining the problem, but not for new ways of examining himself or his own learning process. This approach works well for issues that keep on resurfacing because people have so far not been able to find adequate solutions. These are problems that new perspectives can shed new light on, but that do not find their cause in the person(ality) of the change agent himself.

♦   *Metaparadigmatic*. Here, change agents observe the patterns and fixations in their own learning processes that impede their detecting new perspectives and corresponding new solutions. This is pure second-order learning: the change agent is learning how to learn, thus fueling her own personal development. This approach is very suitable for change agents acting in situations in which, in essence, their personal presence is their intervention tool and where "knowing thyself" and the learning ability of the change agent are of overriding importance. This is also the favored approach of change agents who like to use, or abuse if you will, their profession to further their own personal growth.

Feltman emphasizes that the first, mono-paradigmatic, approach is overly relied on, while the meta-paradigmatic approach is often ignored even though in his view, it is the most effective. We agree with this view. Possibly one of the worst pitfalls for change agents is labeling their observations too quickly. This can happen almost by reflex. You might walk into a room and within minutes find yourself concluding that your discussion partner is not fit for his job, or the organization's problems originate in its dysfunctional management team. In peer review/intervision meetings it is always striking just how difficult it is for the participants to persevere in collecting observations and testing different perspectives. The reflex is to draw conclusions and suggest solutions right from the start: "Why don't you fix it this way?" We suspect that the reason for this is found in the discomfort that often accompanies uncertainty, when we allow confusion to linger for a while, not yet knowing what's going on, seeing multiple realities simultaneously. Ambiguity can be hard to live with even though, in our opinion, recognizing ambiguity is a sign that you are coming to grips with reality. For consultants this pitfall is possibly more present than for other change agents, because clients often seem to desire answers, making many consultants feel incompetent if they cannot supply these quickly. In reality the opposite appears true to us. Any consultant who arrives at an organization and thinks that he has instantly discovered the solution to a problem that the client has been struggling with for ten years displays disdain for the client rather than showing his own competence to that client. In short, the search for a meaningful interpretation, the quest for making sense, is an essential skill. A conflict can cease to be a problem by reframing its significance: "Conflicts are a means to make differences of opinion productive" or "No movement without friction." Human Resource Management can gain stature in an organization by deconstructing beliefs like, "The customer is always right," and "It's only the result that counts." Professionals can contribute to the organization once more if "autonomy" is interpreted as functional when in step with "accountability." Stress can be more easily managed when employees challenge convictions like, "Your colleagues are your friends" and "Your boss has to approve of your actions," or create new distinctions like "Working fast doesn't mean rushing things." These are a few examples from everyday practice. They are not meant to show the best concepts or prescriptions, because many other new frameworks are just as possible, some of which are likely to bring more meaningful perspectives to light. Shepard (1989) considers that this second step in the learning cycle can be once again a reward in itself. He thinks that the search for and the creation of meaningful perspectives will help us to understand the world we live in and to appreciate our place in it.

8.4.3 From Experimentation to Commitment

The third part of the learning cycle is experimentation. In this part we allow ourselves the greatest amount of poetic license. Experimentation is in effect a mini learning cycle in itself: you are busy doing something, reflecting, forming concepts, and so on. We often see variations of the learning cycle, in schools for example, where the word *experimentation* has been replaced with the words *planning* or *intentions*. We think these words are quite relevant. There is a world of difference between thinking and doing, and this gap calls out to be bridged. The change agent retains a host of meanings from the previous conceptualizing phase. There is also a whole world of actions waiting for him in the fourth part of the learning cycle. In between is a time for making decisions: Which choices will we make? What are our priorities? What do we want to achieve in the light of how we made sense of our problems? And is the outcome really worth the effort? Fritz (1990) uses the theory of "structural tension" for this step (see also section 2.3.3.). He argues that there are roughly two ways that people bridge the gap from thinking to doing. One way is productive, the other counterproductive. We will examine both.

The productive way equals the creation of structural tension.
This is done on the one hand by assessing the desired state. What do the actors involved - be they the change agent, the management team, or whoever- really want to achieve? Conrad Busken Huet once wrote, "Passion is the first requirement, passion

the second, passion the third." In other words, the desired state needs to be not something that is artificially constructed but rather something that evokes enthusiasm: it is a desire that is uncovered. Such a desire needs to fit someone's values and norms. This demands gauging whether the desire is grounded in what somebody values in life. If not, the desire requires some fine-tuning. A passion is generally able to evoke images. Nothing as abstract and sterile as, "We want more time." Antoine de Saint-Exupéry wrote, "When you want a ship built, you do not assemble a group of people to collect wood, to draw designs and to allocate tasks but you inspire them to long for the open seas." There are excellent examples of such visions or desired states. Disney, for instance, aims to give "each customer an experience of happiness." And a good friend of ours in the world of theater aspires to be a "singing and dancing manager."

The second element of structural tension is taking a frank look at the current reality, knowing exactly the actual state of affairs. This is not always easy, as it requires not only seeing that the glass is half full but also that it is half empty. It asks you to face what you are not capable of, and that life is, perhaps, not as you had hoped.

The tension between these two elements is structural: If there is a real desire it does not just disappear, and if one is honest enough, one will see clearly how it differs from the current reality. According to Fritz, this difference is the driving force behind the creation of something new, something that fires you up and keeps you going, that makes overcoming all kinds of obstacles worthwhile. It bridges the gap between thinking and acting effectively and thus brings advancement.

The counterproductive way is one of oscillation.
In popular speech this is also called the fight or flight syndrome. It refers to reactive behavior when a vision of the outcome is in fact based more on what you want to get rid of than what you desire. If a client is busy with his fifth reorganization in ten years, you can bet your bottom dollar that people are involved in a "flight" exercise. There are things going on or developing that the client would rather not face and that make him opt repeatedly for stopgap measures. Relief is preferred over creation, solving emotional tension is deemed more important than resolving structural tension. A good example of this dynamic, on an individual level, is dieting. If the intention is to lose weight, the motivation gets weaker with each pound of fat that melts away. As a result, the individual quits his meager meals as soon as an acceptable weight has been reached and gives in to his appetite, even bingeing at times. When sufficient pounds have returned, the motivation to diet and work out comes back. This is oscillating behavior and contrasts with someone whose eating habits are not based on losing weight but geared toward staying healthy.

Reactiveness sometimes assumes a subtle guise: Some intentions seem so logical and rational that nobody could have any objection to them—an organization that wants to expand, a consulting firm that wants to become international, a school that wants to adopt a more professional approach. It all sounds commendable. However, the question is whether these words and the ideas behind them have any real meaning for the people in the organization, whether they make anybody's heart jump. More than once, we have been confronted with visions or missions in organizations that, on closer investigation, turn out to be unknown to employees or deemed of little importance. The problem with these kinds of missions and visions is that few people are willing to consistently put their weight behind achieving them. The goals are sterile and barren. Goals based on reactiveness can be recognized by those involved having great difficulty in dealing with setbacks; the vision is not important and sustainable enough to create the will to succeed.

Fritz is of the opinion that the counterproductive way dominates, but that those involved can often cover it up with all sorts of mental constructs. We recognize this observation, both in our work and in our own lives. "No pain, no gain." This may sound a bit crude, but we don't believe change agents can grow professionally or personally (the gain) if they are not willing to acknowledge their own shortcomings and have the courage to risk making mistakes (the pain). Kierkegaard stated that "Life is lived looking forward but life is learned looking back." We believe that change agents who are unwilling to face their own inadequacies and idiosyncrasies are in trouble. It is part and parcel of the job to assume responsibility for setbacks or problems rather than to seek comfort in blaming others. This might mean facing angry colleagues, dealing with helpless clients, addressing dependency in teams, or facing one's own insecurity when presenting a keynote speech. The paradox is that if a change agent genuinely desires to realize a certain change, the road might be bumpy and confronting but does not need to be experienced as a burden. It resembles the story of the "heroes" who triumph in the face of adversity. There are worse roles to fill, for sure. For this, it doesn't matter whether the adversity is found in us or around us, as long as the change matters to us personally.

What kinds of goals or desires might change agents have when it comes to their own professional development? What sorts of adventures do they seek? These can relate to the kinds of roles they would like to play as change agents or to the kinds of issues they would like to be involved in. Consciously or unconsciously, these intentions crystallize into professional activities, learning activities, and network activities. Help in uncovering one's goals can be found in looking at the roles and competencies of different types of change agents (Tables 8.2 and 8.3.). Table 8.5 can assist in selecting different activities for organizing one's learning. There are deliberately no organization-wide activities like quality control included in this table because these usually lie outside the change agent's direct sphere of influence. Generally speaking, we think that it is extremely helpful to include activities that facilitate receiving feedback from others about one's behavior. Paraphrasing Hersey and Blanchard (1988): only someone

Individual	One-to-One	Groups
– Learning by doing	– Personal networking	– Intercollegial visitation
– Self-tuition/Study	– Master/Apprentice	– Intervision
– Self assessment	relationship	– Clinics/Role play
– Learning assignment	– Internships	– Group assessment
– Product development	– Coaching/Supervision	– Learning assignment
– Publishing/Writing	– Feedback/Evaluation	– Product development
– Sabbatical	talks	– Publications
– External training	– Product development	– Game/Simulation
– Task enlargement	– Joint publications	– Internal training
– Task enrichment		– Work conferences
– Job rotation		– Knowledge centers
– Changing jobs		– Working in
		multidisciplinary teams

Table 8.5 Learning Activities

else can help you uncover where you are unaware of your incompetencies (your "blind spots"), and those are exactly the incompetencies that would allow you to do real damage.

The most important feature of a change agent's goals and intentions is that they must become clearer and less ambiguous over time. It is fine to put these goals and intentions on paper or even to include them in a learning contract with colleagues or superiors if you think this is helpful. However, it is not strictly necessary, for if the goals are vivid and heartfelt, they will not fade away. The activities might change along the way but learning remains somewhat of an adventure anyway. Mistakes will be made, too, but the lessons learned from them can assist the change agent to realize his vision. After all, it is not that hard to remain focused when it regards something you enjoy. Shepard (1989) considers the resulting autonomy of this third phase in the learning cycle its own reward: You will gain the skills and the opportunities to create a life you love.

8.4.4 From Experiencing to (Non) Action

The fourth part of the cycle is "experiencing." We explore it here as "doing" or "acting," the missing link between the preceding step of planning and committing and the subsequent step of observing and reflecting. Acting is important because neither plans nor observations bring a reality into being. Even when a blue-print process is involved, things never turn out exactly as planned. The implementation process is never an irrelevant detail that warrants little attention. Each change process is unique, neither completely predictable nor completely controllable. A "promise on paper" does not create change without "the presence in person" of change agents. In the professional literature, there are roughly two approaches to this phase, and these complement each other nicely as far as we are concerned. They can be characterized by the distinction between "action" and "non-action."

♦   *Action.* Frost (1992) wrote that the best way to solve a problem is by addressing it straight on. This is the decisive or forceful approach, daring to take action, daring to intervene. It adheres to the philosophy that you shouldn't over-analyze situations: "If you are never going to get the answers, all you can do is experiment." It is about taking risks and learning as you go. The Long March began with the first step, as Mao is quoted to have said. This can be seen as true of each professionalization process and each task facing change agents.

♦   *Non-action.* Organization developers in particular often write about easing off when the situation calls for it, about not suggesting a solution immediately but feeling confident that the answers will come, all in good time. This has also to do with not taking responsibility away from the client and not marching in too far ahead of the troops only to find out later that nobody cared to follow. It can be important to set limits for one's self. There is no worse role model than an over-worked and stressed change agent. The real art, in this approach, is trusting others to gain and claim psychological ownership for the change, too, and to become "intrapreneurs." Chaos theory refers to the search for "free order" that can occur in situations full of chaos, a self-organizing ability that exists within any organization but is often not tapped or is even distrusted. Looking at it from a more philosophical stance this approach can be associated with the Taoist *wu-wei* principle, the art of "non-action." This is not to be confused with not taking action. Non-action does not mean sitting back and doing nothing. The *wu-wei* principle means that the actions of an individual should not be driven primarily by his personality but, to use Wilbur's terms, by a desire to serve. It implies that it is not so much the individual change agent who decides to act and claims the result of his work. Rather it is the situation that decides what actions are called for, and the change agent merely discerns this by his intuition and a willingness to be an instrument of service. Consequently the change agent does not feel he acted, but rather that he did not resist the role he was meant to play. It is a distinction that is not easily made. In Wilbur's terms, it requires tapping super-conscious perception: seeing the interconnectedness of what's happening (see section 8.4.1.). This can express itself in the experience that "everything seems to be falling into place," or "you simply knew what you had to do and what not to do," and that "it took place automatically."

What change agents might experience as non-action will be perceived as action by most people around her. Put another way, non-action addresses the state of mind of the person who acts. Seen in this light, action and non-action are not opposites. The decisiveness of action and the faith of non-action are two complementary aspects that the change agent can gradually acquire in her professional life. Both require rapport: with herself, with her environment and, sometimes, with her spirituality. For Shepard, this rapport or resonance is the reason why the fourth part of the learning cycle is in itself a useful exercise: creating connections and relationships that are stimulating, empathetic, responsive, and expansive.

8.5 Trends

We began this book by talking about "change" and have now, at the end, reached "learning." This route, in line with the book's title, refers to the hope that the book will assist readers to learn about change.

We observe a number of trends that, in our opinion, seem to create a demand for books such as this one. Hartman (1985) discerned three trends in his study of the consultant's profession:

◆   *A shift from research assignments to action assignments.* He refers here to clients' requests to realize organizational changes instead of merely submitting reports, and the need for the change agent to assume an active role and share the responsibility for making change happen.

◆   *The unbridled growth of disciplines.* He refers here to the fact that many people have started to call themselves management consultants or change agents. These days, you can find accountants, marketing specialists, architects, software firms, and universities all carrying out work in the consultancy sector. Likewise in organizations, managers, HRM staff, product champions or "empowered" employees regard themselves as change agents.

◆   *Organization-specific vision.* He refers here to the need for change agents to use standardized procedures and solutions only as a starting point after which tailor-made solutions have to be crafted for specific organizations. Made-to-measure might be a fashionable point of departure, but it is no mere fad. The idea is that the increasing complexity that characterizes many changes allows for nothing less.

These trends broaden our reading public. If indeed change agents are less allowed to limit their activities to just a research phase, they remain involved much longer. Thus their involvement as change agents ceases to be of a brief, temporary nature. The second trend implies that change efforts should not be left up to any expertise or any expert elite but should include many people both in and outside the organization and from all kinds of disciplines. The growing cooperation between many disciplines thus increases the number of change agents. These agents must be aware of the limits of their own capabilities and the way in which these various disciplines can complement each other. The demand for tailor-made change processes also swells the ranks of change agents, for if standard measures are rejected, the design of a change process is left to those involved and not to handbook authors like us.

We consider these to be fortunate developments because not only do we find change management an interesting profession, but we also think that the world can become a better place if there are more people with a professional approach or effecting change, regardless of whether the people involved are interested in changes in their personal life, their work life, or the world at large. Given these developments, this book will definitely not be the final word on the subject.

9 Epilogue

A white rabbit is pulled out of a top hat. Because it is an extremely large rabbit, the trick takes many billions of years. All mortals are born at the very tips of the rabbit's fine hairs, where they are in a position to wonder at the impossibility of the trick. But as they grow older they work themselves ever deeper into the fur. And there they stay. They become so comfortable they never risk crawling back up the fragile hairs again. Only philosophers embark on this perilous expedition to the outermost reaches of language and existence. Some of them fall off, but others cling on desperately and yell at the people nestling deep in the snug softness, stuffing themselves with delicious food and drink.

"Ladies and gentlemen," they yell, "We are floating in space!"

But none of the people down there care.

"What a bunch of troublemakers!" they say. And they keep on chatting: "Would you pass the butter, please? How much have our stocks gone up today? What's the price of tomatoes? Have you heard that . . . is expecting again?"

— *Jostien Gaarder, 2001*

We found this quote, a fitting conclusion to this book, in Jostien Gaarder's novel *Sophie's World* (2001). While writing this book, and even after it was finished, we felt as if we were also part of an elaborate conjuring trick. Something emerges, but we're not completely sure how it happened and understand only parts of that process. On the same subject, we see bits and pieces, have our share of experiences, and discern some underlying patterns, but most of all we know that we don't know the big picture. How change works and how it does not work keeps surprising us, and perhaps it is that surprise in itself that allows us to learn.

We, too, feel as if we travel to some outer reaches of language and conceptual insight in our search for new ways to express, to chart, and to bring about an overview. The very process of writing this book has stimulated our thinking. Regularly, we find ourselves floating into space, wondering what to hold on to, and wondering if we will indeed fall.

A book like this is very much a product of its time; a year from now we would probably write a different book. Nevertheless, we hope that people will listen to what we have to say, and that our fate will not be that of Jostien Gaarder's philosophers, but rather that we succeed in stimulating others to explore the wonders of the "change universe" and to challenge the boundaries of their understanding.

There are still many elements and patterns that are not understood in the "universe of change." In fact, it is not a neat and orderly universe at all. Changes happen, both planned and unplanned. They follow each other, but also take place concurrently. They compete with one another, but also support each other. They happen at many levels at the same time, producing both desired and undesirable results. Changes fail because of resistance, but resistance can also initiate change. Resistance can be a type of energy, grumbling can be an expression of vitality, and pocket vetoes can be a means of self-protection and survival. In the end, it is these dialectic tensions and complexities that can inspire us to keep wondering and wandering.

A number of areas of tension, dilemmas and paradoxes connected with change, are mentioned in this book. However, the vast majority are probably missing partly because they have not yet been discovered.

The human being is the crucial element in the universe of change and as yet we have limited knowledge and understanding of that subject.

We have also been "victims" of change processes and have personal experience of what this can lead to. We ourselves have experienced growing resistance and stress; we have dug our heels in, used pocket vetoes, and filled many a garbage can with meaningless decisions. We are as human as anyone else. Perhaps one of the most intriguing mysteries is how people can escape the victim role (the person to whom change happens) and to become the change agents instead, regardless of whether they choose to swim with or against the current. How exactly does that happen?

It is especially our experiences as "victims" that help us to understand why some approaches have a better chance of working than others, and to realize how different these approaches can be, depending on the situation and the people involved.

"When I was still happy and undocumented . . ." is definitely in the past.

Appendix 1
Five Color Glossaries

In this appendix, we present five concise glossaries, one for each color. This is yet another way of distinguishing the ideas and convictions of each of the colors and gaining a better understanding of the various schools of thought.

These glossaries are by no means complete, nor do they need to be. Much work can still be done to map the language used in each paradigm of change. Here they merely provide illustrations of the book's concepts.

We include three categories in each glossary:

1. Typical words: These are words often used by followers of that specific school of thought and will help you to recognize them as such.

2. Catch phrases: These capture favorite approaches or ways of tackling a problem. If you ask, "What should I do?" they might well reply with one or more of these catch phrases.

3. Typical idioms: These are pithy one-liners that express a concept, a dilemma, or a phenomenon originating in common everyday language but also appropriated by the relevant school of thought. They can be seen as metaphors that clarify the colors.

But take care. Even though we feel that the glossaries are fair representations of the relevant schools of thought, these distinctions are not ironclad. Sometimes the meaning of a word is not as it appears at first glance. Words from one school of thought can sometimes be appropriated by others: they undergo subtle changes of meaning and as a result can suddenly support a contrasting view on change. Also, language is sometimes used as "camouflage." For instance, bad news brought by the top (often blue or yellow) can be wrapped in attractive and people-friendly language (often red) to make it more palatable in the hope of raising less resistance.

Yellow-Print Thinking
Typical Words

Agreement	Diplomacy	Policy	Scapegoat
Agenda (Hidden)	Enforce	Politician	Sponsor
Arena	Grass roots	Position	Stakeholder
Alliance	Intention	Power game	Statement
Coalition	Key players	Power base	Status
Code of conduct	Liability	Press release	Tactics
Committee	Loopholes	Pressure-cooker	Time pressure
Compromise	Loss of face	Protocol	Trust and distrust
Conclave	Mandate	Public forum	Win-lose
Connections	Maneuver	Rank and file	Win-win
Consensus	Media	Resign/withdraw	
Convergence	Negotiations	from	
Democracy	Opposition	Responsibility	
De-politicize	Party (Third . . .)	Rules of the game	

Typical Catch Phrases

Maintain confidentiality
Emphasize interdependence
Taking circumstances into account
Agree to disagree
Create sufficient support
Develop a common vision
Search for feasible solutions
Get everyone to think along the same lines
Determine room for negotiating
Induce uncertainties
Start negotiations
Enforce accountability
Create win-win situations
Shelve something
Meet behind closed doors
Assigning blame
Conflict of interests

Typical Idioms

We are all created equal, but some are more equal than others
You scratch my back, I'll scratch yours

If two dogs fight for a bone, the third runs away with it
To pay lip service
To keep something under one's hat
To wear different hats
The buck stops here
You can't please everybody
He butters his bread on both sides
They are using me for target practice
The bigger they are, the harder they fall
Keep your powder dry
Let sleeping dogs lie
Don't show your hand
They are hand in glove
Walking a tightrope
It's not what is said, but who says it
There is strength in numbers
Walk softly, but carry a big stick
There is no such thing as a free ride
Keep your friends close, but keep your enemies closer
Don't fight the system
A bird in the hand is worth two in the bush

Blue-Print Thinking
Typical Words

Accountable	Data	Margins	Reports
Activity	Deadline	Measure	Requirements
Analysis	Decision document	Milestones	Research
Benchmark	Design	Monitoring	Resistance
Budget	Direction	Objectives	Resources
Capacity	Efficiency	Performance	Result
Checklist	Empirical evidence	Plan	Steps
Clarity	Framework	Portfolio	Systems
Concrete	Handbooks	Priorities	Testing
Consistent	Hierarchy	Progress	Transparent
Cost cutting	Indicator	Project	Turnaround
Control	ISO	Quality control	

Typical Catch Phrases

Delineation of responsibilities
Planning and control
Steer activities and people
Cause and effect
Think of the best solution
First define goals, then implement them
Get the best people in
Finish the job
Avoid conflicts
Look before you leap
Think before you act
A deal is a deal
Use proven methods
Good is good enough

Typical Idioms

Actions speak louder than words
It goes like clockwork
It is as right as rain
Mind over matter
No pain, no gain
The man at the helm

Don't put off till tomorrow what you can do today
Keep your eye on the ball
He is a man of his word
To call a spade a spade
A good foundation is half the work
To dot the *i*'s and cross the *t*'s
A man's word is his bond
Let's stick with the facts
First things first
The end justifies the means
There is a time and place for everything
The shortest distance between two points is a straight line
He works like a horse
Hard work never killed anybody

Red-Print Thinking
Typical Words

Assessment	Entice	Outplacement	Sabbatical
Atmosphere	Ethics	Pay for performance	Salary
Attractive	Fair	Perks	Sanction
Bonus	Fringe benefits	Pleasant	Settlement
Business lunch	Headhunter	Potential	Soapbox
Career	HRM	Procedures	Social
Careful	Incentive	Promotion	Status
Cohesion	Job profile	Prospects	Talent
Comfortable	Junior/medior/senior	Regulations	Train
Communication	Loyal	Resume	Working climate
Competence	Motivate	Reward	Working conditions

Typical Catch Phrases

Management by speech
Creating opportunities for people
Tapping talents
Helping each other out
Doing it as a team
Giving people a second chance
Balancing work and private life
Viewing a matter from both sides
Creating commitment to the organization's goals
Searching for an optimal between individuals and the organization
He is the right man in the right place
Putting people at ease
Managing expectations
Arriving at the right moment
We're one big family

Typical Idioms

It doesn't hurt to try
The grass is always greener on the other side of the fence
You need to look at both sides of the coin
Strew someone's path with roses
The glass is always half full
To walk the talk

To sugar the pill
He has his heart in the right place
It is a matter of give and take
Pessimists are right, optimists are successful
Spare the rod, spoil the child
You can't burn the candle at both ends
As you sow, so shall you reap
You should not bite the hand that feeds you
A healthy mind and a healthy body
A good neighbor is better than a distant friend
All work and no play makes Jack a dull boy
One good turn deserves another
Happy landlords mean happy tenants
Am I my brother's keeper?
It's like asking the fox to watch the henhouse
Do unto others as you would have them do unto you
It takes a whole village to raise a child
It's water under the bridge
One finger cannot lift a feather

Green-Print Thinking
Typical Words

Action learning	Double loop	Learning cycle	Respect
Active listening	learning	Learning goals	Role model
Attitude	Didactician	Learning situation	Secondhand
Blind spot	Empathy	Learning	learning
Conscious	Evaluation	organization	Second-order
Clinic	Experimenting	Mental model	learning
Coaching	Experience	Mirroring	Sharing
Concept	Facilitator	Openness	Skills
Corporate	Feedback loops	Organization	Safety
curriculum	Game	development	Skills
Corporate	Group learning	Ownership	Teaching
university	Group setting	Participation	Trainer
Debriefing	Internship	Pilot	Trial and error
Development	Knowledge	Point of view	Try-out
Dips	transfer	Reflection	Unlearn

Typical Catch Phrases

Making people conscious of their incompetence
Asking questions and finding out what works
Learning to learn
Creating a safe environment
Helping others and asking for help
Showing active participation and contribution
Seek translation of lessons learned to everyday work
Linking thinking and actions
Linking theory and practice
Following the learning cycle
Cooperating as a group
Learning from each other
Learning from your mistakes
Developing master-apprentice relationships
Planning organization-development activities
Providing food for thought
Learning on the job

Typical Idioms

Practice makes perfect
That falls on fertile soil

Once bitten, twice shy

The proof of the pudding is in the eating

To put one's cards on the table

He's an old hand at that game

You can't teach an old dog new tricks

Don't judge a man until you've walked a mile in his shoes

The mirror never lies

Don't judge a book by its cover

Help others to help themselves

If you give a hungry man a fish, he will eat for a day; teach him to fish and he will
   never go hungry again

The tree is known by its fruit

That's just growing pains

White-Print Thinking

Typical Words

Adaptive	Ecology	Network	Self-steering teams
Adding meaning	Empowerment	Obstacle	Sense-making
Authenticity	Energy	Open space	Sensing
Autonomy	Evolution	Perception	Space
Catalyze	Feed-forward	Personal growth	Spiritual
Charisma	Heroes	Perspective	Spontaneous
Chaos	Healing	Postmodern	Strength
Coincidence	Identity	Release	Symbol
Complexity	Imagination	Ritual	Transformation
Connectedness	Innovation	Self-confidence	Underlying patterns
Crisis	Movement	Self-determination	Unfold
Dynamics	Nature	Self-organization	Vicious circle

Typical Catch Phrases

Seeing conflicts as opportunities
The purpose resides in the process
Optimal conflict level
Living in the question
Creating your own reality
Accept one's history
Finding the right balance
Recognition of underlying patterns
Living with complexity
In the fullness of time

Typical Idioms

Whatever happens was meant to happen
Seize the day
Que sera, sera
Time will tell
It is only the tip of the iceberg
To be on the side of the angels
Birds of a feather flock together
What goes up must come down
What goes around, comes around
Looks can be deceiving
When life gives you lemons, make lemonade

It's the straw that broke the camel's back
It is always darkest before the dawn
It is a case of the tail wagging the dog
To rise like a phoenix from the ashes
To read between the lines
It's not the destination, but the journey that is most important
We are our own worst enemies
May the force be with you

Appendix 2
A Color Test for Change Agents

Introduction

This test is designed to give you some insight into the ways you are inclined to think about and act during change processes. It will highlight your relative preferences among the five change paradigms, each of which is represented by a different color. The test will also show the degree to which your thoughts and actions are consistent with one another.

The test can be useful for anybody; after all, at times we all try to bring change about in our lives. Whether you are a manager, a consultant, a secretary, a teacher, or a lawyer, we assume that you have more than once attempted to initiate or influence change and thus are a change agent of sorts.

On the following pages pairs of statements are listed that apply to changes within organizations. Please circle the statement in each pair that most reflects your view.

In a number of cases you will find that neither A nor B captures your view accurately. In these cases, choose the statement that most closely resembles your opinion.

Do not take too long to decide on your answers; trust your initial reaction and opt for the statement that makes sense to you at first glance.

Have fun!

Testing Your Thoughts

The first part of the color test is meant to characterize your vision and ideas on change. Read the following statements and choose the statement closest to your viewpoint. The focus here is on your convictions, what you think will work well, what you regard as being a desirable and realistic approach.

Circle your answers:

1. A. Change can be successful only when it is supported by the major players.
    B. Change can be successful only when you tap the energy and the strength of the people involved.

2. A. Things will change if you stimulate people the right way and entice them to come on board.
    B. Things will change if you take power, status, or influence into account and make use of them.

3. A. Organizations change as a result of people holding up mirrors for one another.
    B. Organizations change when you organize around people's energy and strength.

4. A. Things change when you offer those involved a brighter future and a (personally) attractive proposition.
    B. Things change when real dialogue takes place between people.

5. A. A change agent must ensure that the most important players adjust their positions in such a way that they do not counteract each other.
    B. A change agent must ensure that people listen to and learn from one another.

6. A. Organizations change when people develop themselves.
    B. Organizations change when people know what the organization wants to achieve.

7. A. It is important to allow people to link their thoughts and their actions.
    B. It is important to stimulate people and give them incentives.

8. A. You can change organizations only when you first analyze what the best solution is.
    B. You can change organizations only when you can get the most influential people in the organization to agree with a solution.

9. A. Organizations change when you invest in people.
    B. Change should not be dependent on the people who make it happen.

10. A. You should reduce complexity to a minimum during change processes.
    B. You should make full use of the dynamics and complexity of the situation during change processes.

11. A. Time constraints and deadlines are instrumental in pushing important decisions through.
    B. Creating space (by loosening up constricting norms and values or by breaking through entrenched positions) is instrumental in getting things moving.

12. A. For change to succeed, a good atmosphere and team spirit are important.
    B. To bring about change, it is important to form coalitions.

13. A. Change occurs only when a clear result or goal has been determined beforehand.
    B. Change occurs only when individuals put their heart and soul into it.

14. A. In an effective change process there must be scope for consultation and room for negotiations.
    B. For a change process to be effective, the end result must be clear-cut from the start.

15. A. A change agent needs first to create a safe learning environment by clarifying rules and acting as a role model.
    B. A change agent first needs to discern underlying patterns that drive the organization and explicitly make sense of them.

16. A. A change agent should be knowledgeable about the subject matter and ensure that all activities contribute to the intended result.
    B. A change agent should be empathic in order to help create an environment for people to communicate openly and effectively.

17. A. Something changes when you reward the people involved for their contributions to that change.
    B. Something changes when you help the people involved to explore and gain new insights.

18. A. Change requires space; people need to have room to breathe and to explore.
    B. Change needs to be embedded in the organization and its policies; people shouldn't be left hanging.

19. A. A change agent should offer the employees opportunities and perspectives.
    B. A change agent should monitor progress and adjust the planning based on previously determined criteria and standards.

20. A. For organizations to change, policies need to change first.
    B. For organizations to change, people need to change first.

21. A. In order to design interventions, the change agent has to discern the underlying causes behind current problems.
    B. The change agent should have expertise on the problems at hand and be able to handle them systematically.

22. A. The change agent should ensure that the change progresses steadily and controllably.
     B. The change agent should monitor and maintain the balance of power behind a change program.

23. A. Things change when you make it pleasant for people to go along with the change.
     B. Things change when they are framed differently and take on new meaning.

24. A. First and foremost, change agents need to be empathic.
     B. First and foremost, change agents need to exercise care.

25. A. Communication among all those concerned is an indispensable ingredient of a change process.
     B. A thorough analysis carried out beforehand is indispensable if a change is to succeed.

26. A. The change agent must be authentic no matter how confrontational this might seem to others.
     B. The change agent must show empathy to others.

27. A. If the change agent is forced to choose, he or she should give preference to changing a "hard" aspect within the organization, for example, its structure, systems, or strategy.
     B. If the change agent is forced to choose, he or she should give preference to changing a "soft" aspect within the organization, for example, management style, culture, or personnel.

28. A. It is important to offer people support and safety while they are creating and implementing solutions.
     B. It is important to limit the number of options before decision making takes place because agreements are otherwise hard to reach.

29. A. A change agent must ensure that people reach agreements.
     B. A change agent must motivate people.

30. A. A change agent must gain substantial insight into the context of the problem and the networks of people associated with it.
     B. A change agent must gain substantial insight into the underlying patterns that sustain the problem.

Scoring Your "Thinking"

Circle the letter you have chosen for each of the thirty statements

Number	Yellow	Blue	Red	Green	White
1	A				B
2	B		A		
3				A	B
4			A		B
5	A			B	
6		B		A	
7			B	A	
8	B	A			
9		B	A		
10		A			B
11	A				B
12	B		A		
13		A			B
14	A	B			
15				A	B
16		A		B	
17			A	B	
18			B		A
19		B	A		
20	A			B	
21		B			A
22	B	A			
23			A		B
24			B	A	
25		B		A	
26				B	A
27		A	B		
28	B			A	
29	A		B		
30	A				B

303TGIN1e-2

Total number of circled letters for each column	Yellow	Blue	Red	Green	White

Testing Your "Actions"

This second part of the Color Test is designed to characterize the way you act as a change agent.

Before completing this part of the test, think of three change processes in which you have played an important role. The test works best if your role and style in these processes are representative of your behavior during most change processes. Preferably, they should concern change processes that took place within the past two years. First, try to recall the circumstances of the three change processes, the aims of these processes, and your contributions to them.

Now turn your attention to the statements listed below. Base your choice of statement as much as possible on your actual behavior in the three change processes.

Circle your answers:

1. A. I was a role model for others.
    B. I ensured that new role models were given enough space.

2. A. I supported solutions that generated lively interactions.
    B. I supported the best solution.

3. A. I helped management agree with each other on solutions and assisted further implementation from the top down.
    B. I attempted to find and catalyze intrinsic drivers for change wherever I could find them in the organization.

4. A. I encouraged and supported people to make change happen in their own work arenas.
    B. I ensured that the previously formulated outcome was not amended by those carrying out the implementation.

5. A. I held a mirror up to people. I gave them feedback.
    B. I persuaded the staff to act in the right direction.

6. A. In the change process, I supported people in developing their talents.
    B. In the change process, I tried to spot and create new "heroes."

7. A. People remarked on my carefulness and meticulousness when dealing with others.
    B. People remarked on my systematic, planned way of working.

8. A. I ensured that none of the major parties involved suffered loss of face.
    B. I ensured that everyone's performance was rewarded or criticized based on the same procedure and criteria.

9. A. I opted for the best solution.
    B. I opted for the most feasible solution.

10. A. When facilitating groups, I used my position (of authority) when needed.
    B. When facilitating groups, I left the responsibility for the results with them.

11. A. I made clear agreements with all those concerned and made sure that I and everyone else stuck to them.
    B. I allowed people to reach agreement concerning the direction we were going without involving myself too much with the details.

12. A. I always ensured I had room to maneuver.
    B. I always ensured complete openness: Everyone involved knew the score.

13. A. I measured progress using predetermined criteria and norms.
    B. I helped people discuss progress with one another. I concentrated on the way they communicated while doing so.

14. A. During the change process, I helped people develop the competencies that we had identified as crucial.
    B. During the change process, I helped people become aware of the many aspects involved and their interrelationships.

15. A. I created situations that enabled people to work on their own learning goals.
    B. I ensured that there were training programs where specific groups could master predetermined competencies.

16. A. I managed conflicts in order to reach a consensus between the major players.
    B. I optimized conflicts to create dynamics and energy within the organization.

17. A. I strived for the best solution within the stated margins.
    B. I encouraged people to find their own solutions and to implement them.

18. A. I concentrated on neutralizing the forces that block new initiatives and emerging solutions.
    B. I concentrated on clearly defining the desired end result and planning its implementation.

19. A. I stimulated the exchange of ideas and experiences.
    B. I uncovered and shared more fundamental ways of looking at things.

20. A. I strived for open communication and showed empathy.
    B. I guarded my independent position and was self-controlled.

21. A. I attempted to create and retain support for a solution.
    B. I ensured that all activities were goal oriented.

22. A. I carefully recorded my goals and stuck to them.
     B. I constantly reflected on what was going on and based my actions on that from moment to moment.

23. A. I always acted diplomatically in keeping with the situation.
     B. I stuck my neck out and stood up for what I believed in.

24. A. I motivated people by rewarding good performance.
     B. I assisted learning by giving people feedback on their performance.

25. A. I held up a mirror to people.
     B. I stuck to agreements and ensured that others did so as well.

26. A. I acted as an arbiter in conflict situations.
     B. I coached people to improve their communication skills.

27. A. I made the change process manageable.
     B. I created room for change.

28. A. I encouraged people to change their standpoints when doing so would break deadlock situations.
     B. I attempted to create a good atmosphere and to motivate people.

29. A. I aimed at achieving a result that would hurt or compromise no one.
     B. I aimed at achieving the best possible result.

30. A. I aimed at creating a secure learning environment.
     B. I aimed at creating constructive conflicts and dialogues.

Scoring Your "Actions"

Circle the letter you have chosen for each of the thirty statements

Number	Yellow	Blue	Red	Green	White
1				A	B
2		B			A
3	A				B
4		B	A		
5			B	A	
6			A		B
7		B	A		
8	A		B		
9	B	A			
10	A			B	
11	B	A			
12	A		B		
13		A		B	
14			A		B
15			B	A	
16	A				B
17		A		B	
18		B			A
19				A	B
20	B			A	
21	A	B			
22			A		B
23	A				B
24			A	B	
25		B		A	
26	A			B	
27		A			B
28	A		B		
29		B	A		
30				A	B

Total number of circled letters for each column	Yellow	Blue	Red	Green	White

Your Test Result

Enter the "total" scores in the next table. Record the accumulated test scores for each of the colored "thoughts" below the black bar: This tells you how you tend to think about and evaluate specific change processes. The accumulated test scores for your colored "actions" can be recorded above the black bar. This tells you how you generally act in change processes.

An interpretation of the colors is given in Chapter 3 (which predominantly addresses how people think about change) and in Chapters 7 and 8 (which concentrate on how people act as change agents). The cartoons shown here represent stereotypes of the different types of change agents.

Five images of change agents

For further interpretation you can concentrate on two aspects.

How Multicolored Is Your Thinking?

The more experienced change agents are, the more inclined they probably are to develop their own visions on change and show their "true colors." Based on experience and reflection, they consciously choose an approach they feel comfortable with and believe in. This is reflected in their often having only one or two dominant colors. Inexperienced change agents also often have one or two colors dominant in their thinking, but these are generally less a product of conscious and informed choice. If your thinking score is not dominated by one or two colors, chances are you are neither a beginning nor a mature change agent. If you show such eclecticism in your thinking, the time might be ripe to discriminate more and to show your true colors.

Do Your Thoughts Fit Your Actions?

The greater the difference between your scores on "thinking" and "acting," the harder it would be for you to reconcile your thoughts and actions with one another. This can have a number of causes.

One possibility is that you are not quite able to act the way you would like to act. Perhaps you lack the necessary competencies. In this case, the difference in the scores can help you to draw up learning goals.

Conversely, you might already have the desired competencies but not yet be in a position to claim the role you desire. The difference in scores here can help you draw up career goals.

A third possibility is that your thoughts and actions seem to live separate lives. They are loosely coupled (see Chapter 2, section 2.1.2.). This might be the case when the outcome of the test is a complete surprise to you. Such "separate lives" can occur when you as a change agent do not reflect sufficiently on your own actions. As a result your thinking might represent somewhat of a fantasy world while your actions give a more realistic indication of what you actually believe in. For instance, white-print thinking is very popular at the moment. It is a socially acceptable way of thinking. At the same time, however, we have noticed that when organizations get serious about change, they rarely put their trust in this approach. They don't put their money where their mouth is. Such actions demonstrate more clearly than their words what they really believe in, which might be yellow-print thinking. If your thoughts and actions are loosely coupled, feedback from others can help you bring the two (back) in line with each other.

Aggregated Results

• Enter the scores from the scoring tables 'Thinking' and 'Acting' in the table below:
  The scores for 'Thinking' under the black bar and those for 'Acting' above it.
• Color the columns black, and put the score above the column

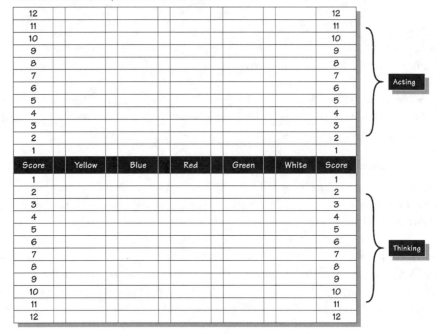

Score	Yellow	Blue	Red	Green	White	Score
12						12
11						11
10						10
9						9
8						8
7						7
6						6
5						5
4						4
3						3
2						2
1						1
Score	Yellow	Blue	Red	Green	White	Score
1						1
2						2
3						3
4						4
5						5
6						6
7						7
8						8
9						9
10						10
11						11
12						12

Acting

Thinking

Bibliography

Abell, D. F., and J. S. Hammond, *Strategic Market Planning: Problems and analytical approaches*. Englewood Cliffs, NJ: Prentice Hall (1979).

Ackerman, L. S., "Development, transition or transformation: The question of change in organizations." *OD Practioner* (1986) 4:1-8.

Aken, J. van, L. Hop, and G. Post, "De virtuele onderneming: Begripsafbakening en evaluatie." *Holland Management Review* (1997) 53:26-35.

Aken, J. E. van, "De virtuele organisatie en andere organisatienetwerken." *Bedrijfskundig Vakblad* (1998) 1:10-15.

Alberdingk Thijm J., and J. Jansen, "Strategieën voor succesvolle organisatieveranderingen", *Holland Management Review* (1996) 50:32-38.

Amelsfoort, P. van and G. Scholtes, *Zelfsturende teams: Ontwerpen, invoeren en begeleiden*. Oss: ST-groep (1994).

Andrews, K. R., "The concept of corporate strategy." In: H. Mintzberg, J. B. Quinn, *The strategy process: Concepts, contexts, cases*. 2nd edition, Englewood Cliffs: Prentice Hall (1991), pp. 44-52.

Ansoff, J., *Corporate strategy*. New York: Penguin Books (1987).

Argyris, Ch., *Intervention theory and method: A behavioral science view*. London: Addison-Wesley (1970).

Argyris, Ch., and D. A. Schön, *Organizational learning: A theory of action perspective*. Reading, MA: Addison-Wesley (1978).

Argyris, Ch., *Leren in en door organisaties*. Schiedam: Scriptum Management (1996).

Argyris, Ch., and D. A. Schön, *Organizational learning II: theory, method, and practice*. Reading, MA: Addison-Wesley (1996).

Bandura, A., *Social learning*. Englewood Cliffs, NJ: Prentice Hall (1977).

Bandura, A., "Self efficacy: Towards a unifying theory of behavior change." *Psychological Review* (1977) 84:191-215.

Bateson, G., *Steps to an ecology of mind*. New York: Ballantine (1972).

Bateson, G., *Het verbindend patroon*. Amsterdam: Bert Bakker (1984).

Bateson, G., *Mind and nature: A necessary unity*. London: Fontana Paperbacks (1985).

Beckhard, R., and R. Harris, *Organizational transitions*. 2nd edition, Reading, MA: Addison-Wesley (1987).

Beckhard, R., and W. Pritchard, *Changing the essence: The art of creating and leading fundamental change in organizations*. San Francisco: Jossey-Bass (1992).

Beer, M., *Organization change and development: a systems view*. Dallas: Scott, Foresman (1980).

Beer, M., "The critical path for change: Keys to success and failure in six companies." In: R. H. Kilmann and T. J. Covin (eds.), *Corporate transformation: Revitalizing organizations for a competitive world*. San Francisco: Jossey-Bass (1988).

Bekke, H., and P. Kuypers (eds.), *Afzien van macht*. Den Haag: SDU (1990).

Bekman, A., *Bewogen organisaties: Het klantproces als bron voor vernieuwing en vermaatschappelijking van organisaties*. Assen: Van Gorcum (1998).

Belbin, R. M., *Management teams. Why they succeed or fail*. London: Heinemann (1981).

Bennis, W. G., K. D. Benne, and R. Chin, *Strategieën voor verandering*. Deventer: Van Loghum Slaterus (1979).

Bennis, W. G., K. D. Benne, and R. Chin, *The planning of change*. New York: Holt, Rinehart and Winston (1985).

Bhagavad Gita: "The song of God." 14th edition, Hollywood, CA: Vedanta Press (1987).

Bicker Caarten, A., *Chaos en stress. Stressoren die op kunnen treden bij spontane organisatieveranderingsprocessen bekeken vanuit de chaostheorie*. Scriptie vakgroep Arbeids-en Organisatiepsychologie. Amsterdam: Universiteit van Amsterdam (1998).

Blake, R. R., and J. S. Mouton, *Consultation*. Reading, MA: Addison-Wesley (1976).

Blake, R. R., J. S. Mouton, and R. L. Allen, *Spectacular teamwork: How to develop the leadership skills for team success*. New York (1987).

Blake, R. R., J. S. Mouton, and R. L. Allen, *Teamwork: Het ontwikkelen van vaardigheden om succesvol in teams te werken*. Utrecht: Het Spectrum (1988).

Blanchard, K., and T. Waghorn, *Mission possible: Vandaag bouwen aan een organisatie van wereldklasse*. Schiedam: Scriptum (1997).

Blanchard, K., T. Waghorn, and J. Ballard, *Mission possible: Becoming a world-class organization while there's still time*. New York: McGraw-Hill (1997).

Blanken, G. J., *Het curriculum vitae*. Den Bosch: Projectteam Arbeidsmarkt Consultants (1994).

Blau, P., *The dynamics of bureaucracy*. Chicago: University of Chicago Press (1963).

Block, P., *Flawless consulting; A guide to getting your expertise used*. Johannesburg: Pfeiffer & Company (1981).

Bohm, D., *Wholeness and the implicate order*. London: Ark Paperbacks (1992).

Bohm, D., *Heelheid en de impliciete orde*. Rotterdam: Lemniscaat (1985).

Bomers, G. B. J., *De lerende organisatie*. Breukelen: Nijenrode (1989).

Bomers, G. B. J., "De lerende organisatie." *Harvard Holland Review* (1990) 22:21-31.

Bono, E. de, *Six thinking hats*. Harmondsworth: Penguin Books (1985).

Boons, A. A. M., H. J. E. Roberts, and F. A. Roozen, *Activity based costing*. Deventer: Kluwer (1991).

Boonstra, J. J., *Integrale organisatie-ontwikkeling: vormgeven aan fundamentele verandering-sprocessen in organisaties*. Utrecht: Lemma (1992)

Brug, J. van der, and K. Locher, *Ondernemen in de levensloop: een route naar inspiratie en vernieuwing in het werkleven*. Vrij Geestesleven, Zeist (1995)

Bruijn, J. A. de, E. F. ten Heuvelhof, and R. J. in 't Veld. *Procesmanagement. Over procesontwerp en besluitvorming*. Schoonhoven: Academic Service (1998).

Bruining, G. R. P. and J. T. Allegro, "Organisatie-ontwikkeling." In: P. J. D. Drenth e.a. (ed.), *Handboek Arbeids-en Organisatiepsychologie*. Deventer: Van Loghum Slaterus (1981) 4.9 bru 1-36.

Buijs, J. A., *Innovatie en interventie*, proefschrift. Deventer: Kluwer (1984).

Buijs, J. A., *Innovatie en interventie: Een empirisch onderzoek naar effectiviteit van een procesge-oriënteerde adviesmethodiek voor innovatieprocessen*. Deventer: Kluwer (1987).

Buijs, J. A., "Innovatie, een bijzonder verschijnsel." *M&O* (1988) 4:209-234.

Buijs, J. A., and R. Valkenburg, *Integrale produktontwikkeling*. Utrecht: Lemma (1996).

Bunker, B. and B. Alban: *Large group inventions: Engaging the whole system for rapid change.* San Francisco: Jossey-Bass (2000).

Busken Huet, C. "Quotation." In: A. Witteveen, *M.A.W.-Citaten voor managers*. Amsterdam: Management Press (1992), pp. 58, 146.

Caluwé, L. de, and M. Petri, *School en verandering: Gedachten over en ervaringen met veranderingen van scholen*. Van school naar middenschool, deel 4A (pgBERK katernen). Hoevelaken: Vereniging de Samenwerkende Landelijke Pedagogische Centra (1981).

Caluwé, L. de, *Koppelen en ontkoppelen: Een alternatieve zienswijze*. Handboek Schoolorganisatie, Alphen aan den Rijn: Samsom (1984), p. 1530-1/19.

Caluwé, L. de, and M. Petri, "*De school als vuilnisvatorganisatie."* Handboek Schoolorganisatie, Alphen aan den Rijn: Samsom (1985), p. 1520-1/13.

Caluwé, L. de, and B. E. M. Gielen, "De rol van de spelleider." In: P. van Wierst en J. Geurts: *Opleiders in organisaties* (1991) 7:93-101.

Caluwé, L. de, "Gaming: Ervaringen uit de praktijk." *Opleiding & ontwikkeling* (1992) 13:13-18.

Caluwé, L. de, J. Geurts, and A. Stoppelenburg, *Changing organisations with gaming/simulation*. Elsevier bedrijfsinformatie bv, 's-Gravenhage/Twynstra Gudde Amersfoort (2000).

Caluwé, L. de, *Veranderen moet je leren; Een evaluatiestudie naar de opzet en effecten van een grootscheepse cultuurinterventie met behulp van een spelsimulatie*. Den Haag: Delwel; Amersfoort: Twynstra Gudde (1997).

Caluwé, L. de, and H. Vermaak, "Nestoren kijken terug op het adviesvak: Een bijdrage leveren in gebrokenheid." M&O (1997) 1:56-64.

Caluwé, L. de, and J. Geurts. "The use and effectiveness of gaming/ simulation for strategic culture change." In: D. Saunders and J. Severn (eds.), *Simulation and games for strategy and policy planning*. London: Kogan Page (1999).

Caluwé, L. de, H. Vermaak, and J. van der Woude, *In search of corporate learning: The archipelago of learning,*" Amersfoort: Twynstra Group (1999).

Camp, P., and F. Erens, *Meer dan 500 managementstijlen*. Amsterdam: Contact (1994).

Camp, P., *De kracht van de matrix; Een model om veranderingsprocessen in beeld te brengen en doeltreffend aan te pakken.* Amsterdam: Contact (1996).

Capra, F., *Het levensweb.* Kosmos-Z&K, Utrecht: (1996)

Cohen, M. D., J. G. March, and J. P. Olsen, "A garbage can model of organizational choice." *Administrative Science Quarterly* (1972) 11:1-25.

Cornelis, A., *Logica van het gevoel.* Amsterdam: Essence (1995).

Cornelissen, V., *Hoe til ik mezelf aan mijn schoenveters op.* Doctoraalscriptie Katholieke Universiteit Brabant: Tilburg (1999).

Cozijnsen, A. J., and W. J. Vrakking, *Ontwerp en invoering; Strategieën voor organisatieverandering.* Alphen aan den Rijn: Samsom (1995).

Cummings, T. G., and C. G. Worley, *Organization development and change.* Minneapolis, MN: West (1993).

Delden, P. van, *Professionals: Kwaliteit van het beroep.* Amsterdam: Contact (1995).

Dillen, R. J. C., and A. G. L. Romme, "Leren door organisaties: Analyse van verleden en heden." *M&O* (1995) 3:160-182.

Doppler, K., and C. Lauterburg, *Change mangement; Vormgeven aan het veranderingsproces.* Amsterdam: Addison-Wesley (1996).

Drucker, P., *Managing for results.* London: Heinemann (1964).

Drukker, E., and F. Verhaaren, "Paradoxen in het organisatie-advies proces." *Tijdschrift voor Agologie* (1980) 3:361-379.

Duke, R. D., *Gaming, the future's language.* Beverley Hills, CA: Sage (1974).

Eijbergen, R. van, *De invoering en het effect van zelfsturende teams in organisaties,* Proefschrift, Leiden: Rijksuniversiteit van Leiden (1999).

Eisenhower, D. D., *The wisdom of Dwight D. Eisenhower: Quotations from Ike's speeches & writings, 1939-1969.* Selected by Stephan E. Ambrose, Eisenhower Center, New Orleans (1990).

Erikson, E. H., *The life cycle completed, a review.* New York/London: Norton (1982).

Evered, J. F., and J. E. Evered, S*hirt-sleeves management.* New York: Amacom (1989).

Feltmann, C. E., "Help! Een manager! Waar is de professional???" *TAC* (1993) 7/8: 16-23.

Feltmann, C. E., *Adviseren bij organiseren; een studie over interventiekunde ten behoeve van organisatie-ontwikkeling en maatschappij-geörienteerd organiseren.* Amsterdam: Perscombinatie (1984).

Ford, J. D., and L. W. Ford, "The role of conversations in producing intentional change in organizations." *Academy of Management Review* (1995) July:541-570.

French, W. L., C. H. Bell, and R. A. Zawacki, *Organization development: Theory, practice and research.* Homewood, IL: BPI-Irwin (1978).

French, W. L., and C. H. Bell, *Organizational development, behavioral science interventions for organization improvement.* 3rd edition, Englewood Cliffs, NJ: Prentice Hall (1984).

Fritz, R., *De weg naar de minste weerstand; Over de kunst van het creëren.* Deventer: Ankh-Hermes (1990).

Fritz, R., *Corporate tides.* San Francisco: Berret-Koehler (1996).

Frosch, R. A., and N. E. Gallopoulos, "Strategies for manufacturing." *Scientific American* (1989) p. 144.

Frost, R. In: *Quotation*. A. Witteveen, *M.A.W.—Citaten voor managers*, Amsterdam: Management Press (1992), pp. 51, 153.

Fruytier, B., and J. Paauwe, "Competentie-ontwikkeling in kennisintensieve organisaties." *M&O* (1996) 6:424-529.

Fry, R., I. Rubin, and M. Plovnik, "Dynamics of groups that execute of management policy." In: R. Payne and C. Cooper (eds.), *Group at work*, New York: John Wiley (1981), pp. 41-57.

Fullan, M., *The meaning of educational change*. New York: Teachers College Press (1982).

Gaarder, J., *Sophie's world*. London: Orion Books (2001).

Gerrichhauzen, J., A. Kampermann, and F. Kluytmans (eds.), *Interventies bij organisatieverandering*. Deventer: Kluwer Bedrijfsweten-schappen (1994).

Geschka, H., "Introduction and use of idea-generating methods." *Research Management* (1978) 3:25-28.

Geursen, G., *Virtuele tomaten en conceptuele pindakaas*. Deventer: Kluwer Bedrijfswetenschappen (1994).

Geurts, J., and J. Vennix, *Verkenningen in beleidsanalyse: Theorie en praktijk van modelbouw en simulatie*. Zeist: Kerckebosch (1989).

Geurts, J. L. A., *Omkijken naar de toekomst, lange termijn verkenningen in beleidsexercities*. Inaugurele rede KUB. Alphen aan den Rijn: Samsom (1993).

Geus, A. P. de, "Planning as learning." *Harvard Business Review* (1988) 2:70-74.

Giddens, A., *The constitution of society*. Berkeley: University of California Press (1984).

Gielen, E. W. M., *Transfer of training in a corporate setting*. Proefschrift. Enschede: Universiteit Twente (1995).

Goossens, W. M. J., "De lerende organisatie leert." *Doelmatige Bedrijfsvoering* (1992) 11:4-6.

Greiner, L., "Evolution and revolution as organizations grow." *Harvard Business Review* (1972) 4:37-46.

Greiner, L., and V. Schein, *Power and organization development: Mobilizing power to implement change*." Reading, MA: Addison-Wesley (1988).

Groote, G. P., C. J. Hugenholtz-Sasse, and P. Slikker, *Projecten leiden*. Utrecht: Het Spectrum/Marka (1995).

Hamel, G., and C. K. Prahalad. *Competing for the future*. Boston: Harvard Business School Press (1994).

Hammer, M., and J. Champy, *Reengineering the corporation: A manifesto for business revolution*. London: Nicholas Brealey (1993).

Handy, C., *Understanding voluntary organizations*. Harmondsworth: Penguin Books (1988).

Hanson, E. M., *Educational administration and organizational behavior*. Boston: Allyn and Bacon (1996).

Hartman, G. J. C., "Zich profileren als organisatie-adviseur." *M&O* (1985) 1:69-85.

Heijden, Th. J. van der, H. F. Reidinga, R. J. Schutte, and A. B. Volz, *Competentiemanagement: Het verzilveren van human talent*. Deventer: Kluwer Bedrijfswetenschappen (1999).

Henderson, B. D., *Henderson on corporate strategy*. Cambridge, MA: Abt (1979).

Heraclitus: "Quotation". In: L. D. Eigen, J. P. Siegel, *The manager's book of quotations*, Rockville, MD: American Management (1989), p. 29.

Hersey, P., and K. H. Blanchard, *Management of organizational behavior*. Englewood Cliffs, NJ: Prentice Hall (1988).

Hofstede, G., *Cultures and organizations: Software of the mind*. New York: McGraw-Hill (1997).

Hofstede, G., *Allemaal andersdenkenden*. Amsterdam: Contact (1998).

Homans, G. C., "Social behavior as exchange." *American Journal of Sociology* (1958) 62:597-606.

Hugenholtz-Sasse, C. J., "Risicoanalyse." In: G. P. Groote, P. Slikker, C. J. Hugenholtz-Sasse, *Projecten leiden*, Utrecht: Het Spectrum/Marka (1995), pp. 109-119.

Humble, J. W., *Management by objectives in action*. London: McGraw-Hill (1970).

Kanter, R. M., *The changing masters*. New York: Simon & Schuster (1983).

Kanter, R. M., *The change masters: Corporate entrepreneurs at work*. London: Routledge (1992).

Kanter, R. M., B. Stein, and T. D. Jick, *The challenge of organizational change: How companies experience it and leaders guide it*. New York: Free Press (1992).

Kaplan, R. S., and D. P. Norton, "*Translating strategy into action: The balanced scorecard*." Boston: Harvard Business School Press (1996).

Kapteyn, B., "Diagnose van organisatieproblemen." In: J. Gerrichhauzen, A. Kampermann, F. Kluytmans, *Interventies bij organisatieverandering*, Deventer: Kluwer Bedrijfswetenschappen; Heerlen: Open Universiteit (1994), pp. 67-95.

Kessels, J., "Dialectiek als instrument in de vorming van een lerende organisatie," *M&O* (1994) 5:452-477.

Kessels, J. W. M., and C. A. Smit, *Organisaties lerend veranderen: Organisatieverandering en opleiden*. Deventer: Kluwer Bedrijfswetenschappen (1992).

Kessels, J. W. M., *Towards design standards for curriculum consistency in corporate education*. Proefschrift. Enschede: Universiteit Twente (1993).

Kierkegaard, S. "Quotation". In: A. Witteveen, *M.A.W.—Citaten voor managers*. Amsterdam: Management Press (1992), pp. 79, 96.

Kim, D. H., *The link between individual and organizational learning*. Cambridge: Sloan Management Review (1993).

Kim, D. H., "Het verband tussen individueel leren en het leren van organisaties." *Holland Management Review* (1994) 38:104-116.

Kloosterboer, P., *Leidinggeven aan verandering*. Deventer: Kluwer Bedrijfswetenschappen (1993).

Kloosterboer, P. P., and R. M. Sterk, "Tussen centraal en decentraal." *M&O* (1996) 1:5-24.

Kluytmans, F., "Organisatie-opvattingen door de jaren heen." In: J. Gerrichhauzen, A. Kampermann, F. Kluytmans, *Interventies bij organisatieverandering*, Deventer: Kluwer Bedrijfswetenschappen (1994), pp. 21-38.

Knibbe, H., *Rusten in Zijn*. Utrecht: Servire (1996).

Knip, H., *Organisatiestudies in het onderwijs*. Utrecht: Drukkerij Elinkwijk (1981).

Koeleman, H., *Interne communicatie als managementinstrument*. Houten: Bohn Stafleu Van Loghum (1992).

Koesler, A., *The ghost in the machine*. London: Hutchinson (1967).

Kolb, D., and A. Frohman, "An organization development approach to consulting," *Sloan Management Review* (1970) 12:51-65.

Kolb, D., I. M. Rubbin, and J. S. Osland, *Organization behavior, an experiential approach*. Englewood Cliffs, NJ: Prentice Hall (1991).

Koning, C. de, *Goed bestuur. De regels en de kunst*. Deventer: Kluwer (1987).

Kor, R., "Veranderen van organisaties vraagt delicaat samenspel." *Holland Management Review* (1993) 36:69-76.

Kor, R., and G. Wijnen, *50 checklists for project and programme managers*. Gower: Aldershot/Brookfield (2000).

Kor, R., G. Wijnen, and M. Weggeman, *Management en motiveren*. Deventer: Kluwer (1997).

Korteweg, H., and J. Voigt, *Helen of delen: Over de transformatie van mens en organisatie*. Amsterdam: Contact (1986).

Kotter, J., and L. Schlesinger, "Choosing strategies for change." *Harvard Business Review* (1979) 2:106-114.

Kotter, J., *A force for change: How leadership differs from management*. New York: Free Press (1990).

Kouwenhoven, V. P., *Publiek private samenwerking*. Delft: Eburon (1991).

Krijger, N. L., "Coaching van gedrag: Management-coaching." In: J. Gerrichhauzen, A. Kampermann, F. Kluytmann, F. Klytmans, *Interventies bij organisatieverandering*. Deventer: Kluwer Bedrijfswetenschappen. Heerlen: Open Universiteit (1994), pp. 139-156.

Kübler-Ross, E., *Leven met stervenden*. Baarn: Ambo (1981).

Kuipers, H., and P. Amelsfoort, *Slagvaardiger organiseren. Inleiding in de sociotechniek als integrale ontwerpleer*. Deventer: Kluwer (1990).

Kuypers, B. C., *Group development patterns: An emerging perspective for the study and change of training groups*. Utrecht: Rijksuniversiteit Utrecht (1986).

Lao Tse, *Tao te ching: The classic book of integrity and the way*. New York: Bantam (1990).

Lap, H. H. M., "Resultaatgericht management." *Handboek Human Resource Management* (1992) II.A.4.1-201/212.

Leeuw, A. C. J. de, "Bureaucratische zegeningen." *M&O* (1997) 1:92-11.

Lewin, K., "Frontiers in group dynamics. Concept, method and reality in social science: Social equilibria and social change." *Human Relations* (1947) January:5-41.

Lewin, K., "Frontiers in group dynamics. Channels of group life: Social planning and action research." *Human Relations* (1947) January: 143-153.

Lewin, K., *Field theory in social science*. New York: Harper & Bros. (1951).

Lewin, K., "Quasi-stationary social equilibra and the problem of permanent change." In: W. G. Bennis, K. D. Benne, R. Chin, *The planning of change*. New York: Holt, Rinehart and Winston (1961), pp. 235-238.

Lievegoed, B. C. J., *De levensloop van de mens*. Rotterdam: Lemniscaat (1981).

Lippit, R., J. Watson, and B. Westley, *The dynamics of planned change: A comparative study of principles and techniques* . New York: Harcourt, Brace & World (1958).

Loman, J. B., *Verkenning toepassingsmogelijkheden chaos-theorie*. Amersfoort: Twynstra Gudde (interne publicatie)(1998).

Lorentz, E. N., "Deterministic non-periodic flow." *Journal of the Atmospheric Sciences* (1963) 20:130-141.

Lynn, G. T., "Levels of development for OD consultants: Moving from self-acceptance to mastery." *OD Practioner* (1986) 2:14-16.

Machiavelli, N., *De beheerser*. Amsterdam: Atheneum-Polak and Van Gennep (1976).

Machiavelli, N., and G. Inglese, *Il principe*. Torino: Einaudi (1995).

Maister, D., *Professional service firm management*. Seminar van de ROA, July (1991).

Maister, D. H., *Managing the professional service firm*. New York: Free Press (1993).

Marquez, G.G., "Toen ik nog gelukkig was en ongedocumenteerd". *Journalistiek Proza* nr. 5, Meulenhoff, Amsterdam (1978).

Maslow, A. H., *Motivatie en persoonlijkheid*. Rotterdam: Lemniscaat (1976).

Maslow, A. H., and R. Frager, *Motivation and personality*. New York: Harper & Row (1987).

Mastenbroek, W. F. G., *Conflicthantering en organisatie-ontwikkeling*. Alphen aan den Rijn: Samsom (1986).

Mayo, E., *The human problems of an industrial civilization*. New York: Macmillan (1933).

McGregor, D., *The human side of enterprise*. New York: McGraw-Hill (1960).

Mintzberg, H., *Structure in fives: Designing effective organizations*. Englewood Cliffs, NJ: Prentice Hall (1983).

Mintzberg, H., *Power in and around organizations*. Englewood Cliffs, NJ: Prentice Hall (1983).

Mintzberg, H., *Mintzberg on management: Inside our strange world of organizations*. New York: Free Press (1989).

Mol, C. J. B., J. B. G. Born, and C. W. Vroom, "De paradox van cultuur verandering: Beïnvloedt de verandering de cultuur of de cultuur de verandering." *M&O* (1994) 5:494-506.

Morgan, G., *Images of organizations*. Newbury Park, CA: Sage (1986).

Moursund, J., *The process of counseling and therapy*. 3rd edition, Englewood Cliffs, NJ: Prentice Hall (1993).

Nadler, D., *Feedback and organizational development: Using data-based methods*. Reading, MA: Addison-Wesley (1977).

Nadler, D., "Managing organizational change: An integrative perspective." *Journal of Applied Behavioral Science* (1981) 2:191-211.

Nadler, D., and M. Tuhsman, "Organizational framebending: Principles for managing reorientation." *Academy of Management Executive* (1989) 3:194-204.

Naisbitt, J., *Megatrends*. London: McDonalds (1984).

Ofman, D., *Bezieling en kwaliteit in organisaties*. Cöthen: Servire (1992).

Oss, L. van, *Cosmos uit chaos: How can I know what I think until I see what I say?* Utrecht: Universiteit van Utrecht (1997).

Otto, M., and A. C. J. de Leeuw, *Kijken, denken, doen; Organisatieverandering: Manouvreren met weerbastigheid.* Assen: Van Gorcum (1994).

Overduin, B. R., "Managers en transfer van training: Opleiden in een sadistisch universum?" *Opleiding & Ontwikkeling* (1995) 12:5-11.

Paauwe, J., "Kernvraagstukken op het gebied van strategische HRM in Nederland." *M&O* (1995) 5:369-389.

Palmer, H., *Creativism: The art of living deliberately.* Longwood, FL: Star's Edge (1990).

Parsons, T., *Social systems and the evolution of action theory.* New York: Free Press; London: Collier Macmillan (1977).

Parsons, T., *Action theory and the human condition.* New York: Free Press; London: Collier Macmillan (1978).

Pedler, M. (ed.), *Action learning in practice.* Aldershot, UK: Gower (1983).

Perrow, C., *Organizational analysis: A sociological review.* Belmont, CA: Wadsworth (1970).

Peters, T., and R. Waterman, *In search of excellence.* New York: Harper & Row (1982).

Petri, M. W., *Samen vliegeren, methodiek en resultaten van interactieve schooldiagnose.* Leuven: Acco (1995).

Pfeffer, J., *Power in organizations.* London: Pitman (1981).

Popcorn, F., *The Popcorn report.* New York: Doubleday (1991).

Porter, M. E., "How competitive forces shape strategy." *Harvard Business Review* (1979) 2:137-145.

Prigogine, I., *Orde uit chaos.* Amsterdam: Bert Bakker (1985).

Pirgogine, I., and I. Stengers, *Order out of chaos: Man's new dialogue with nature.* London: Flamingo; publ. by Fontana paperbacks (1986).

Quinn, R. E., *Beyond rational management: Mastering the paradoxes and competing demands of high performance.* San Francisco: Jossey-Bass (1988).

Rapmund, R., and G. Wijnen, *Bezeten van je vak.* Deventer: Kluwer (1990).

Richards, D., *Artful work—Awakening, joy, meaning and commitment in the workplace.* San Francisco: Berret-Koehler (1995).

Roethlisberger, F. J., and W. J. Dickson, *Management and the worker.* Cambridge, MA: Harvard University Press (1939).

Roethlisberger, F. J., *Management and morale.* Cambridge, MA: Harvard University Press (1941).

Russo, J. E., and P. Schoemaker, *Beslis(t) beter.* Schiedam: Scriptum Management (1989).

Russo, J. E., and P. Schoemaker. *Decision traps: Ten barriers to brilliant decision-making and how to overcome them.* New York: Doubleday/Currency (1989).

Sadler, P., and K. Miller, *The talent-intensive organisation.* London: The Economist Intelligence Unit (1993).

Saint Exupéry, A. de, "Quotation." In: A. Witteveen, *M. A. W.—Citaten voor managers,* Amsterdam: Management Press (1992), p. 131.

Sas, H., F. Verberne, G. Postma, H. Vermaak, M. Mieras, and M. Taiti, *Project Ontwikkeling Milieumanagement*. Amsterdam: IMSA (1989).

Saxe, J. G., *The blind men and the elephant*. Kingswood, Surrey: World's Work (1964).

Schein, E., and W. G. Bennis, *Personal and organizational change through group methods*. New York: John Wiley (1965).

Schein, E. H., *Organizational culture and leadership: A dynamic view*. New York/London: Harcourt Brace Jovanovich (1985).

Schlenger, S., and R. Roesch, *How to be organized in spite of yourself*. New York: NAL Meridian (1991).

Schmuck, R. A., and M. B. Miles (eds.), *OD in schools*. La Jolla, CA: University Associates (1971).

Schoemaker, M. J. R., *Managen van mensen en prestaties. Personeelsmanagement in moderne organisaties*. Deventer: Kluwer Bedrijfswetenschappen (1994).

Schön, D. A., *The reflective practitioner. How professionals think in action*. New York: Basic Books (1983).

Schonberger, R., *Japanese manufacturing techniques*. New York: Free Press (1982).

Selznick, P., *TVA and the grass roots*. Berkeley: University of California Press (1949).

Senge, P. M., *The fifth discipline: The art & practice of the learning organization*. New York: Doubleday/Currency (1990).

Senior, B., *Organisational change*. London: Pitman (1997).

Shepard, H. A., "Life planning." In: W. L. French, C. H. Bell, R. A. Zawacki, *Organization development, theory, practice and research*. 3rd edition. Homewood, IL: BPI-Irwin (1989).

Sitter, L. U. de, "Moderne sociotechniek," *Gedrag en organisatie* (1989) 4/5:222-252.

Skinner, B. F., *Beyond freedom and dignity*. New York: Knopf (1972).

Soeters, J., "Organisatiecultuur: Inhoud, betekenis en veranderbaarheid." In: J. J. Swanink, *Werken met de organisatiecultuur: De harde gevolgen van de zachte factor*, Vlaardingen: Nederlands Studie Centrum (1988), pp. 15-27.

Soeters, J., "Cultuurbeïnvloeding." In: J. Gerrichhauzen, A. Kampermann, and F. Kluytmans (eds.), *Interventies bij organisatieverandering*, Deventer: Kluwer Bedrijfswetenschappen; Heerlen: Open Universiteit (1994), pp. 99-121.

Sprenger, C. C., C. H. van Eijsden, S. ten Have, and F. Ossel, *Vier competenties van de lerende organisatie*. Den Haag: Delwel (1995).

Stacey, R. D., *Complexity and creativity in organizations*. San Francisco: Berrett-Koehler (1996).

Steyaert, C., "Teambuilding en teamontwikkeling." In: J. Gerrichhauzen, A. Kampermann, and F. Kluytmans (eds.), *Interventies bij organisatieverandering*, Deventer: Kluwer Bedrijfswetenschappen; Heerlen: Open Universiteit (1994), pp. 209-226.

Stoker, J., *Leiding geven aan zelfsturende teams*. Assen: Van Gorcum (1999).

Stroes, H. J., and M. E. Egberts, *Veranderen met resultaat*. Deventer: Kluwer (1996).

Sutherland, J. (ed.), *Management handbook for public administrators*. New York: Van Nostrand Reinhold (1978).

Swieringa, J., and A. F. M. Wierdsma, *Op weg naar een lerende organisatie*. Groningen: Wolters Noordhoff (1990).

Taylor, F. W. *The principles of scientific management*. New York: Harper and Row (1913).

Thierry, H. K., P. Koopman, and H. van der Flier, *Wat houdt mensen bezig?* Utrecht: Lemma (1992).

Thijssen, J., "To be or not to be: Organizational learning in learning organizations." *Opleiding & Ontwikkeling* (1992) 7:47-52.

Tichy, N. M., *Managing strategic change: Technical, political and cultural dynamics*. New York: John Wiley (1983).

Tichy, N., and M. Devanna, *The transformational leader*. New York: John Wiley (1986).

Trompenaars, F., and C. H. Hampden-Turner, *Riding the waves of culture: Understanding cultural diversity in business*. London: Brealey (1997).

Trompenaars, F., and C. H. Hampden-Turner, *Over de grenzen van cultuur en management*. Amsterdam: Contact (1998).

Tushman, M., W. Newman, and D. Nadler, "Executive leadership and organizational evolution: Managing incremental and discontinuous change." In: R. Kilmann, T. Covin, *Corporate transformation: Revitalizing organizations for a competitive world*. San Francisco: Jossey-Bass (1988), pp. 102-130.

Vandendriessche, F., *De input-output manager*. Tielt: Lannoo (1996).

Ven, A. H. van de, and M. S. Poole, "Explaining development and change in organizations." *Academy of Management Review* (1995) 3:510-540.

Verhallen, H. J. G., *Veranderaars veranderen: Organisatieadviseurs over hun werk*. Alphen aan den Rijn: Samsom (1979).

Vermaak, H. "Men zegt dat professionals niet te managen zijn". *Nijenrode Management Review* (1997) 7:12-27

Vermaak, H., and M. Weggeman. "Conspiring fruitfully with professionals: New management roles for professional organizations." *Management Decision* (1999) 37/1:29-44.

Vermaak, H. "Wat is een goede carrière? Zin en onzin van levensfasen in het advies-vak." *M&O* (2000) 54/5-6:217-236.

Vermaak, H. "Managers leren groen concurreren," *Holland Management Review* (1994), 40:64-71

Vermaak, H., and Westerveld, H. *De werelden die schuil gaan achter de zorg; Een nieuw taalspel voor het richten, inrichten en veranderen van gezondheidszorginstellingen*. Twynstra Gudde (2001).

Vinke, R., *Motivatie en belonen*. Deventer: Kluwer (1996).

Vinkenburg, H. H. M., *Stimuleren tot perfectie. Kritieke factoren bij het verbeteren van dienstver-lening*. Deventer: Kluwer Bedrijfswetenschappen (1995).

Vlist, R. van der, J. T. Allegro, and M. I. Demenint, "Organisatie veranderkunde: Een theoretisch overzicht." In: J. J. Boonstra, Demenint, M. I. and H. O. Steensma (eds.), *Organiseren en veranderen in een dynamische wereld: Begeleiden van veranderingsprocessen binnen organisaties*. Culemborg: Lemma (1989), pp. 35-53.

Vlist, R. van der, *Visies op organisatiecultuur: Een multidisciplinair perspectief*. Utrecht: Lemma (1992).

Vlist, R. van der, "Geplande verandering van organisaties en organisatie-ontwikkeling in de jaren negentig." *Nieuw Hanboek A&O psychologie* (1993), p. 4.5-1/54.

Vroemen, M., *Werken in teams. Samen denken en doen.* Deventer: Kluwer (1995).

Waterman, R. H., T. J. Peters, and J. R. Philips, "Structure is not organization." *Business Horizons* (1980) 3:14-26.

Watson, G. W., "Resistance to change." In: G. W. Watson (ed.), *Concepts for social change.* Cooperative Projects for Educational Development Series (1). Washington, DC: NTL (1969).

Watzlawick, P., J. H. Weakland, and R. Fisk, *Het kan anders.* Deventer: Van Loghum Slaterus (1974).

Weggeman, M., *Collectieve ambitie ontwikkeling.* Tilburg: University Press (1995).

Weggeman, M., *Leidinggeven aan professionals.* Deventer: Kluwer (1997).

Weggeman, M., G. Wijnen, and R. Kor, *Ondernemen binnen de onderneming. Essenties van organisaties.* Deventer: Kluwer (1997).

Weick, K. E., *The social psychology of organizing.* Reading, MA: Addison-Wesley (1969).

Weick, K. E., "Educational organizations as loosely coupled systems." *Administrative Science Quarterly* (1976) 1:1-19.

Weick, K. E., *Sensemaking in organizations.* Thousand Oaks, CA: Sage (1995).

Weisbord, M. R., "Towards a new practice theory of OD: Notes on snapshooting and moviemaking." *Research in Organizational Change and Development* (1988) 2:59-96.

Weisbord, M. R., *Discovering common ground: How future search conferences bring people together to achieve breakthrough innovation, shared vision, and collaborative action.* San Francisco: Berrett-Koehler (1992).

Westra, E., and E. van de Vliert, "Waarden en adviesstijlen." *Mens en Onderneming* (1989) 2:145-154.

Wijnen, G., and R. Kor, *Managing unique assignments: A team approach to projects and programmes.* Gower, UK: Aldershot/Brookfield (2000).

Wijnen, G., *Multiprojectmanagement.* Utrecht: Het Spectrum (1997).

Wijnen, G., W. Renes, and P. Storm, *Projectmatig werken.* Utrecht: Spectrum (1998).

Wijnen, G., M. Weggeman, and R. Kor, *Verbeteren en vernieuwen van organisaties.* Deventer: Kluwer (1999).

Wilber, K., *The Atman project: A transpersonal view of human development.* Wheaton, IL: Theosophical Publishing House (1980).

Wolfe, D. W., "Developing professional competences in the applied behavioral sciences." In: *New directions for experimental learning,* San Francisco: Jossey-Bass (1980).

Zaltman, G., and R. Duncan, *Strategies for planned change.* New York: John Wiley (1977).

Zee, H. van der, "De vijf denkparadigma's binnen het opleidings—en ontwikkelingsveld." *M&O* (1995) 2:107-134.

Zuijderhoudt, R. W. L., "Principes van synergie en zelfordening: Introductie van de chaostheorie binnen de organisatiekunde." *M&O* (1992) 1:15-40.

Zwart, C. J., *Gericht veranderen van organisaties: Theorie en praktijk van het begeleiden.* Rotterdam: Lemniscaat (1993).

List of Figures

List of Tables

Index

About the Authors

Léon de Caluwé (1950) is senior partner with the Twynstra Group, management consultants, and part-time professor at the Free University in Amsterdam. He studied social psychology at the University of Utrecht and received his science degree in 1975 and his Ph.D. in 1997 at Tilburg University. He was appointed Professor in Amsterdam in 2000. Working for all types of clients in government and industry, he leads the Center for Research on Consultancy at the Free University, which is part of an international network, and regularly works as an expert for the OECD and the Council of Europe.

At Twynstra Gudde, where he's been affiliated since 1988, de Caluwé is a member of the company think tank and specializes in change, conflict resolution, quality of coop-eration, culture interventions, and facilitation of policy development sessions. He works regularly with games and gaming methods as an intervention for advanced learning.

He has published more than 80 articles and more than 15 books, several of which are in English, including *Changing Organizations With Gaming/Simulation* (2000). His doctoral dissertation, *Veranderen moet je leren* (1997), received the "Best Book of the Year" award from the Dutch Association of Management Consultants. His subjects are change, consultancy, and interventions.

De Caluwé is a member of the Academy of Management, editor of several scientific journals, and lecturer in many postgraduate and master's programs.

Hans Vermaak (1961) studied chemistry and organizational psychology in Utrecht and Florida and received his degree in Utrecht in 1985. He worked as a faculty member in both the science and the psychology departments of the University of Utrecht between 1982 and 1987. For many years a social activist, he worked with the Institute of Environmental and Systems Analysis from 1987-1992, where he mediated conflicts of (mostly) multinational industries or trade houses with governments and environmental groups. He also helped these companies to set up strategic environmental management.

Vermaak completed different course programs in psychotherapy and counseling. Since 1987, he has taught counseling and still works part-time as a psychotherapist. In 1990, he began teaching yoga classes and was the interim manager of a spiritual center in 1992 and 1993.

Taking a master's degree in management consulting from the Free University in Amsterdam in 1994, Vermaak has worked as a management consultant with the Twynstra Group since 1993, where he is a partner. His principal area of consulting concerns the diagnosing, planning, and implementing of organizational change in professional firms and institutions. He does most of his work as a process consultant, working in many different kinds of organizations. Generally, a substantial part of his work takes place in an international context. He trains and coaches change agents, and he heads the Change Management knowledge center of the Twynstra Group.

Vermaak has been a guest lecturer at several universities and has published articles and books on change management, dilemmas of professional organizations, environmental issues, coaching and counselling, group systems, visions of the future, and approaches to learning. He has received several publication awards. His English publications include *Conspiring Fruitfully With Professionals: New Management Roles for Professional Organisations; Managers Learning to Be Green Competitors*, and *In Search of Corporate Learning: The Archipelago of Learning.*